Basic to Brilliant, Y'all

BASIC TO
Brilliant,
Y'ALL

150 Refined Southern Recipes and Ways to Dress Them Up for Company

Virginia Willis

Photography by Hélène Dujardin

TEN SPEED PRESS

Berkeley

Contents

Foreword by Anne Willan

I vividly remember the day Virginia walked into our kitchen, and our lives. The day was warm, the sun shining, and Virginia appeared smiling in the doorway, fresh as a daisy off the train from Paris after an overnight flight from Atlanta. Within minutes she had introduced herself all around. An hour later I found her prepping dinner with the rest of the trainees as if she'd been there for weeks. And after dinner, praise be, she was first at the sink without being asked—the acid test of successful traineeship at Château du Feÿ in Burgundy.

The chefs accepted her as one of their own as soon as they discovered she could dice carrots into tiny *brunoise* cubes and stir up a satin-smooth *crème anglaise* without further instruction. We always had a head trainee, one who guided the others through what could be long days spent inside and outside the kitchen, starting at the bakery for still-warm baguettes at 7:00 a.m. and ending with 8:30 p.m. dinner on the terrace overlooking the fields of wheat and corn as the sun went down. Virginia was the one who stood firm when the hollandaise curdled (start again with a new egg yolk) or the garden lettuces had worms in them (just avert your eyes). She would pilot novices through their first run on gougères, the cheese choux puffs that we served with a glass of the local sparkling Crémant to each of our many visitors.

Virginia soon realized the importance of what she was learning, that basics like stock and *pâte brisée* must be followed to the letter, but that white wine butter sauce is just a starting point, it's up to the chef to make each variant of the sauce his own. One recipe of hers remains in my mind. After testing an obscure recipe for gumbo (not a success), we were left with nearly a whole crate of okra. Okra is not exactly on the front burner in Burgundy but in a French kitchen nothing, ever, is thrown away. The chefs were nonplussed, but Virginia's grandma's corn-fried okra was the hit of the season (a tough call) at Château du Feÿ and made it into my next cookbook, with permission of course.

I guess corn-fried okra is pure southern, but I like to think that recipe—with its French insistence on getting deep frying just right—bridged the culinary gap that Virginia has navigated so adroitly here. Dishes such as Southern Ratatouille, Shrimp Rillettes, Garlic-Stuffed Prime Rib Roast, Winter Greens and Butternut Squash Gratin, and Bittersweet Chocolate Bread Pudding sum up the best of both worlds. Virginia came to France for three months and stayed with us for three years. She helped with books in the editorial office, she oversaw much of what we ate (a pleasure for us all!), and little by little she became a lifelong friend.

Since those early days at Château du Feÿ, Virginia and I have shared many happy experiences. We've worked on booksful of photo shoots, with Virginia styling and me running the set. We've stood side by side on the cooking platform many a time, sometimes with an audience, others in front of a camera. We've often cooked together, and occasionally we've just talked—we're both very good at that! In one case, I appeared solo in a one-hour cooking special produced by Virginia, and the anchor of her beaming face beside the cameraman ensured the success of the show. She did not hesitate to tweak my hair or powder my nose, nor to tell me "that won't do"—so refreshing!

In *Basic to Brilliant Y'all,* Virginia brings us the best of both worlds. Her love of cooking goes go back to her grandmother in the South. Onto that rich history she has grafted the techniques and recipes—the reduction sauces and seasonal vegetables—she found in France. She has applied her own imagination to the vivid palate of her native southern ingredients. For anyone who loves French food or southern cooking, either one or both, this book calls out an irresistible welcome. I can't wait to try Kale Omelet and Burnt Caramel Cake. "Basic to Brilliant" is a great concept, too, summing up the idea that you can leave a simple recipe alone, or take and run with it to create a festive dish. As for the "Y'all," Virginia has me there. No way, ever, will I be able to pronounce the tongue-twister. So, I'm reverting to a third language to wish you all as much joy in the kitchen as Virginia and I have had together, with a resounding, multi-national "Bon Appétit"!

Introduction

I've been cooking as a professional for a little more than fifteen years, but my passion actually started when I wasn't tall enough to reach the counter in my grandmother's country kitchen. I called her Meme, and she was the light of my life. The kitchen never really changed much. There never was enough space for everything. The overhead light hummed. My grandmother's recipes were posted on the inside of the cabinet, some written in her old-fashioned, loopy, spidery penmanship directly on the wood.

My grandmother and I spent hours together in that kitchen. There are photos of me as young as three years old standing on a stool "helping." As dinner cooked, we'd roll out the biscuits, and she'd let me make a handprint with the scraps of dough. The tiny fingers on my biscuit would cook very dark in the heat of the oven, taking on a slightly bitter, almost nutty taste. I know that's where my love for cooking took root, working at her side on her linoleum countertop, in the gentle breeze of the oscillating fan.

Oh, my grandmother could cook. Her pound cake was legendary. She'd wake in the early morning before the heat of the day and prepare fried chicken, buttermilk biscuits, old-fashioned butter beans, creamed corn, okra, and tomatoes.

Many of the vegetables were grown in my grandfather's garden. My grandfather Dede was a patient man. She would call outdoors and make the man take his shirt off so she could wash it. That never made a lick of sense to me. He'd mumble quietly under his breath "Lawd, have mercy," but he would have moved a mountain range for her.

The very last time I saw my grandmother was on Mother's Day in 2000. She had a sore throat, went to the doctor, and was diagnosed with cancer. She was 91 and conceded defeat when she heard that ugly word. When I returned to that simple country kitchen, our tables were turned, and I cooked for her. There's still hardly a day that goes by that I don't think of her. I often wish I could be in the kitchen with her, smelling her chicken frying just one more time.

My mother, Virginia, known as Jenny, grew up in Columbia County, Georgia. She returned there almost twenty-five years ago and now lives less than a mile from the house where she was raised. When asked where I am from, I generally reply, "My family is from Evans, Georgia." I haven't lived there since I was three years old, and I've lived dozens of places since. However, home is far more complex than a mailing address. My deep roots in the South and family history continually help me define my journey, what I will be, and where I will go.

My maternal grandparents, Sam and Louise Baston, bought fifty acres near Evans, Georgia, in 1938. She was the lady and he was the tall, handsome, strapping country boy with dark hair and crystal clear blue eyes. He swept her off her feet, they fell in love, and scandalously, they eloped. (I feel compelled at this point to point out for my grandmother's honor that their first child was not born shortly thereafter.) Together they made a family, helped start a community, built a church, and most importantly, left a long-lasting legacy of what home really is.

I spent much of my childhood with my grandparents. Dede always seemed to be working outdoors. There are photos of me as a toddler, chubby legs covered in dirt from tagging along behind him in the garden. He, my sister, and I would pick berries in the woods and bring them to Meme to make Sweet Biscuits with Stewed Blackberries (page 235) or some form of cobbler. I remember being in the steamy kitchen with my apron-clad grandmother, before central heat and air was installed, listening to her cook, and taking in every last sight and scent. The gentle burbling of Meme's Chicken and Rice (page 214) in the cast-iron Dutch oven; the sweet, sticky cake batter licked from the spatula; the gentle hum of the electric mixer beating the icing for Dede's Burnt Caramel Cake (page 253) and the pitched whistle of the pressure cooker emitting the meaty smell of bacon and green beans fresh from the garden are the tastes, smells, and sounds of my childhood.

When I was a teenager, I didn't hang out in the Dairy Queen parking lot with the other kids on Friday nights. I stayed at home in the kitchen with Mama. My parents divorced the summer between my junior and senior year. That same summer, the school

I attended closed. I was sixteen, and it was hard. Mama and I leaned on each other, and it was then that our "grown-up" friendship really started as we spent time in the kitchen together. Instead of attending my senior year of high school, I started college. Mama never let on she was worried. She believed in me, and if she had any hesitation about her sheltered, bookish daughter starting college at sixteen, she never said a word.

After a great start, I sputtered a bit and got lost. I realized the one constant, the one place I always sought, whether a scared teenager leaving Mama, or in a flat in London, or in Athens, Georgia, at my college commune-of-sorts, or as a lonely university grad in Charleston, South Carolina, the one place that had been my constant home was the kitchen. That realization started me on my way.

My first job cooking was on a TV cooking show with Nathalie Dupree. I learned to make Sally Lunn Bread (page 227) and enjoyed the infinite pleasure of feeling crust tearing beneath my bite to reveal the moist, yeasty crumb inside. I attended culinary school at L'Academie de Cuisine in Bethesda and was taught to make earthy, fragrant soups. I tasted delicate, clear consommés that belied the complexity within. I discovered an infinite world of sauces beyond the familiar gravy, and learned about reductions, seasoning, and balance. I remember my first taste of the slick, iron-rich demi-glace and the brittle, bony minerality of court-bouillon.

Shortly thereafter I moved to France. I was supposed to be at La Varenne in Burgundy with Anne Willan for three months and was there for nearly three years. At La Varenne I felt like I actually tasted the warm, grassiness of butter for the first time. I explored cheeses I had never known—some heady and thick with animal aroma, others delicate, pure suspensions of fresh, sweet milk. The vegetables from the garden reminded me of home: voluptuous tomatoes bursting with savory flavor; sweet, tender squash; and musky, honeyed melon fully ripened by the hot summer sun.

My kitchen home grew increasingly larger; I felt I'd been given keys to the culinary castle. Learning through the French emphasis on basic, fundamental techniques, I tasted and saw food as I had never seen it before. I also began to realize how important those years of learning by Meme's and Mama's sides had been.

Returning stateside, I was the TV kitchen director for Bobby Flay, then Martha Stewart. With *Epicurious* television I ate freshly caught grilled octopus on an Aeolian beach, the fire spitting steam and seawater. I made pungent, eye-watering *moutarde au vin* in Dijon, and pressed deliciously biting olive oil with a media heiress in Sonoma. During my extended time in Europe, while traveling in the United States and abroad, and while living in New York, I was exposed to brilliant food, simple to complex creations—made in people's homes, through my work, or prepared in restaurants by some of the world's most celebrated chefs.

Then, on 9/11, I was trapped in Manhattan as the towers burned. People were huddled around cars with doors and windows open at every street corner, listening to the radio. The sound of sirens and the gnawing pull of fear were omnipresent. At one point I could see the towers smoldering and smoking against the cerulean blue sky, and then they were gone. Just gone. In the economic aftermath, I lost my job with *Epicurious*. Months later, walking down the West Side Highway with tears streaming down my cheeks, the sounds of sirens still permeating the air, I realized I wanted to go home after nearly ten years away from the South.

Like many expatriates, I returned home with a better sense of place than I would have ever had if I had never left. In my travels, I had built upon what my grandmother and mother had taught me, a solid repertoire of basic fundamental techniques. My eyes had been wondrously opened to just how brilliant the world of food—and home—could be. I continue my journey, still building my collection of stories with every bite, every word, every scent.

I've always devoured books and still do. Words are magic to me. What I hope to share with you is a collection of recipes and recollections that you will devour, that you will find magical. I am offering a body of basic recipes that can stand on their own, but they can be transformed to brilliant by a short recipe, presentation tip, or technique—all accomplished without "dumbing down" the basic to make the brilliant work, and without the overuse of expensive or hard-to-find ingredients. I like to think of the Basic recipes as what you might prepare on a weeknight for supper with family, a simple recipe I might teach in a cooking class. The Brilliant versions are more chef inspired, something to prepare for dinner guests on the weekend, something I might prepare for you if you were a guest in my home, the culinary version of the fine Southern tradition of dressing up for company. I believe in letting the goodness of the food shine through—refined Southern cuisine.

This is what home means to me—talking for hours with my mother, fresh garden vegetables, pulling the wishbone with my sister just like we did when we were young, and sharing sweet kitchen memories. Around the world and home again. Welcome, once again, to my Southern kitchen. Pull up a chair.

1

Fundamental Recipes

Fundamental recipes are the cornerstone of cooking by technique, not simply cooking by a recipe. Julia Child supposedly once said, "If you understand the technique, you don't need a recipe." Outfitted with a foundation of solid techniques and fundamental recipes, a cook can accomplish many things. Now, most of us aren't going to grow up and become Julia Child, but what she said is true. A recipe should be a guide, not a ball and chain.

For example, something as simple as using a bouquet garni is a technique. A bouquet garni is a sachet of aromatics, often tied in cheesecloth for easy removal, added to a stew, soup, or sauce to contribute and enhance flavor. Traditionally in French cooking it is made of a few sprigs of parsley, thyme, a bay leaf, and peppercorns. It's a simple, innocuous, but important layering of flavor. Take that same concept and tailor it to the recipe and bells start to go off. With a Latin-inspired soup, try using cilantro and coriander seeds instead of parsley and peppercorns. With an Asian-inspired dish, try using star anise or a cinnamon stick instead of bay leaves and thyme.

Subtle layering of flavor is what transforms good food to great food. When I was in culinary school at L'Academie de Cuisine, one of my textbooks, and an indispensable guide in the years since, was *Le Répertoire de la Cuisine.* It's a basic guide to the cuisine of Antoine Escoffier, a premier chef in the late 1800s and early 1900s, perhaps the most important leader in the development of modern French cuisine. Much of Escoffier's technique was based on that of Antoine Carême, impressively referred to as the "chef of kings and the king of chefs." Prominent in the early nineteenth century, Carême was the very first celebrity chef and was famous for elaborate *pièces montées* of pastry and spun sugar, and cooked for both the czar of Russia and the Rothschilds, possibly the wealthiest family in the world at that time. His recipe for vol-au-vent—made with cocks' combs and testicles, lamb sweetbreads and brains, calves' udders and truffles—has stood the test of time (see page 107). Ahem. Think Martha Stewart meets Tony Bourdain, with a dash of Elizabeth Falkner and Andrew Zimmern.

Escoffier modernized, codified, and organized Carême's haute cuisine, forming the basis for much modern French cooking and the foundation of western foodways. *Le Répertoire* is a thin, unassuming book whose appearance obscures the treasure inside. It claims more than seven thousand recipes, but it's not a recipe book in the traditional sense with a list of ingredients, measurements, and cooking times. A "recipe" might be only one or two sentences. The recipe for Sauce Maltaise reads "Hollandaise sauce with zest and juice of blood oranges." *C'est tout.* That's it.

Le Répertoire assumes the reader and cook knows the fundamentals, the basic techniques. My experiences at both L'Academie de Cuisine and La Varenne were all about learning these fundamentals. Peering over her spectacles, Anne Willan, the director of La Varenne, once wisely told me, "Learn the scales before you play the music. Cooking is about creativity, but it's important to acquire discipline first."

Here are a few harmonious notes to get you started.

Chicken Stock

I am often asked about the difference between stock and broth. Many of the chicken, beef, and vegetable stock products available in the grocery store are labeled "broth," which is at odds with the definition of many chefs. Chefs view broth as liquid in which meat, fish, or vegetables have been cooked when the goal is also to consume the meat, fish, or vegetables.

Stock, on the other hand, is the liquid in which meat, fish, bones, or vegetables are simmered for a relatively long period. All the flavor, taste, and texture are cooked out of the ingredients, which are then discarded. The remaining liquid is then used as a base for preparing soup, gravy, or sauces.

Chicken feet make an absolutely excellent gelatinous chicken stock. Generally, you can find chicken feet in Asian markets and grocery stores.

2 pounds chicken wings, bones, or well-washed feet

14 cups water

3 celery stalks, coarsely chopped

3 onions, preferably Vidalia, coarsely chopped

3 carrots, scrubbed and coarsely chopped

2 bay leaves, preferably fresh

2 sprigs flat-leaf parsley

2 sprigs thyme

4 to 6 whole black peppercorns

In a large soup pot, combine the chicken, water, celery, onions, carrots, bay leaves, parsley, thyme, and peppercorns. Bring the mixture to a boil over high heat. Decrease the heat to low and simmer for $1^1/2$ hours, skimming the foam off the top as it rises. Strain through a colander, reserving the stock and discarding the chicken and vegetables. (Some people think this is wasteful and insist the chicken be picked off the bone and used for chicken salad. My response is that all the flavor is in the stock. If you want tasteless, mushy chicken salad, then go right ahead.)

Store in an airtight container in the refrigerator for up to 1 week, or freeze for up to 3 months. Before using, skim off and discard any fat that has risen to the surface.

☙ Beef Stock

MAKES ABOUT 10 CUPS

You know when you roast a chicken and put it in the fridge and the next day when you take it out there's this sort of meat Jell-O around the bones? That's a result of collagen. Both beef and veal may be used as a base for soups, stews, and as a braising liquid. (Veal stock is a good deal richer than beef stock, so keep that in mind and season and taste as you go.)

Store-bought beef broth tastes precious little like homemade beef stock. The USDA only requires commercial beef broth to be 1 part beef to 135 parts water. That is one thin broth. The concentrated pastes are only marginally better, and both versions are full of sodium. If you are going to prepare a beef stew or a dish in which beef stock plays a primary role, it is worth it to first take a day to make homemade beef stock.

6 pounds veal or beef bones, cut into 2-inch pieces

3 carrots, scrubbed and coarsely chopped

3 onions, preferably Vidalia, skins on, coarsely chopped

3 celery stalks, coarsely chopped

1 head garlic, halved, skin on

1 (6-ounce) can tomato paste

4 sprigs flat-leaf parsley

4 sprigs thyme

2 bay leaves, preferably fresh

10 whole black peppercorns

2 cups dry red wine

4 1/2 quarts water, or as needed

Preheat the oven to 400°F. Place the bones in a roasting pan. Roast, turning them occasionally, until they start to brown, about 15 minutes. Add the carrots, onions, celery, garlic, and tomato paste. Stir to combine. Continue roasting until the vegetables are brown, an additional 20 to 30 minutes.

Using a slotted spoon so the fat remains in the roasting pan, transfer the bones and vegetables to a large stockpot. Discard the fat and place the roasting pan on the stovetop. Add the wine to loosen any brown bits remaining in the pan. Tip the wine and any brown bits into the stockpot. Add the parsley, thyme, bay leaves, and peppercorns. Add the water to cover. Bring the mixture to a boil over high heat. Decrease the heat to low and simmer, skimming the foam off the top as it rises, until the broth is rich and dark, 4 to 8 hours for beef and preferably 10 hours for veal stock.

Strain the liquid through a colander, reserving the stock and discarding the solids. Store in an airtight container in the refrigerator for up to 1 week, or freeze for up to 3 months. Before using, while still cold, skim off and discard any fat that has risen to the surface; the fat will lift off easily.

Have Another Go

Remouillage is defined as "rewetting." It is a second stock made from the bones that have been used once for a primary stock. It's a weaker stock, of course, but gets every little bit of goodness out of those bones.

Vegetable Stock

Making stock is a great way to use vegetable trimmings that would otherwise be tossed into the compost or trash can. Having said that, a stockpot is not a garbage pail, so use only clean trimmings that are free of soft, rotten spots and blemishes. I save bits and pieces of zucchini and carrot ends, celery leaves, and onion peels, covered and refrigerated, and add them to a batch of stock when needed.

1 tablespoon pure olive oil

1 onion, preferably Vidalia, coarsely chopped

2 carrots, scrubbed and coarsely chopped

2 celery stalks, coarsely chopped

8 ounces white button or cremini mushrooms, sliced

10 cloves garlic, with peels, smashed

2 tablespoons tomato paste

8 sprigs flat-leaf parsley

6 sprigs thyme, or 1/2 teaspoon dried thyme

2 bay leaves, preferably fresh

14 cups cold water

Heat the olive oil in a stockpot over medium-high heat. Add the onion, carrots, celery, and mushrooms. Cook, stirring often, until caramelized, about 10 minutes. (The richer the color, the richer the flavor, but take care not to burn it.) Add the garlic, tomato paste, parsley, thyme, bay leaves, and water. Bring to a boil. Lower the heat and simmer, partially covered, for 45 minutes.

Remove from the heat and strain the stock through a fine-mesh sieve, pressing on the vegetables to extract the juices. Discard the vegetables. Refrigerate the stock in an airtight container for 3 to 4 days, or freeze for up to 3 months.

The Five Mother Sauces

French chef Antonin Carême created an intricate methodology by which hundreds of sauces were classified under one of five "mother sauces."

Béchamel is a white sauce made by stirring heated milk into a butter-flour roux. The thickness depends on the proportion of flour and butter to milk. The proportions for a thin sauce are 1 tablespoon each butter and flour per 1 cup milk; a medium sauce uses 2 tablespoons each butter and flour; a thick sauce, 3 tablespoons each. A thick béchamel is the base for a savory soufflé. Béchamel is one of the most useful sauces.

Velouté is a stock-based white sauce. (White simply means the ingredients are not browned.) I often laugh because it really is what most Southerners call gravy. It is made by stirring chicken, veal, or fish stock into a butter-flour roux. It's important that the stock in velouté and the milk in béchamel are heated before you add them to the roux. If the liquids are not heated, the starch in the flour will set, and you will have lumpy gravy.

Brown sauce, or *espagnole*, is traditionally made of meat stock, often beef with a mirepoix of browned vegetables (most often a mixture of diced onion, carrots, and celery), plus ham or bacon and a nicely browned roux, herbs, and sometimes tomato paste.

Hollandaise is an emulsion of egg yolks and fat. Hollandaise is made with butter, egg yolks, and lemon juice, often in a double boiler to prevent overheating, and served warm. It is generally served with vegetables, fish, and egg dishes, such as the classic eggs Benedict.

Sauce Tomate is made with a purée of tomatoes (or strained tomatoes) with savory vegetables and other seasonings (page 228). *Sauce tomate* is more closely associated with Italian cooking, but it is still a major part of French cuisine, as well. It can be used on pasta, as a sauce on its own, or as a component in other dishes.

Seafood Stock

This all-purpose seafood stock is much more flavorful than bottled clam juice, which is best used only in a pinch. If you are using fish carcasses, do not use oily fish such as salmon or mackerel; use lean fish, such as halibut, barramundi, or sea bass.

5 cups water

1/2 cup dry white wine

2 onions, preferably Vidalia, chopped

2 carrots, scrubbed and coarsely chopped

2 celery stalks with leaves, coarsely chopped

10 whole black peppercorns

4 sprigs flat-leaf parsley

2 bay leaves, preferably fresh

2 sprigs thyme

1-inch strip lemon zest

2 pounds shrimp shells with heads, if possible, or fish heads and bones, rinsed, or a combination

Combine the water, wine, onions, carrots, celery, peppercorns, parsley, bay leaves, thyme, and lemon zest in a medium to large stockpot. Add the shrimp shells. Bring to a boil over high heat, then decrease the heat to simmer. Simmer for 20 minutes, skimming occasionally.

Transfer to a rack to cool, during which time the bits and bones will settle to the bottom of the pot. Then ladle out and strain the stock through a fine-mesh sieve, leaving the bits and bones in the bottom of the pot. For the clearest stock possible, do not press on the solids, but simply discard. Transfer to an airtight container and refrigerate for 3 days, or freeze for up to 3 months.

❧ Shallot Vinaigrette

There's been a whole lot of talk about culinary "apps" (as in smartphone applications, not starters or nibbles) and cooking by ratio, not by recipe. Vinaigrette is an excellent example of this premise. To make a proper vinaigrette, that is, one that is a perfect balance of smooth and creamy to acidic and tart, a certain ratio of ingredients must be followed: one part acid to three parts oil. The recipe emerges from the technique when the acid is sherry versus balsamic vinegar, or lemon juice versus a combination of white wine vinegar and champagne vinegar. One could also use apple cider, white wine, or red wine vinegar, each vinegar with a different flavor profile. The recipe continues to unfold when the oil is chosen. Is it a full-flavored vinaigrette for tomatoes and cold meats with some of the garlic oil (from below), extra-virgin olive oil, a milder combination of corn and olive oil, or even milder still, with grapeseed or canola oil?

Shallot vinaigrette isn't just for lettuce greens and is excellent with lentil salad (page 62), wild rice salad (page 161), or even as a dipping sauce for crudités. Salt doesn't dissolve in oil, so it must be added to the vinegar or lemon juice.

2 large shallots, finely chopped

1 tablespoon Dijon mustard

2 tablespoons vinegar

Coarse salt and freshly ground black pepper

6 tablespoons oil

In a small bowl, whisk together the shallots, mustard, and vinegar. Season with salt and pepper. Add the oil in a slow stream, whisking until emulsified. Taste and adjust for seasoning with salt and pepper. Store in an airtight container in the refrigerator for up to 2 weeks.

❧ Garlic Confit

There are lots of recipes for garlic cooked in foil in the oven, and I do love the roasted garlic taste. But, time and time again, I return to simmering garlic in oil on the stovetop. It creates two ingredients to use in the kitchen—the soft, tender garlic cloves and the fragrant, flavorful oil. It's an excellent use of garlic if you have purchased a large container of peeled cloves in bulk, and they are on their way out.

1 cup garlic cloves

1¼ cups canola, grapeseed, or pure olive oil

Put the peeled garlic in a small saucepan and add the oil. It should cover the garlic completely. Set over low to medium-low heat and bring to a simmer, about 210°F, just hot enough to blurb and bubble gently. Cook until the garlic is tender and opaque, 35 to 40 minutes.

Transfer to a bowl to cool. Transfer the cloves and oil to separate airtight containers. Store each in the refrigerator for up to 3 weeks.

Mayonnaise

MAKES 1 CUP

I love a hand-whisked mayonnaise. It's softer than the machine-blended version and one can control the flavors. Canola and grapeseed oils produce very mild versions. Olive oil results in a more full flavored mayonnaise. Chose which oil to use depending on what the end result will be. The Southern Salad Macédoine (page 49), for example, would be best with a mild oil to let the flavor of the vegetables shine through. An olive oil–based mayonnaise would be better suited for Jona's Tomato Pie (page 187) since tomatoes and olive oil are a natural marriage. I once did a commercial for Duke's mayonnaise with my friend Mary Moore, owner of The Cook's Warehouse. She made a fancy chicken salad with roasted red peppers, and I made a classic version with tarragon. Our whole point was that the chicken salads can be different, but our choice of mayonnaise was the same. I said, "If it's not homemade, it's got to be Duke's." Turned out, they used this as the tagline.

I heard a rumor that the side of an eighteen-wheeler had a photograph on it of Mary and me holding our chicken salads. I told my sister, who dryly commented, "That would make me run off the road."

2 large egg yolks

1 teaspoon Dijon mustard

Juice of 1/2 lemon or 2 tablespoons white wine vinegar

1 cup oil (such as canola, grapeseed, olive, or a combination), at room temperature

Coarse salt and freshly ground black pepper

Whisk the egg yolks, mustard, and lemon juice together in a bowl until smooth and light. In a slow, steady stream, whisk in the oil, a drop at a time, until the mixture starts to stiffen and thicken. As the mixture thickens, you may add the oil slightly faster. Season with salt and pepper. Use immediately or store in an airtight container in the refrigerator for up to 2 days.

Mix It Up

You've probably noticed that when you combine oil and vinegar in a bowl they form separate layers. If you whisk the mixture it will combine for only a brief period, then separate out again. The secret to a creamy, emulsified dressing or vinaigrette is mustard. Mustard helps thicken liquid sauces by absorbing some of the liquid and allows the suspension of one liquid in another.

An emulsion is a fine dispersion of minute droplets of one liquid in another in which it is not soluble or mixable, meaning it won't combine smoothly, such as oil and water. This fine dispersion is achieved by slowly adding one ingredient to another while rapidly mixing or whisking, suspending droplets of one liquid throughout the other.

Many mixtures can be emulsions, including house paint; but in the kitchen, an emulsion is usually a combination of eggs, some kind of fat, and an acid, such as vinegar or lemon juice. Often, mustard is also added, because mustard is an emulsifying agent, and also because mustard lends a distinctive flavor.

When making an emulsion, the key to success is being careful and not adding the oil too quickly. A slow, steady stream is best. If the oil is added too quickly, it will cause the emulsion to "break," and the mixture will have a curdled appearance.

Crème Fraîche

MAKES 2 CUPS

Crème fraîche translates to fresh cream, but it is actually a soured cream with about 28 percent butterfat. The high fat content allows crème fraîche to be heated without curdling, and the nutty, complex flavor is delicious.

2 tablespoons cultured buttermilk

2 cups heavy cream (pasteurized, but not ultrapasteurized or sterilized)

Combine the buttermilk and cream in a saucepan and heat only to tepid (not more than 85°F on an instant-read thermometer). Pour into a clean glass jar. Partially cover and let stand at room temperature (between 65°F and 75°F) for 8 to 24 hours, or until thickened. Stir and refrigerate for at least 24 hours before using. The cream will keep for about 2 weeks in an airtight container in the refrigerator.

French Pie Crust *Pâte Brisée*

PASTRY FOR 1 DOUBLE- OR 2 SINGLE-CRUST (9- TO 10-INCH) PIES

Making pie crust is terrifying for many people, but the difference between a homemade crust and a manufactured butterless tube of tasteless dough is night and day. If you like to cook, it's very much worth overcoming your fears. Try the real thing.

2¹/2 cups all-purpose flour

1 teaspoon fine sea salt

1 teaspoon sugar

1 cup (2 sticks) unsalted butter, chilled and cut into small pieces

¹/4 to ¹/2 cup ice water

In a food processor fitted with a metal blade, combine the flour, salt, and sugar. Add the butter and process until the mixture resembles a coarse meal, 8 to 10 seconds.

With machine running, add ¹/4 cup of the ice water in a slow, steady stream. Pulse until the dough holds together without being sticky; be careful not to process for more than 30 seconds. To test, squeeze a small amount together: if it is crumbly, add more ice water 1 tablespoon at a time. You may not use the entire ¹/2 cup.

Transfer the dough to a lightly floured work surface and shape into 2 disks. Wrap the disks in plastic wrap and transfer to the freezer; chill until firm, about 30 minutes. Alternatively, refrigerate for at least 1 hour, or up to 2 days. The dough may be frozen, tightly wrapped in plastic, for up to 1 month.

To make a baked pie shell, follow the instructions for rolling out the dough, forming a single crust, and blind baking on page 18.

La Varenne Sweet Pie Pastry *Pâte Sucrée*

"Thwack, thwack" reverberated off the kitchen wall as Anne Willan demonstrated softening butter with a rolling pin. Now, that was scary. Who needs a microwave when you can bully the butter into soft submission? It was my first week in France, and I had certainly never seen that technique before. By the end of that first summer at La Varenne and endless fruit tarts later, Anne assured me that I could "thwack" with the best of them.

Traditionally, this pie crust is made by hand, not in a machine. I think it's important to learn things by hand to learn what they should feel like. But, there's potential for a real mess here, with making a well, beating butter with a rolling pin, and the push-me pull-me *fraiser* technique. So, you'll find instructions for both techniques.

11/2 cups all-purpose flour, plus more for rolling

1/3 cup sugar

1/2 teaspoon fine sea salt

3 large egg yolks, at room temperature, lightly beaten

1/2 teaspoon pure vanilla extract (optional)

6 tablespoons unsalted butter, slightly softened

To prepare in a food processor, combine the flour, sugar, and salt in a food processor fitted with a metal blade and pulse until combined. Add the butter and process until the mixture resembles coarse meal, about 10 seconds. With the processor running, add the yolks and vanilla through the feed tube, and pulse until the dough just holds together (no longer than 30 seconds).

Transfer the dough to a lightly floured work surface and shape into a disk. Wrap the dough in plastic wrap and transfer to the freezer; chill until firm, about 30 minutes. Alternatively, refrigerate for at least 1 hour, or up to 2 days. The dough may be frozen, tightly wrapped in plastic, for up to 1 month.

To prepare by hand, sift together the flour, sugar, and salt into a bowl. Make a well in the center and add the egg yolks, vanilla extract, and butter. Using the fingertips of one hand, gradually pull in the flour until the dough starts to form large crumbs. Turn the dough out onto a clean work surface and blend by pushing it away with your palm. (The French term for this technique is *fraiser*.) Gather the dough and flatten, forming a disk. Wrap the dough in plastic and chill in the freezer until firm, about 30 minutes. Alternatively, refrigerate for at least 1 hour (or up to 2 days), or freeze for up to 1 month.

Pat yourself on the back. As Anne would say heartily, "Well done!"

To make a baked pie shell, follow the instructions for rolling out the dough, forming a single crust, and blind baking on page 18.

All-American Pie Crust

PASTRY FOR 1 (9-INCH) PIE CRUST

This is a pie crust with "training wheels" that I learned at the side of my friend, teacher, and mentor Nathalie Dupree. Butter makes a delicious pie crust, but is far trickier to work with than shortening. Nathalie, blessed with "cold pastry hands," used to fuss at me, "Get your hot little hands off that pie dough." Warm hands, cold heart? Hmmpf.

For a double-crust pie, simply double the amounts and divide the dough before rolling out.

1 1/4 cups all-purpose flour, plus more for rolling

1/2 teaspoon fine sea salt

1/4 cup solid vegetable shortening, preferably Crisco, chilled and cut into pieces

1/4 cup (1/2 stick) unsalted butter, chilled and cut into pieces

3 to 8 tablespoons ice water

In a food processor fitted with a metal blade, combine the flour and salt, then add the vegetable shortening and butter. Process until the mixture resembles coarse meal, 8 to 10 seconds.

Add the ice water, 1 tablespoon at a time, pulsing to mix, until the dough holds together without being sticky or crumbly. Shape the dough into a disk and wrap in plastic wrap. Chill in the freezer until firm, about 30 minutes.

Flour a clean work surface and a rolling pin. (If you are making a double-crust pie or two pie shells, work with one disk at a time, keeping the second disk chilled.) Place a dough disk in the center of the floured surface. Starting in the center of the dough, roll to, but not over, the upper edge of the dough. Return to the center, and roll down to, but not over, the lower edge. Lift the dough, give it a quarter turn, and lay it on the work surface. Continue rolling, repeating the quarter turns, until you have a disk about 1/8 inch thick.

Ease the pastry into a 9-inch pie plate. To keep your crust from shrinking or tearing, snuggle your dough into the pie plate by lifting the edges and letting the weight settle it into the plate contours. Trim 1 inch larger than the diameter of the pie plate; fold the overhanging pastry under itself along the rim of the plate. For a simple decorative edge, press the tines of a fork around the folded pastry. To make a fluted edge, using both your finger and thumb, pinch and crimp the folded dough. Chill in the freezer until firm, about 30 minutes.

To blind bake, preheat the oven to 425°F. Crumple a piece of parchment paper, then lay it out flat over the bottom of the pastry. Weight the paper with pie weights, dried beans, or uncooked rice. This will keep the unfilled pie crust from puffing up in the oven.

For a partially baked shell that will be filled and baked further, bake for 20 minutes. Remove from the oven and remove the paper and weights. (You can reuse the rice or beans for blind baking a number of times.) The shell can now be filled and baked further, according to recipe directions. For a fully baked shell that will hold an uncooked filling, bake the pie shell until it is a deep golden brown, about 30 minutes total.

Quick Puff Pastry

MAKES ABOUT 2 POUNDS

Classic puff pastry begins with a basic dough called a *détrempe,* which is then rolled out and wrapped around a slab of butter. As the dough is repeatedly rolled, folded, and turned, the butter is distributed in thin sheets throughout the dough. When it bakes, the moisture in the butter creates steam, causing the dough to puff and separate into many flaky layers. It takes a lot of time to make because the dough needs lengthy rests between its many turns. Quick puff pastry abbreviates the process by cutting the butter into the flour as if you were making pie crust, but instead of simply rolling out the crust, you give the dough a quick series of turns and folds as you would for classic puff pastry.

2 1/2 cups all-purpose flour

3/4 teaspoon fine sea salt

1 1/2 cups (3 sticks) unsalted butter, chilled and cut into
  1/2-inch cubes

3/4 cup cold water

Sift together the flour and salt by pulsing in a food processor fitted with a metal blade. Add the butter and pulse three to five times, until the butter pieces are about the size of large lima beans. Add the water to the mixture and pulse again about three times until the dough is slightly moistened.

Turn the crumbly mass onto a lightly floured work surface. Using a rolling pin and bench scraper, shape the mass into a long rectangle. Using the bench scraper, carefully flip one-third of the rectangle toward the center. Then, flip the other end to the center, like folding a business letter. Rotate the dough 90 degrees.

Reshape and roll the dough into a rectangle. Repeat the folding and rotating process three more times for a total of four turns. If the dough becomes soft or sticky during this process, immediately refrigerate until firm. You can stop midturn.

After four turns, wrap the dough in plastic wrap so the dough can rest and the moisture will be evenly distributed throughout the dough. With your finger, make four indentations in the dough—one for each time the dough has been turned. You need to keep track of how many times the dough has been turned. Refrigerate the dough for at least 30 minutes, or until firm.

Unwrap the dough and discard the plastic. Keep your work surface and rolling pin well floured. Press down on each of the four sides of dough to seal its shape. With the rolling pin at the center of the dough, roll away from you. Return to the center and roll toward you. Repeat the folding and rotating process of the dough two times for a total of six times. Lightly roll the dough to flatten.

Wrap the dough in plastic wrap and chill for at least 2 hours before using it. It can be kept, refrigerated, for up to 2 days, or frozen for up to 3 months. Defrost in the refrigerator overnight before use.

Basic Crème Anglaise

MAKES 3 CUPS, OR 2 CUPS ICE CREAM WHEN FROZEN

Crème anglaise, or English custard, is a classic dessert sauce that can also be churned and transformed into ice cream. Vanilla is the classic recipe, but add peaches and a bit of peach purée and you have peach, adding melted chocolate and cocoa produces chocolate, and so on. Crème anglaise is a very versatile kitchen fundamental.

Whenever I make ice cream I am reminded of an experience years ago. My colleague Marnie and I had to pick up ice cream from a boutique gelateria to take to Connecticut for taping. It was the peak of summer. We packed the precious cargo in our cooler surrounded by dry ice to keep it frozen. (Dry ice is solid carbon dioxide and when it sublimates—not exactly the same as melting, but almost—it produces the white, wispy vapor sometimes used for dramatic effect at Halloween.) As we headed north for the hour-long drive to the studio, I started to feel light-headed. And Marnie did, too. Turns out we were DUI—of dry ice! That wispy vapor displaces the oxygen in the air, and if the concentration is too high, it can be dangerous. We made it safely, but lesson learned!

Pinch of fine sea salt, plus more for the ice

2 cups whole milk

1 vanilla bean, split and scraped or 1 tablespoon pure
   vanilla extract

6 large egg yolks

1/4 cup sugar

To prepare an ice bath, fill a large bowl halfway with ice cubes; toss salt generously among the cubes, and add a bit of water. Set aside.

Bring the milk almost to a boil in a saucepan. Add the vanilla seeds and bean. Cover and leave in a warm place to infuse vanilla flavor, about 15 minutes. Remove the bean, wash it to use again, and reheat the milk to boiling.

In a second saucepan, blend together the egg yolks, sugar, and a pinch of salt with a wooden spoon until thick and light, being careful not to make the mixture foamy. (Add pure vanilla extract, if using.) Whisk in half the hot milk, then whisk the mixture back into the remaining milk.

Heat gently, stirring constantly with a wooden spoon. Continue stirring the custard until the mixture is thick enough to coat the back of the spoon and it reaches 180°F on an instant-read thermometer. Remove from the heat.

Set a sieve over a large clean bowl, and pass the custard through the sieve.

Place the bowl in the ice bath and stir the custard until it has completely cooled. Lay a piece of plastic wrap directly on the surface of the custard to prevent a skin from forming. Store the custard, refrigerated, for up to 24 hours. Use as a dessert sauce or process according to machine instructions for French vanilla ice cream.

Pastry Cream *Crème Pâtissière*

MAKES 2 1/2 CUPS

Crème Pâtissière may sound fancy, but this is essentially vanilla pudding. I have always been more of a chocolate kind of girl, but Mama loves vanilla. She's had quarts of Mexican vanilla extract in her baking pantry for as long as I can remember. This can be served as pudding, as the base for a tart, or layered between crepes or even the *dacquiose* (page 240).

This recipe may seem excessively old school, so stuffy French. Many hot-shot chefs would scoff—there's no foam or espuma in sight. You know what? Taste it. It's delicious. Sometimes old-school is the way to go—and Mama is usually right

2 cups whole milk

1 vanilla bean, split and scraped, or 1 tablespoon pure
   vanilla extract

6 large egg yolks

1/2 cup sugar

1/3 cup all-purpose flour

Pinch of fine sea salt

Bring the milk almost to a boil in a saucepan. Add the vanilla seeds and bean. Cover and leave in a warm place to infuse the vanilla flavor, about 15 minutes. Remove the bean, wash it to use again, and reheat the milk to boiling.

In a bowl, beat the egg yolks and the sugar with a wooden spoon, until thick and light. Stir in the flour and the pinch of salt to make a smooth paste. (Add the vanilla extract, if using.) Whisk the scalded milk into the egg mixture, blending well, then return the mixture to the pan. Place over low heat and whisk until boiling. (Make sure the cream is perfectly smooth before letting it come to a boil!) Cook the cream, whisking constantly, for 2 minutes.

Strain the cream into a bowl. To use immediately, cool over an ice bath, stirring often, until cooled completely. If refrigerating for later use, to prevent a skin from forming, press a piece of buttered plastic wrap onto the surface and refrigerate until cool, several hours or overnight. Store for up to 2 days in the refrigerator.

Caramel Sauce

MAKES ABOUT 1 1/2 CUPS

Meme always made her caramel sauce in a cast iron skillet. The heavy-duty pan is helpful in preventing burning. Now, I'm not saying Meme was wrong—because she made many a caramel in her day—but it's hard to tell the color in a dark pan. My suggestion is to use a heavy-duty stainless steel pan to play it safe.

A drizzle of this would taste good over red Georgia clay, it's so delicious. Sometimes I use soft goat cheese instead of the heavy cream to create Chevre Caramel Sauce, something truly out of this world. It's perfect with dark chocolate and full-flavored desserts.

1 cup sugar

1/2 cup water

Juice of 1/2 lemon

1/2 cup (1 stick) unsalted butter

1/2 cup heavy cream or fresh goat cheese

1 vanilla bean, split and scraped, or 1 tablespoon pure vanilla extract

Pinch of fine sea salt

In a heavy saucepan, combine the sugar, water, and lemon juice. Heat over low heat, swirling the pan occasionally, until the sugar dissolves. Increase the heat to high and bring to a boil. Continue to boil, without stirring, until it begins to turn golden around the edges. (It is important not to stir, or the syrup may crystallize).

Meanwhile, combine the butter and cream in a small saucepan. Heat until the butter melts. Keep warm. When the syrup begins to color, lower the heat, and continue boiling to a deep golden color. It will darken rapidly. Remove the pan from the heat and add the butter and cream. (Be very careful because the syrup will furiously bubble up in the pan.) Return the pan to the heat and stir until the caramel is completely dissolved. Add the vanilla and a pinch of salt. Stir to combine.

Serve warm or at room temperature. Store the sauce in an airtight container in the refrigerator for up to 1 month; it will solidify. Reheat it over a double boiler or in a heavy saucepan over very low heat, adding a bit of warm water if it is too thick and not of sauce or pouring consistency.

Sugar Stages

When I was in culinary school, our chef made us test the temperature of sugar syrups with our fingers. French masochist. Only a few dared, but I certainly wasn't going to be intimidated. We foolish few held our fingers in ice water until it was time to make the quick dip to test the stage of the syrup. I managed to do it, but I got still got burned. One of my fellow students who was too timid (and wise) to work with her fingers accidentally drizzled sugar on my finger from her wooden spoon. My finger burning, I instinctively put my finger in my mouth instead of the adjacent bowl of ice water—and burned my mouth in the process. It was one of those "can't win for losing" moments. I suggest you forgo the daredevil routine; it's dangerous. Get yourself a candy thermometer.

The key to sugar work is temperature. The final texture of candy depends on the sugar concentration. As the syrup boils, water evaporates, the sugar concentration increases, and the boiling point rises. A given temperature corresponds to a particular sugar concentration. The stage refers to the reaction of a spoonful of sugar syrup drizzled into cold water.

Thread Stage: 230°F to 235°F

At this relatively low temperature, there is still a lot of water left in the syrup. When you drop a little of this syrup into cold water to cool, it forms a liquid thread that will not ball up, but simply dissolves in the water. Cooking sugar to this stage simply produces syrup, not candy.

Soft-Ball Stage: 234°F to 242°F

At this temperature, sugar syrup dropped into cold water will form a soft, flexible ball. Fudge, classic pralines, and fondant are made by cooking sugar to the soft-ball stage.

Firm-Ball Stage: 244°F to 248°F

Drizzle a little of this syrup in cold water. It will form a firm ball that will retain its shape when you take it out of the water, but will remain pliable and will flatten when squeezed between your fingers. Caramels are cooked to the firm-ball stage.

Hard-Ball Stage: 250°F to 266°F

At this stage, the syrup will form thick threads as it drips from the spoon. Very little water remains and the sugar concentration is rather high. The syrup drizzled into cold water will form a hard ball. If you take the ball out of the water, it won't flatten, but you can still change its shape by squashing it. Nut brittles, nougat, marshmallows, and divinity are cooked to the hard-ball stage.

Soft-Crack Stage: 270°F to 290°F

As the syrup reaches the soft-crack stage, the bubbles on top of the boiling syrup will become smaller and closer together. When you drop a bit of this syrup into cold water, it will solidify into threads that, when removed from the water, are flexible, not brittle. They will bend slightly before cracking and breaking. Butterscotch is cooked to the soft-crack stage.

Hard-Crack Stage: 300°F to 310°F

The hard-crack stage is the highest temperature before caramel. If you spoon a little of the molten syrup into cold water, it will form hard, brittle threads that crack and break when bent. Toffee and lollipops are cooked to the hard-crack stage.

Caramel: 330°F to 350°F

At the lower end of the temperature range of caramel, all the water has boiled away and the pure sugar is liquid and light amber. As the temperature rises, the sugar becomes richer and darker. Caramelized sugar is used for spun sugar and also can be used to give a candy coating to nuts, or made into Burnt Caramel Icing (page 253). Above 350°F caramel tastes burnt and bitter.

2

Starters and Nibbles

Impeccable petite appetizers make ideal bites to serve as nibbles with predinner drinks. As full-on cocktail fare, small and savory nibbles are perfect for the shaken and stirred crowd. Hors d'oeuvres used to be considered before or outside the meal, but have increasingly become part of the meal, or sometimes the meal itself.

The trend today is to call little bites tapas, the term for a wide variety of appetizers, or snacks, in Spanish cuisine. It is as if the term *hors d'oeuvres* is as outdated as the formerly de rigueur party dish, bacon-wrapped water chestnuts. Somehow it doesn't seem right to call a very traditional Southern nibble, such as pigs in a blanket, a tapa. Technically, I think it would be a canapé, but that doesn't seem quite right either. I've seen pigs in a blanket range from Vienna sausages and canned biscuit dough to artisan-made sausage wrapped in puff pastry. The phrase "lipstick on a pig" comes to mind. However, there's one truth no one, myself included, can deny. As sure as death and taxes, people may look down their tapas-sniffing noses at pigs in a blanket, but you can bet money it's the first empty platter on the buffet.

That truism aside, a party menu needs to be a balance of dishes: some that can be made ahead and served chilled or at room temperature, some freshly assembled or prepared, and some basic dishes that are perhaps as simple as opening a mason jar. Boring and basic are not the same thing. The most interesting bites are those that are a little out of the proverbial (cracker) box.

I prefer homemade and handmade, but I am a cook. It's what I do. I'd be telling a tale, though, if I didn't reveal to you that I also buy premade products. I try to buy the best quality, but I do buy what some overachieving hosts might deem shortcuts. Heck, even my former boss, Martha Stewart, the doyenne of DIY, suggests in her *Hors d'Oeuvres Handbook* to serve bowls of edamame or pistachio nuts.

Let the guests help themselves; there's no need to stuff, spread, and frantically fill your way into a tired tizzy. This isn't a bridge group or your grandmother's tea party. Put the doilies away. Please.

I generally have a Southern-kissed hors d'oeuvres platter made with quality store-bought ingredients, such as olives, pickled okra, tomato confit, and pickled green beans. I love the look of a whole country ham surrounded by a mountain of biscuits on a wooden board with bowls of room temperature sweet butter and pungent mustard. And, if you don't want to make the Mini Country Ham Cheddar Biscuits (page 40), buy them from a local bakery or restaurant. I know for a fact that one of Atlanta's top hostesses serves Mary B's tea biscuits, and no one is the wiser.

In this chapter, I've included recipes to create more informal and relaxed menus that satisfy the guests without sacrificing you, the host. They marry ease and elegance, flavor and finesse, and of course, each Basic recipe has a Brilliant alternative.

Welcome your guests. Focus on flavor and good ingredients. *À votre santé*—and relax and enjoy.

Southern Ratatouille

SERVES 4 TO 6

The French have ratatouille; the Sicilians, caponata; the Basque, pipérade; Indians, chutney; and Southerners have relish. All nationalities have gardens brimming full with fresh vegetables at the height of a hot summer. Southerners generally consider relish a cooked or pickled vegetable or fruit that is typically used as a condiment, starter, or nibble. It has always been an obligatory component of major feasts in my family. China cabinets across the South are filled with ornate cut-glass relish trays, multichambered vessels for holding various relishes. Relish was fairly recently perceived as a relic from an elderly relative's dinner table, but with the resurgence of home canning, relishes have returned.

2 tablespoons pure olive oil

1 onion, preferably Vidalia, chopped

2 cloves garlic, finely chopped

1 large eggplant (about 2 pounds), cut into 3/4-inch cubes

2 zucchini (about 2 pounds), cut into 1-inch cubes

Coarse salt and freshly ground black pepper

3/4 cup water

1 red bell pepper, cored, seeded, and chopped

3 tomatoes, cored, seeded, and chopped, or 1 (28-ounce) can whole tomatoes with juice

1 pound small tender okra, ends trimmed

1 teaspoon chopped fresh thyme

1/2 cup chopped fresh basil

Heat the oil a large, heavy saucepan with a tight-fitting lid over medium heat. Add the onion and cook, stirring occasionally, until translucent, 3 to 5 minutes. Add the garlic and cook until fragrant, 45 to 60 seconds. Stir in the eggplant and zucchini; season generously with salt and pepper. Add the water; cover, and simmer, stirring once, until the vegetables are beginning to soften, about 5 minutes. Stir in the bell peppers; simmer, covered, until softened, about 5 minutes. Stir in the tomatoes, okra, and thyme; bring to a boil.

Decrease the heat to medium-low. Partially cover; simmer, stirring often, until the vegetables are tender, 15 to 20 minutes. Remove from the heat.

Just before serving, stir in the basil. Taste and adjust for seasoning with salt and pepper. Serve warm, at room temperature, or cold.

Brilliant: Short Recipe
Crispy Cornmeal Cups

Lots of things can be used as a vessel for that perfect hors d'oeuvre bite, including those store-bought pastry and phyllo cups available in the freezer section of most grocery stores and markets. What's really Brilliant? A simple cornmeal crust that pairs wonderfully with the savory vegetable relish.

Position a rack in the center of the oven and preheat to 350°F. In the bowl of a heavy-duty mixer fitted with the paddle attachment, combine 6 tablespoons unsalted butter and 3 ounces room-temperature Neufchâtel or cream cheese. Combine 1 cup all-purpose flour, 1/2 cup fine cornmeal, and a pinch of fine sea salt in a small bowl. Add gradually to butter mixture, mixing constantly until well incorporated. Divide the dough into 1-inch balls and press into a nonstick mini muffin tins, using your thumbs to form cups that come up the sides. Make the dough cups as even as possible. Bake until pale golden brown, about 18 minutes. Transfer to a rack to cool. Store in an airtight container for up to 1 week. Makes about 30.

To serve, spoon 1 tablespoon of the vegetables into the cups and serve immediately. You will use about 2 cups of the ratatouille.

Butter Bean Croustades

MAKES ABOUT 32

Butter beans are one of my very favorite things on earth. I love them. There is an expression, "what grows together, goes together," and that sums up how I prefer to cook. I am particular about combining flavors, and even though I blend my Southern tradition with my French training, I think fusion is more akin to con-fusion. In my mind, flavors have to make sense together in a flavor as well as in an emotional sense. What thrives at the peak of a smoldering hot Southern summer? Tender butter beans and fragrant basil—both love the heat.

2 cups shelled fresh butter beans (about 1 1/2 pounds unshelled) or frozen butter beans

4 cups water, plus more if needed

1 onion, preferably Vidalia, halved

2 tablespoons canola oil

Coarse salt and freshly ground black pepper

1 baguette, sliced diagonally 1/4 inch thick

2 tablespoons extra-virgin olive oil, for the bread

1 shallot, finely chopped

2 cloves garlic, halved, for the toasts, plus 1 clove garlic, very finely chopped

1 small jalapeño, cored, seeded, and chopped

Finely grated zest and juice of 1/2 lemon

6 large fresh basil leaves

16 grape tomatoes, halved

Combine the butter beans, water, onion, and 1 tablespoon of the canola oil in a saucepan over medium-high heat. Season with salt and pepper. Bring to a boil, then decrease the heat and simmer, occasionally skimming the scum that floats to the top, until the beans are tender, 35 to 45 minutes for fresh or according to package instructions if frozen.

Meanwhile, position an oven rack 4 inches below the broiler and preheat the broiler. To make the toasts, arrange the baguette slices on a baking sheet and brush one side with some of the olive oil. Broil until brown, 2 to 3 minutes. Turn the toasts and broil the other side until brown, 2 to 3 minutes. Remove the toasts from the oven and while warm, rub one side of each toast with the cut surfaces of the halved garlic cloves. Transfer to a rack to cool.

Reserve 1 cup of the cooking water. Drain the beans in a colander and shake well to remove excess moisture. Remove and discard the onion or set aside for another use. Set the beans aside to cool.

In the now-drained saucepan, heat another 1 tablespoon of the canola oil over medium-low heat. Add the shallot and cook until translucent, about 3 minutes. Add the chopped garlic and cook over low heat until fragrant, 45 to 60 seconds. Add the jalapeño and cook for 1 minute longer.

Transfer the drained beans and the shallot mixture to a food processor fitted with a metal blade. Add the lemon zest, lemon juice, and basil. Season with salt and pepper. Purée until smooth, adding a little of the reserved cooking water, if necessary.

Taste and adjust for seasoning with salt and pepper. Spread some of the bean mixture on the prepared toasts. Drizzle lightly with any remaining olive oil. Top with the tomatoes. Sprinkle with a little salt and pepper to finish.

Making Ahead The toasts can be made up to 2 days ahead and stored at room temperature in an airtight container. And, if you have time, make the spread a day ahead, too. The flavors marry and blend nicely if refrigerated overnight in an airtight container. Taste and adjust for seasoning before proceeding with the assembly.

Brilliant: Short Recipe
Basil Oil

Layering on the flavor of the sun-kissed basil elevates the Basic Butter Bean Croustades to Brilliant.

To make the basil oil, heat $1/2$ cup pure olive oil in a small saucepan over medium-low heat until very warm. Combine the heated oil, the leaves of 4 large sprigs basil, and $1/4$ teaspoon sugar in a blender. Purée until smooth and well combined. Pour into a bowl, cover, and chill for 2 hours to let the flavor develop, then strain through a fine-mesh sieve lined with cheesecloth. Makes $1/2$ cup. Store in an airtight container for up to 2 weeks. Using a small spoon or squeeze bottle, drizzle over the croustades and serve.

Anne's Roasted Pepper and Cheese Gratin

SERVES 6

Sometimes roasted red pepper can be overpowering, but this is a full-flavored combination that is reminiscent of French country cooking. This simple yet delicious combination can be achieved at a moment's notice with a well-stocked pantry. Having a jar of peppers in your pantry is not a sin, nor is using a jar of best-quality store-bought tomato sauce. If you do use bottled red peppers, I suggest draining and rinsing them under cold running water.

I like serving this in individual portions for a first course (pictured at left of photo). The gratins can be put together a day ahead and held in the refrigerator. Just let them come to room temperature before baking.

1 tablespoon extra-virgin olive oil, for the gratin dish

2 red bell peppers and 1 poblano pepper, or 1 (12-ounce) jar roasted red peppers

10 1/2 ounces fresh goat cheese, thickly sliced

2 teaspoons fresh rosemary leaves, finely chopped

2 teaspoons chopped fresh oregano

1 1/2 to 2 cups Sauce Tomate (page 228) or best-quality store-bought pasta sauce, at room temperature

30 Niçoise or brine-cured black olives, pitted

Freshly ground black pepper

Garlic Toasts (page 80), for serving

Position the oven rack about 5 inches below the broiler and preheat. Brush a medium gratin dish with the olive oil.

If you are using fresh peppers, place the peppers directly on a gas burner over high heat or on a grill. As each side turns puffy and black, turn the peppers with tongs. (If you don't have a gas stove or grill, place the peppers on a rimmed baking sheet and broil in the oven, turning as each side becomes charred.) When the peppers are charred on all sides, transfer them to a large bowl and immediately cover with plastic wrap. The steam will help loosen the skins. Let the peppers sweat until they are cool enough to handle, about 10 minutes.

Transfer the peppers to a clean cutting board. Peel off the blackened skin and discard. Halve the peppers and open them flat. Use the blade of a paring knife to remove the seeds, hard seed cluster, stem, and whitish ribs. Slice the cleaned peppers lengthwise into strips about 1 inch wide. Avoid rinsing the home-charred

peppers since it dilutes the smoky sweet flavor of the peppers; instead, wipe clean with paper towels. If using jarred peppers, rinse and cut into strips.

Scatter the roasted red pepper strips and sliced goat cheese slices on the bottom of the prepared gratin dish. Top with a sprinkling of half of the herbs. Spoon over the tomato sauce to coat evenly. Top with the olives and the remaining herbs. Season with black pepper.

Transfer the gratin to the oven. Broil until bubbling and hot, about 5 minutes. Serve with the garlic toasts.

Brilliant: Short Recipe
Cheese-Stuffed Roasted Red Peppers

Put in just a few minutes in additional preparation of the peppers and you will have a showstopping Brilliant dish (pictured at right of photo).

Increase the number of peppers to 6 or, for an extra-special presentation, use a smaller chile such as Fresno or baby bell peppers. Roast them as directed in the Basic recipe, but instead of slicing the roasted, peeled peppers into strips, cut a lengthwise slit in each pepper; discard the seeds, leaving the stems intact. (If it tears a little don't worry, it can be coated in sauce.) Set aside. Preheat the oven to 400°F. Combine the goat cheese and herbs in a bowl. Season with salt and freshly ground black pepper. Divide into 6 portions and shape each portion into a cylinder. Slip 1 cheese cylinder into each prepared pepper. Transfer the peppers to the prepared baking dish. Spoon the sauce and olives over the peppers. Bake until heated through, about 10 minutes. Serve with garlic toasts.

Pickled Vegetables

SERVES 6 TO 8

Southerners are fond of pickles, but we're not alone. There's been an enormous resurgence of canning and "putting up" across the country. In French cooking, the term *à la grecque* refers to vegetables, most often mushrooms, lightly pickled in a seasoned mixture of oil, lemon juice, and water, and served cold. In this recipe I've combined a basic American-style refrigerator pickle made with vinegar and spices, and the French version made with lemon and oil.

Pickled vegetables are a traditional accompaniment to cured meats. The vinegary impertinence of the pungent pickle cuts the fat of the meat; the richness of the meat mellows the piquancy of the vegetables. Serve these quick pickles with the Pork Terrine (page 37), or pick up some country ham, pâté de campagne, salumi, or saucisson sec at a local gourmet market.

2 teaspoons coriander seeds

1 teaspoon mustard seeds

1 teaspoon allspice berries

3/4 cup dry white wine

1/2 cup apple cider vinegar

1/2 cup water

Freshly grated zest and juice of 1 lemon

1/3 cup pure olive oil

Coarse salt and freshly ground black pepper

8 ounces small white button mushrooms, stems trimmed

8 ounces small cremini mushrooms, stems trimmed

8 ounces haricot verts or young tender green beans, ends trimmed

1/2 cauliflower, cut into florets

8 ounces small tender okra, ends trimmed

2 teaspoons finely chopped fresh flat-leaf parsley

Combine the coriander seeds, mustard seeds, and allspice berries in a piece of cheesecloth. Place in a very large pot with the wine, vinegar, water, lemon zest, lemon juice, and olive oil; season with salt and pepper. Bring to a boil over medium-high heat.

Add the mushrooms and vegetables, stirring to combine. Cover the pot and bring to a simmer over medium heat, gently shaking the pan a few times during the first few minutes of cooking. Simmer gently, covered, until the vegetables are just tender, about 8 minutes.

Using a slotted spoon, remove the mushrooms and vegetables from the pot to a bowl. Set aside. Increase the heat under the liquid to high. Bring to a boil, uncovered, and simmer until the liquid is reduced by half, about 8 minutes. Remove from the heat. Pour the reduced liquid into a bowl over a bowl of ice. Stir until cool. Once cooled, pour over the vegetables. Taste and adjust for seasoning with salt and pepper.

Serve garnished with the parsley. Store in an airtight container in the refrigerator up to 6 days.

Brilliant: Short Recipe
Basil Aioli

Elevate the Basic Pickled Vegetables to Brilliant with Basil Aioli as a dipping sauce, or for a more interesting presentation, spoon some of the sauce into the bottom of short glasses and top with the vegetables.

To make the basil aioli, whisk to combine 2 large egg yolks, 1 teaspoon Dijon mustard, finely grated zest and juice of 1 lemon, and 1 finely chopped garlic clove in a bowl until smooth and light. In a slow, steady stream, whisk in the oil, a drop at a time, until the mixture starts to stiffen and thicken. Add 2 tablespoons very finely chopped fresh basil. Taste and adjust the seasoning with coarse salt and freshly ground white pepper. Store in an airtight container in the refrigerator for up to 2 days. Makes 1 cup.

Shrimp Rillettes

SERVES 6

Rillettes are found throughout France, but they are a specialty of the Loire Valley, traditionally made with pork or duck; they are essentially pulverized confit: shredded meat smashed with fat to produce a rich, rustic paste for spreading on bread. First the meat is cooked slowly over low heat until very tender—this is the *confit*—then it is raked into small shreds and blended with the warm cooking fat to form a rustic paste—the *rillettes.* Rillettes, like confit, were originally a means of preservation. The meat could be stored in crocks under a layer of fat in a cool place. The thing to remember is that pâtés and rillettes aren't considered upscale delicacies in France; they are simple everyday food.

Sometimes I prepare free nibbles for book signings. You could offer cotton balls on toothpicks, and people would devour every fluffy bite. However, when I offered this recipe, there was a veritable stampede. Be warned.

1 tablespoon canola oil

2 shallots, chopped

1 bay leaf, preferably fresh

8 ounces large shrimp (21/25 count), peeled and deveined

1/4 cup dry white wine

Coarse salt and freshly ground white pepper

3 tablespoons unsalted butter

4 ounces Neufchâtel or cream cheese, at room temperature

Finely grated zest and juice of 1/2 lemon

2 tablespoons chopped fresh chives

Belgian endive, cored and separated into individual leaves, crackers, or croutons, for serving

Heat the oil in a large skillet over medium heat. Add shallots and bay leaf. Cook until the shallots are translucent, about 3 minutes. Add the shrimp and wine. Season with salt and white pepper and cook until the shrimp are pink and cooked through, about 3 minutes. Remove and discard the bay leaf. Transfer the mixture to a food processor fitted with a metal blade.

Add the butter and Neufchâtel. Purée until smooth. Add the lemon zest and juice, chives, and salt and pepper to taste. Pulse to mix and transfer to a 1 1/2-cup crock or to 3 small jars. Cover with plastic wrap, pressing the plastic wrap directly onto surface of shrimp mixture to prevent a skin from forming.

Refrigerate for at least 8 hours or up to 3 days. Let stand at room temperature for 30 minutes before serving with Belgian endive, crackers, or croutons.

Brilliant: Short Recipe
Fennel Flatbread

Serving the Shrimp Rillettes with store-bought crackers is Basic; homemade crackers are definitely above and beyond but scrumptious and Brilliant. This recipe is based on the flatbread served at Canoe, in Atlanta, and was shared with me by chef Carvel Gould. She told me that one of her regular patrons had placed the dough between two baking sheets and run over it in her car to flatten it. I suggest a rolling pin and a little elbow grease.

Preheat the oven to 350°F. Brush a rimmed baking sheet with olive oil. In the bowl of a food processor fitted with a metal blade, combine 2 1/4 cups bread flour, 1/2 teaspoon fine sea salt, 1/4 cup fresh thyme leaves, and 1 tablespoon fennel seeds. Pulse to combine. Add 3/4 cup cold water and pulse until the dough comes away from the sides of the bowl, 45 to 60 seconds. Turn the dough out onto a silicone baking sheet or lightly floured surface and knead until smooth and elastic, 5 to 7 minutes. Form the dough into a ball. Portion the dough into ten 2-ounce balls. One at a time, working on a silicone baking sheet and using a lightly floured rolling pin, roll each ball as flat as possible. Season with salt and pepper, then give the dough one more roll. Place two or three at a time on the prepared baking sheet. Bake until golden brown, about 20 minutes. Remove to a rack to cool. Repeat with the remaining dough. Makes 10.

Curried Chicken Wings with Peach Dipping Sauce

MAKES ABOUT 24

Madras curry is a fairly hot curry blend, most often deep red from a heavy amount of powdered chile. Oddly enough, for a region that until recently considered any flavor other than bacon fat to be exotic, there is a history of curry in the South, which entered our region through the seaports of Savannah and Charleston. Curried chicken salad was once considered a very proper Southern Junior League sort of ladies tea or lunch delicacy. Some of those ladies might not consider a wing to be an appropriate nibble for party guests. In my opinion, with that built-in handle, chicken wings are perfect.

Wings

3 pounds chicken wings (12 to 14 whole wings)

1 teaspoon Madras or spicy curry powder

1/2 teaspoon ground turmeric

1/4 teaspoon cayenne pepper, or to taste

2 tablespoons soy sauce

2 tablespoons canola oil

2 to 3 jalapeños, cored, seeded, and very finely chopped, plus more for garnish

2 cloves garlic, very finely chopped

Coarse salt and freshly ground black pepper

Dipping Sauce

1/2 cup plain low-fat or whole-milk Greek-style yogurt

3 tablespoons peach preserves

1/4 teaspoon hot sauce, or to taste

Coarse salt and freshly ground black pepper

Cilantro sprigs, for garnish

To prepare the chicken wings, cut off the wing tips (reserve to make stock), and halve the wings at the joint. In a large bowl, combine the wings, curry powder, turmeric, cayenne, soy sauce, canola oil, jalapeños, garlic, salt, and pepper. Toss to coat. Cover and refrigerate for at least 1 hour, or overnight.

Meanwhile, to make the sauce, combine the yogurt, preserves, and hot sauce. Season with salt and pepper. Cover and refrigerate until serving.

Remove the marinated wings from the refrigerator and let come to room temperature.

Preheat the oven to 400°F. Line a rimmed baking sheet with aluminum foil, then set a large wire rack on the foil. (I don't like to use a nonstick baking liner on the baking sheet in this instance because the curry can stain the silicone.)

Transfer the wings without crowding to the prepared baking sheet.

Bake until the wings are deep brown and the juices run clear, turning once, 15 to 20 minutes per side. (If you like charred bits, after the 40 minutes, turn the oven on to broil for about 5 more minutes.)

Taste the yogurt dipping sauce and adjust for seasoning with salt and pepper. Garnish with cilantro and serve the hot wings with the dipping sauce on the side.

Brilliant: Technique
Chicken "Lollipops"

I first learned this watching Jacques Pépin on television. It's impossible to watch him without learning something. This converts regular old chicken wings to Brilliant hors d'oeuvres.

To prepare the "lollipops," cut off the wing tips (reserve to make stock), and halve the wings at the joint. (This will leave you with the drumette and flat.) Using a paring knife, cut the tendons at the narrower end of each drumette joint. Hold that end with a kitchen towel and scrape down the meat as far as possible toward the thicker end to make a plump lollipop shape. Then, take each flat and cut through the cartilage at one end of each piece, separating the bones. Scrape the meat down the larger bone to make a lollipop shape; remove and discard the smaller bone. Proceed with the Basic recipe to marinate as instructed.

Sautéed Spiced Chicken Livers

SERVES 4 TO 6

I love liver. Mama and my sister prefer gizzards, but when you chew them, they bounce back while you are chewing a little too much for me. I once brought my mother a large can of duck gizzard confit from France. I didn't have to purchase it in a specialty store. *Confit de gibier* is a merely a few steps from canned tuna and crackers in a typical French grocery store. Perhaps more interesting is that duck gizzards are available in those number 10 cans we're more accustomed to for pork and beans stateside. Mama's response to her savory snack? You would have thought there was an Hermès scarf in that tin.

Quatre épices means "four spices," although some versions contain a mixture of five; it is a traditional French ground spice blend that usually contains a combination of both white and black peppercorns, cinnamon, nutmeg, ginger, and cloves. If you don't want to make your own, or order it online, McCormick's sells Chinese five-spice powder, with a similar flavor profile, which makes it a perfectly acceptable substitute.

1 tablespoon canola oil

1 onion, preferably Vidalia, finely chopped

1 clove garlic, very finely chopped

1 pound chicken livers, tough membranes and fat removed

1 sprig thyme

1/2 cup dry white wine

1 teaspoon quatre épices

Coarse salt and freshly ground black pepper

Toasted brioche, for serving

Heat the oil in large, heavy skillet over medium heat. Add the onion and cook until translucent, 3 to 5 minutes. Add the garlic and cook until fragrant, 45 to 60 seconds. Increase the heat to medium-high and add the chicken livers and thyme. Sauté until lightly browned, 2 to 4 minutes. Add the wine and cook until most of the liquid evaporates, about 3 minutes. Remove from the heat and remove the thyme sprig. Taste and adjust for seasoning with salt and pepper.

Spoon the livers onto warmed serving plates and accompany with the toasted brioche.

Brilliant: Short Recipe
Chicken Liver Pâté

Some folks won't touch liver, but pâté? That's Brilliant.

To make the pâté, transfer the sautéed livers to a food processor fitted with a metal blade. Add 1/2 cup (1 stick) unsalted butter; purée until smooth and creamy. Taste and adjust for seasoning with salt and pepper. (It can be a little on the salty side because it will be served cold, which slightly dulls the seasoning.) Transfer to several small crocks or ramekins. Press a piece of plastic wrap directly onto the surface of the pâté and refrigerate until firm, about 4 hours or overnight. Serve with toasted brioche. Because of the richness, it's also nice to serve piquant cornichons or Pickled Vegetables (page 32) alongside. Serves 4 to 6.

In the Pink

Sel rose (also known as pink salt), a mixture of sodium chloride, potassium nitrate, and natural red coloring, is a preserving salt that helps meats keep their rosy color. It is available online and in gourmet markets. To use, place the livers in a bowl and toss with 1 teaspoon sel rose. Proceed with the recipe. The livers do not brown in the pan, but stay pink and the resulting Brilliant pâté is pink, as well.

Pork Terrine

Containing three different forms of pork, this is a real country pâté—country French and country Southern. When I first moved to France, the weekly farmer's market was a menacing combination of pleasure and pain. My eyes were seeing food for the first time as I had never seen it, but my Southern ears struggled with the thick country French accents, and let me just say my honeyed drawl and the French "r" are not friends. The worst part of all was the elderly French women who would run rough-shod over me. I'd be standing at the counter, wanting to order terrine, and everyone would be mumbling, waiting for me to decide. At best, the bevy of pinched face women would not-so-gently press me forward; at worst, they would literally push me out of the way. It was if I was mute, no amount of *excusez–moi* mattered. All I really wanted to do was cuss out one of them, which I would have never done, but just thinking about it made me feel better.

In my effort to take the fear out of pâté and be as polite as possible to you, I want to make this simple. Make sure to use shoulder so the mixture will contain enough fat. Don't be intimidated, just think of it as meat loaf.

10 to 12 thin slices bacon

1½ pounds pork shoulder, cut into cubes

4 ounces country ham, skin and fat removed, cut into
   cubes or strips

4 ounces chicken livers

1 tablespoon unsalted butter

1 onion, preferably Vidalia, chopped

Pinch of ground allspice

Pinch of cayenne pepper

2 large eggs, lightly beaten

2 tablespoons bourbon

2 bay leaves, preferably fresh

2 sprigs thyme

Coarse salt and freshly ground black pepper

Preheat the oven to 350°F. Line a 12½ x 4-inch terrine mold with the bacon, reserving several slices for the top.

Combine the pork, ham, and liver in a bowl. Transfer the meats to the freezer until quite firm but not frozen, 15 to 20 minutes.

While the meats are chilling, begin making the filling. Heat the butter in a small frying pan over medium heat. Add the onion and sauté until translucent, 3 to 5 minutes. Set aside to cool.

Work the chilled meats and cooled onion through the coarse plate of a meat grinder into a large bowl, or process a little bit at a time in the bowl of a food processor fitted with a metal blade. Stir in the allspice, cayenne, eggs, and bourbon. (Sauté a spoonful of the mixture in a bit of oil and taste. It should be quite spicy, as it will be served cold later.) Adjust the seasoning of the mixture, as needed. Spread the mixture in the terrine mold and smooth the top. Cover the top with the remaining bacon, trimming it to fit the mold. Put the bay leaves and thyme sprigs on top and cover the terrine with the lid.

Make a water bath by filling a roasting pan half full with hot water and bring to a boil on the stovetop. Add the terrine. Transfer the roasting pan to the oven and bake until the temperature registers 165°F on an instant-read thermometer, 1 to 1½ hours.

Remove the terrine from the water bath and let it cool to tepid. (For safety purposes, leave the hot water in the oven to cool completely before removing.) Remove the lid and set a 2-pound weight on top to compress the filling. A brick tightly wrapped in plastic wrap is an ideal size for many terrines. Or, cut a piece of cardboard and wrap in aluminum foil, then set a couple of cans on top. Chill the terrine until cold and

CONTINUED

firm, about 12 hours. Remove the weight, cover the mold again with the lid, and store in the refrigerator, preferably for 1 to 3 days before serving.

Brilliant: Short Recipe
White Wine Mustard
(Moutarde au Vin Blanc)

What could be more Brilliant than homemade mustard to go with the terrine?

Combine 1/3 cup yellow mustard seeds with 1/2 cup white wine and 2/3 cup white wine vinegar in a glass or stainless-steel bowl. Let sit for 48 hours. In a second bowl, combine 1/2 cup mustard powder and 1/2 cup water and mix until smooth. Let rest for 20 minutes. Transfer the seeds and their soaking liquid to a food processor. Process until the seeds become creamy, 4 to 6 minutes. (It's important to really process until smooth; this takes an entire 4 to 6 minutes.) Add the mustard-water mixture, 2 teaspoons sugar, 1/2 teaspoon ground allspice, and a pinch of ground turmeric. Process until well combined. Store in an airtight container in the refrigerator for at least 1 week before using to let the flavors develop. Store the mustard in an airtight container in the refrigerator for up to 1 month. Makes 2 cups.

Pigs in a Blanket Bites

MAKES 36

The smoky flavor of highly spiced andouille is a cornerstone of Cajun cuisine, and is featured in classic dishes such as jambalaya, gumbo, and red beans and rice. LaPlace, Louisiana, about 30 miles outside of New Orleans, is "the place" to find the authentic Cajun sausage made from pork shoulder, garlic, peppery seasoning, and pecan smoke.

I'm putting some of that aforementioned lipstick on these pigs in a blanket. Puff pastry is the pastry equivalent of a pashmina scarf. Wrapped around andouille sausage and dusted with cornmeal and whole mustard seeds, these have a crispy, toothsome bite. Regardless of how fancy I've made it, this little nibble is still dead easy and your guests will love it, although they may think you've gone a bit high on the hog.

1 pound Quick Puff Pastry (page 19) or 1 (14-ounce) box
    store-bought puff pastry

All-purpose flour, for rolling out

1 large egg

1 tablespoon water

18 ounces (6 sausages) fully cooked andouille sausage

2 tablespoons yellow mustard seeds

2 tablespoons very fine yellow cornmeal

Creole mustard, for serving

Preheat the oven to 400°F. Line a rimmed baking sheet with a silicone baking liner or parchment paper.

Place the puff pastry on a lightly floured work surface. Sprinkle the pastry with a little flour, and roll out to a thickness of 1/8 inch. Brush away any excess flour and trim the edges to form a 12-inch square. Slice in half horizontally, then again in thirds vertically to make six 4 x 6-inch rectangles. (Layer the resulting scraps on top of one another—don't bunch them all together—and save for another use. Wrap in plastic wrap and store in the freezer for up to 3 months.)

In a small bowl, whisk together the egg and water. Brush the rectangles with the egg wash. Place 1 cooked sausage along the long edge of a rectangle (its tips will extend out either end). Roll up the pastry around the sausage and press the edge to seal. Place on the prepared pan. Repeat with the remaining sausages; set aside the remaining egg wash. Refrigerate until firm and chilled, about 30 minutes up to overnight.

Combine the mustard seeds and cornmeal in a shallow baking dish. Working with 1 roll at a time,

brush the outside of the pastry all over with the reserved egg wash. Roll in the seed-cornmeal mixture, then place on the prepared baking sheet. Repeat with the remaining rolls. (If the pastry becomes warm or soft, return the rolls to the refrigerator to firm up.) Using a sharp knife, trim the ends of the sausage that protrude from the pastry to make 4-inch rolls and discard the ends. Cut the rolls about 2/3-inch thick to make 6 pieces. Return to the prepared baking sheet, placing the pieces about 1 1/2 inches apart. Return to the refrigerator to chill and firm, if necessary.

Bake until a rich golden brown on the bottom, about 10 minutes. Using an offset spatula, flip each disk and continue baking until rich golden brown on both sides, an additional 8 to 10 minutes. Remove to a rack to cool slightly. Transfer to a warmed serving platter. Serve hot or warm, topped with a small dollop of Creole mustard.

Brilliant Presentation

Served on Skewers

Talk about going high on the hog—our humble finger food is transformed into Brilliant, and perfect for passing at a party, with a wooden skewer. Once the sausage has been cut into pieces, insert a 6-inch skewer into the side of each disk. Place the sausage on the prepared baking sheet, alternating the orientation so the skewers don't touch the dough as it expands while baking. Bake as directed. Serve hot or warm with Creole mustard on the side for dipping.

Mini Country Ham Cheddar Biscuits

MAKES ABOUT 30

When I was a little girl, one of my favorite breakfast meals was cheese toast biscuits. Mama would halve biscuits, leftover from supper the night before, and I would take that familiar plastic-wrapped orange slice and bend it until it broke into four equal pieces. I topped each half biscuit with a quarter of a slice before placing it on the bent and battered baking tray she used to make toast. Sometimes Mama would place a thin slice of ham under the cheese. She then placed it under the broiler. The cheese would bubble and melt, and the biscuit edges would toast and brown. I especially liked it when she cooked the cheese to a deep chocolate color so that I could remove the nutty burnt skin and enjoy it separately first, leaving the cheese creamy and soft underneath. (Mama used to make cheese toast every morning for our dachshund, as well. But that's another story for another day.)

2 cups all-purpose flour, plus more for rolling out

1 tablespoon baking powder

1/2 teaspoon fine sea salt

1/4 teaspoon freshly ground black pepper

1/2 cup (1 stick) unsalted butter, chilled and cut into
   1/2-inch pieces

1/3 cup shredded sharp Cheddar cheese (11/4 ounces)

1/3 cup finely diced country ham (13/4 ounces)

1/2 cup buttermilk, plus more for brushing

2 large eggs

Preheat the oven to 400°F. Line a baking sheet with a silicone baking liner or parchment paper.

To prepare by hand, whisk together the flour, baking powder, salt, and pepper in a bowl. Using a pastry cutter or two knives, cut in the butter until it's the size of large peas. Stir in the cheese and ham and make a well in the center. In a small measuring cup, whisk together the buttermilk and eggs. Pour the liquid into the well and quickly stir until the dough is moistened.

To prepare in a food processor fitted with a metal blade, combine the flour, baking powder, salt, and pepper in the food processor and pulse to combine. Add the butter and pulse until it is the size of peas. Pulse in the cheese and ham. Then, pour in the buttermilk mixture and pulse to combine. The dough will pull away from the sides of the bowl.

Turn the dough out onto a lightly floured work surface and knead two or three times, just until it holds together. Using a lightly floured rolling pin, roll the dough out to a thickness of 3/4 inch. Cut out rounds of dough with a 11/2-inch round cutter dipped in flour; press the cutter straight down without twisting so the biscuits will rise evenly when baked. Place the biscuits on the prepared baking sheet. If the biscuits are baked close together the sides will be moist. If the biscuits are baked farther apart, the sides will be crisp.

Gently press the remaining scraps together and cut out more biscuits. (These are more worked and will be a little tougher and likely not as pretty, but they still taste good!) Transfer the biscuits to the prepared baking sheet.

Using a pastry brush, lightly brush the biscuit tops with buttermilk. Bake until golden brown and risen, 15 to 17 minutes. Serve hot.

Brilliant: Short Recipe
Honey Bourbon Butter

Honey and butter on a biscuit is Basic, but being a good Southern girl, I am of the mind that adding bourbon to a situation is always Brilliant.

Combine 1/2 cup (1 stick) room-temperature unsalted butter with 1/4 cup honey and 2 tablespoons bourbon in a bowl. Season with salt and freshly ground black pepper. Whisk until smooth. (It will look like it will never come together, but it will; just keep whisking. Makes 3/4 cup. To serve, split the warm biscuits and spread with Honey Bourbon Butter. Serve immediately.

Apple Roquefort Turnovers *Petite Chaussons au Roquefort*

MAKES ABOUT 12

Chausson is French for "slipper," and *chausson aux pommes* is a classic triangle-shaped pastry filled with tender slices of apple. While I was working in France at La Varenne, it was tradition every Bastille Day for the *stagiares* to make hundreds of bite-size morsels for the town festival. We'd work for a week preparing *pâte feuilletée*, then subsequently bake *bouchées, palmiers, sacristains,* and *chaussons,* all bite-size puff pastry hors d'oeuvres, canapés, and *mignardises.* Repetition may seem monotonous, but it can be the key to real learning.

The most widely available version of store-bought frozen puff pastry is available in a 17.3-ounce box and does not contain a bit of butter. Considering puff pastry is nothing more than flour, butter, and water, that's pretty significant. My Quick Puff Pastry is fundamental and worth making. Honestly? Shh, don't tell but I rarely have time to make my own and most often use Dufour's, a fine product made from real butter. It is available in 14-ounce containers online and at many Whole Foods Market locations.

1 pound Quick Puff Pastry (page 19) or 1 (14-ounce) package store-bought puff pastry

1 large egg yolk

2 tablespoons heavy cream

2 Granny Smith apples, peeled, cored, and finely chopped

1/4 cup crumbled Roquefort cheese (see sidebar page 42) or best-quality blue cheese

2 teaspoons chopped fresh thyme

Freshly ground black pepper

Preheat the oven to 400°F. Line a rimmed baking sheet with parchment paper or a silicone baking liner.

Place the puff pastry on a lightly floured work surface. Sprinkle the pastry with a little flour, and roll out to a thickness of 1/8 inch. Brush away any excess flour and trim the edges to form a 9 x 12-inch rectangle. Cut the pastry into twelve 3-inch squares, and transfer them to the prepared baking sheet. (Layer the scraps on top of one another, don't bunch them all together—and save for another use. Wrap in plastic wrap and store in the freezer for up to 3 months.)

Combine the egg yolk and heavy cream in a small bowl and whisk together with a fork. Neatly brush a little of the egg wash along two adjoining edges of each square. Place a spoonful of the apple just below the center of each square, top with a teaspoon of cheese, sprinkle with thyme, and season with pepper. Fold down the unwashed edges to enclose the mixture and form a triangle. Using your fingers, gently but firmly press the pastry edges together to seal. Then, using the back of a paring knife, create a scalloped edge.

Place the baking sheet in the freezer for 20 minutes, or until the pastry is chilled. Remove from the freezer and brush the tops liberally with the remaining egg wash. Bake until the pastries are puffed and golden brown, about 15 minutes. Store warm or at room temperature. These nibbles are best served the day of baking; if you want to prepare ahead, assemble to the point just before the final egg wash and baking. Cover the baking sheet tightly with plastic wrap and refrigerate overnight.

CONTINUED

Apple Roquefort Turnovers, *continued*

Brilliant: Short Recipe
Spiked Apple Butter

Even though the pastries are filled with fine cheese and made with puff pastry, our *chaussons* are simply Basic pocket sandwiches. So, to take our little slippers to Brilliant, serve with a drizzle of Spiked Apple Butter.

To make the apple butter, heat ³/4 cup apple butter in a saucepan. Add 2 tablespoons Calvados, applejack, or brandy. Cook until bubbly and warm. Remove from the heat. Using a whisk, stir in 1 tablespoon unsalted butter. Makes 1 scant cup. To serve, spoon the enhanced butter onto a plate. Top with 2 pastries set at an angle to one another and serve immediately.

AOC

Certain French products have a protected designation of origin, known as *Appellation d'Origine Contrôlée* (AOC), which translates as "controlled term of origin." Similar cheeses are produced elsewhere, but European and French law dictate that only those cheeses aged in the natural Combalou caves of Roquefort-sur-Soulzon may bear the name Roquefort. The AOC certification of authenticity is granted to certain French wines, cheeses, butters, and other agricultural products, all under the very powerful auspices of the government bureau *Institut National des Appellations d'Origine*.

Black Pepper Cheese Shortbread

MAKES ABOUT 4 DOZEN

This aromatic shortbread is a twist on Dede's cheese straws, a Southern classic I have enjoyed my entire life. It is very appropriately spiced, too, as he loved black pepper. The French have a tradition of nibbles such as this with an *apéritif* before dinner. The word is derived from the Latin verb *aperire*, which means "to open." An *apéritif* is served before a meal to stimulate the appetite, contrasting with *digestifs*, which are served at the end of a meal to aid digestion. Dede never had an *apéritif* in his life.

1 1/2 cups all-purpose flour

1 tablespoon freshly ground black pepper, or to taste

1/2 teaspoon fine sea salt

Pinch of cayenne pepper, or to taste

1/2 cup (1 stick) unsalted butter, at room temperature

8 ounces sharp white Cheddar cheese, at room temperature, grated

Position the oven racks in the top and bottom third of the oven. Preheat the oven to 375°F. Butter two baking sheets or line them with silicone baking liners or parchment paper.

Combine the flour, black pepper, salt, and cayenne in a food processor fitted with a metal blade and pulse to combine. Add the butter and cheese and process until smooth. Cover the work bowl with plastic wrap and set aside to rest for about 15 minutes.

Transfer the dough to a clean work surface. To shape the dough, work it in your hands; it should be soft and pliable (like Play-Doh). Shape the dough into two equal cylinders and wrap tightly in plastic wrap. Transfer to the refrigerator and chill until firm, about 30 minutes. Then, working with 1 cylinder at a time, using a utility knife, cut into 1/4-inch-thick slices and place 1 inch apart on the prepared baking sheet. Repeat with remaining dough.

Bake the shortbreads, rotating the baking sheets once, until lightly browned on the edges, about 20 minutes. Remove the baking sheets to a rack to cool slightly. Using an offset or slotted spatula, remove the individual shortbreads to a rack and cool completely.

Making Ahead Store the savory shortbread at room temperature in an airtight container between sheets of waxed paper. They will keep for 2 to 3 weeks.

Brilliant: Short Recipe
Pecan Garnish

It's all about accessorizing. To lift our simple cheese nibble to Brilliant, garnish with pecans (pictured on page 24). Prepare the dough as directed in the Basic recipe. Roll the edges of each cylinder in 1 cup chopped pecans to coat. Then, when you are ready to bake, slice the shortbread and place on the prepared baking sheets. Top each slice with a perfect pecan half. Bake as directed.

3

Salads and Slaws

When I was a little girl, we would occasionally go to the Piccadilly Cafeteria after church on Sundays. It was a family treat, intended to give Mama a break from cooking. One of the things I remember most about the experience was the salad section. Hunks of iceberg lettuce and a wedge of pale tomato shoulder to shoulder to shoulder with rows of plastic dishes filled with limp, shredded carrot spotted with raisins, flanked by turquoise bowls of dull, dry canned beets. The plastic vessels were the only things vibrant and bright about those salads. They were unseasoned and seasonless. And, these tasteless offerings were positioned directly adjacent to the dessert section, with a rainbow of bouncy cubes of Jell-O, creamy chocolate pudding, and cloudlike pillows of lemon meringue pie. I swooshed right past the salads to the dessert.

What would *you* do? It wasn't because I was a green-opposing brat. I have loved vegetables all my life. Believe me, I have never had problems with a dislike of vegetables, salads and slaws included. One of my favorite dishes of all time is a green bean salad. When I was little, I would help Dede in the garden, eating tomatoes right off the vine, the warm juices running down my suntanned arms. To this day, I think one the most electrifying experiences is to eat a vegetable pulled straight off the vine; you can feel the life in it.

Not much has changed as I have grown older, and tomatoes remain one of my greatest culinary loves. A good salad is a wonderful thing. I adore the usefulness of arugula—part herb, part lettuce. I almost always have a box or bag in the fridge. Ironically, sometimes it can be hard to find regular pedestrian head lettuce in the grocery store. The aforementioned arugula is de rigueur for any upscale market. Some bags of prepared salad add mâche to the mix. There are all shapes and sizes of endive and escarole, the inevitable bag of "Italian Blend," and you can top off your salad with a "cherry" in the form of deliciously bitter and red radicchio. The choices are extensive and amazing. No reason anymore to push the tray quickly past the salads to the desserts.

Combine a base of greens with seasonal vegetables or farm-fresh produce for a superior salad. Honest, fresh ingredients make the best salads and slaws. Assembled at the height of the season and treated with respect, they can create a low-maintenance lunch, satisfying supper, simple side dish, or perhaps a Brilliant bed for an even better bite. Use really good ingredients in your salad and do as little to them as possible so as not to mess them up. It's a very French approach to cooking. What better way to feature the freshness of vegetables than just a hint of cooking or serving them raw, letting the clean flavors of the food shine through? Sometimes less is, indeed, more.

Assembling a great salad is an art. There are certain techniques that must be followed: proper washing, balanced vinaigrette, and the right poise of textures and flavors. The goal is a well-balanced salad that is a marriage of sour, salty, bitter, sweet, and savory, as well as a perfect blend of crisp and creamy, tender and crunchy. Add a contrast in temperature, and you have a very special treat.

In this chapter I share some of my favorite combinations. Let the seasons and what's available at the market be your guide. Basic to Brilliant, I hope you enjoy every fresh, electrifying bite.

Summer Squash Slaw

SERVES 4 TO 6

As a teacher I always caution my students to "season as they go." If all the salt is added at the beginning of cooking, it will not taste right, and if it is all added at the end, it will be equally incorrect. In this slaw, the vegetables are seasoned, the dressing is seasoned, and then they are tossed together and the slaw is seasoned again. Seasoning food and assessing how it tastes is a constantly developing process. The same is true in life. Every now and then we need to assess and make adjustments.

Although the end result will taste the same, the vegetables are much prettier sliced into julienne matchsticks on a mandoline instead of grated on a box grater or in a food processor.

3 small zucchini, grated

3 small yellow squashes, grated

2 carrots, grated

Coarse salt and freshly ground black pepper

Finely grated zest and juice of 2 lemons

2 shallots, finely chopped

1 teaspoon Dijon mustard

1/2 cup pure olive oil

1/4 cup chopped mixed fresh herbs (such as flat-leaf parsley, tarragon, and mint)

Pinch of sugar

Combine the zucchini, yellow squashes, and carrots in a bowl. Season with salt and pepper.

In a small bowl, whisk together the lemon zest and juice, shallots, and mustard. Season with salt and pepper. Add the olive oil in a slow, steady stream until creamy and emulsified. Add the herbs and sugar.

Just before serving, pour the dressing over the vegetables and toss to coat. Taste and adjust for seasoning with salt and freshly ground black pepper. Serve immediately on chilled plates.

Brilliant Presentation

Shaved Raw Mushrooms

There's a restaurant in Sens, France, about twenty miles from where I lived and worked. The chef-owner, Patrick Gaulthier, periodically taught at La Varenne. He once made a mushroom salad that was the simplest thing possible, yet it made such an impression, it still resonates with me years later. His approach, and the approach of successful chefs, is to do even the simplest tasks as perfectly as possible. He handled those lowly *champignons de Paris* as if they were the finest *cèpes*.

To follow his example, remove the stems from 8 ounces white button mushrooms. Then, using a paring knife, grasp the bottom edge of the mushroom and pull to peel; the outer skin will come off in strips, leaving the mushroom perfectly white. Slice the mushrooms lengthwise as thinly as possible. Spread the mushrooms out on chilled plates and drizzle each with a squeeze of lemon. Drizzle with the best-quality extra-virgin olive oil and mound a spoonful of the squash slaw in the center. Serve immediately.

Southern Salad Macédoine

SERVES 4

Corn, butter beans, and green beans are summer staples in the south. Macédoine refers to a mixture of cut fruits or vegetables of different colors. The key in this salad is everything is cut about the same size. This salad is found on menus of little cafés throughout France, but unfortunately it is sometimes the French version of "airline food," a hodgepodge of overcooked vegetables held together with mayonnaise. Now, that sounds like a Southerner's dream, doesn't it? Southerners have embraced mayonnaise, practically making it a food group. In my version, the vegetables are cooked to crisp and just coated in a light mayonnaise dressing, blending the best of both worlds.

2 ears fresh sweet corn, shucked and silk removed

1 cup freshly shelled butter beans (about 12 ounces unshelled) or thawed frozen butter beans

6 ounces green beans, ends trimmed and cut into 1/4-inch lengths (about 1 cup)

2 carrots, diced (about 1 cup)

1/2 cup mayonnaise (page 15)

1/4 cup chopped mixed fresh herbs (such as tarragon, flat-leaf parsley, and basil)

Coarse salt and freshly cracked black pepper

8 ounces mesclun salad greens

2 tablespoons extra-virgin olive oil

Juice of 1/2 lemon

Prepare an ice-water bath by filling a large bowl with ice and water. Line a plate with paper towels.

To cook the corn, bring a large pot of salted water to a rolling boil over high heat. Add the corn and cook until tender, 2 to 3 minutes. Remove with tongs to the ice water to cool, and then transfer to the towel-lined plate to drain.

To cook the butter beans, add them to the simmering water and simmer until tender but not mushy, about 20 minutes. (Taste one and see how tender it is; the cooking time will depend on their freshness.) About 15 minutes into the cooking, add the green beans and carrots. Meanwhile, cut the corn kernels from the cobs and place in a large bowl.

Drain the vegetables well in a colander, and then set the colander with the vegetables in the ice-water bath (to set the color and stop the cooking), making sure the vegetables are submerged. Lift out of the water, shake well to remove the excess water, then transfer the vegetables to the bowl with the corn.

Add the mayonnaise and herbs. Taste and adjust for seasoning with salt and pepper.

Place the greens in a large bowl. Add the olive oil and lemon juice and toss to coat. Season with salt and pepper. Divide the greens equally among chilled serving plates. Top with equal portions of the macédoine salad. Serve immediately.

Brilliant: Short Recipe
Served in Artichoke Bottoms

In classic French cooking, the use of an artichoke bottom as a *garniture* is termed *châtelaine*, also a term for the mistress of a château, indicating something very elegant. In this case, serving our Basic salad in an artichoke bottom is not only elegant, it's Brilliant.

Using a sharp kitchen knife, trim all but an inch of the stem from 4 artichokes. Cut off the top two-thirds, leaving about 1 1/2 inches at the base. Hold the artichoke upside down and pare away the leaves, leaving just the pale green center. Rub the cut surface with lemon juice to prevent discoloration. Holding the bottom in the palm of one hand, scoop out the fuzzy choke with a spoon. Place in a bowl of water with the

CONTINUED

Southern Salad Macédoine, *continued*

juice of a lemon to reduce oxidation and browning until you are ready to cook.

To cook, heat 4 cups salted water in a heavy pot over medium-high heat to a gentle boil. Add 1 halved lemon, 2 sprigs thyme, and 1 bay leaf, preferably fresh, and the prepared artichoke bottoms. Cover with a smaller lid or heatproof plate to weigh down and keep the bottoms submerged. Cook over medium heat until the hearts are tender when pierced with knife, about 30 minutes. Remove with a slotted spoon to a bowl of ice water to cool. When cool, remove and pat dry. Drizzle with pure olive oil and season with coarse salt and freshly ground black pepper When you are ready to serve, lightly dress the artichoke bottoms as well as the mesclun greens. Place one on each chilled serving plate, trimming if necessary so it sits flat. Top with the greens and a spoonful of the chilled vegetable mixture. Season with finishing salt (see sidebar) and freshly ground pepper. Serve immediately.

Salt

I get lots of questions about salt. Glancing over at my stovetop, I can see at least ten different salts on my work surface, and I know there are at least a few more in the cupboard. In general, I cook with kosher salt. Sea salt is harvested from evaporated seawater and receives little or no processing, so it still contains the minerals from the water it came from. Salt harvested from the coast of France is going to be different from salt from the coast Spain, or Georgia, if we harvested salt. I like to use smoked salts, too, because they allow for smoky bacon flavor without the saturated fat. Most often smoked salts are made from large-flake sea salt. Some premier sea salts, such as fleur de sel, are considered finishing salts that add something special when applied to food. They are a bit more expensive and are added at the end of cooking.

Summer Tomato Salad

SERVES 4 TO 6

The simplest of Southern salads is a plate of sliced tomatoes, seasoned with a little salt and pepper. No fancy olive oil. No herbs. Usually next to it on the table is an equally old-fashioned combination of thinly sliced Vidalia onions and cucumbers seasoned with a bracing splash of white vinegar whisked together with "salad oil." As pedestrian as that may sound, when the vegetables are garden fresh, there's nothing better.

The combination of watermelon and tomato would be considered weird at worst, or "fancy gourmet" at best, on a great many Southern tables. I can envision my grandmother's puzzled face if I had suggested adding watermelon to her tomato salad. It may not be traditional, but once again, it embraces the winning Basic combination of sour, salty, bitter, and sweet that satisfies our palates. To give this salad a burst of umami flavor, just before combining everything, add 1 to 2 ounces thinly sliced cured sausage, such as saucisson, salami, or sopressata.

2 large ripe tomatoes, preferably heirloom, cored and
    cut into eighths

2- to 3-pound piece watermelon, cut from the rind and
    cubed (about 1 pound/1 quart, cubed)

1 cucumber, peeled, if necessary, halved lengthwise,
    seeded, and sliced into 1/4-inch crescents

1 banana or yellow wax pepper, sliced into 1/4-inch rings,
    with seeds

1 small bunch watercress, tough stems removed

1/2 small onion, preferably Vidalia, very thinly sliced

3 tablespoons red wine vinegar

2 tablespoons extra-virgin olive oil

1/4 cup chopped mixed fresh herbs (such as basil, mint,
    and flat-leaf parsley)

Coarse salt and freshly ground black pepper

1/4 cup microgreens (such as basil, arugula, or beet), optional

Combine the tomatoes, watermelon, cucumber, pepper, watercress, and onion in a large bowl. Whisk together the vinegar and olive oil. Drizzle it over the salad. Add the herbs and season with salt and pepper. Toss to combine. Serve on chilled plates and garnish with the microgreens.

Brilliant: Short Recipe
Pickled Cherry Tomatoes

One of the methods chefs employ to elevate a dish to restaurant quality is layering flavor. In this dish, the flavor of the fresh tomato is juxtaposed with with a pop of deliciously sour in the Brilliant. This chic little pickle (pictured on page ii) comes from Steven Satterfield, chef-owner of Miller Union in Atlanta. Peeling cherry tomatoes is a bit fussy, but that extra step is what makes them Brilliant.

First, in a sterilized 1 quart jar, place 1 sprig thyme, 6 peppercorns, 2 whole cloves, and 1 bay leaf, preferably fresh. Set aside. Then, with a sharp knife, score the bottom of 4 cups cherry tomatoes with an "x" shape, being careful not to pierce too deeply into the flesh. Drop them into a pot of boiling water for 10 seconds and then shock in ice water to stop them from cooking. Using your fingers or a paring knife, remove the skins gently, being careful not to break the fruit. Discard the skins. Add the peeled tomatoes to the jar, with very thin onion slices between each layer of tomatoes. Heat 1 cup Champagne vinegar, 3/4 cup water, 1/4 cup sugar, and 2 tablespoons kosher salt in a medium saucepan over medium high heat until boiling. Remove from heat and ladle the liquid into the jar. (You may have some liquid leftover; it depends on the size of the tomatoes.) Refrigerate overnight. Remove the pickled tomatoes from the brine with a slotted spoon. Makes 1 quart. Serve as a garnish.

Chilled Haricots Verts with Crème Fraîche

SERVES 4 TO 6

My mother has never met a green bean she didn't like. She "got it honest" because her father, Dede, felt the same. He and my grandmother would grow bushels and bushels in their garden, and throughout the summer we would eat them fresh, as well as put them up in mason jars. Dede would close the seals so tightly with his strong, brawny hands that he was the only one who could open them. More than ten years after his death, we sold the house Meme, Dede, and, subsequently, Mama lived in. I found cases and cases of his canned beans in the eaves of the attic.

Don't chop the nuts too finely or they will turn the mixture dry, absorbing all of the creaminess.

1¹/2 pounds haricots verts or other thin green beans, ends trimmed

¹/2 cup crème fraîche (see page 16) or sour cream

¹/2 cup almonds or walnuts, toasted and coarsely chopped

2 tablespoons chopped fresh basil

Coarse salt and freshly ground black pepper

1 to 2 tablespoons low-fat or whole milk, if needed

Make an ice-water bath by filling a large bowl with ice and water. Line a plate with paper towels.

To cook the beans, bring a large pot of salted water to a rolling boil over high heat. Add the beans and cook until crisp-tender, about 3 minutes. Drain well in a colander, then set the colander with the beans in the ice-water bath to set the color and stop the cooking, making sure the beans are submerged. Once chilled, remove the beans to the prepared plate. Pat dry with paper towels and transfer to a bowl.

Combine the crème fraîche, almonds, and basil. Season with salt and pepper. Pour over the beans and toss to coat. Taste and adjust for seasoning with salt and pepper. If the dressing seems too thick, drizzle on the milk and toss again to coat. Serve at room temperature or chill and serve cold.

Brilliant: Short Recipe
Porcini Crumbs

One of my goals in this book is to show home cooks that a recipe can be elevated from Basic to Brilliant, made more chef inspired, without "dumbing down" the Basic, shaving a truffle, or drizzling copious amounts of duck fat over everything. However, sometimes special and more expensive ingredients *are* needed to take a recipe to the top, and this is one of them. Mushrooms and green beans have an affinity for one another—there's a reason that old-fashioned green bean casserole with cream of mushroom soup topped with crispy onions tastes so good.

To prepare the porcini crumbs, coarsely chop 4 to 6 slices sourdough bread and combine with 3/4 ounce dried porcini mushrooms in a food processor fitted with the metal blade. Pulse until coarse crumbs form. Heat 1 tablespoon each pure olive oil and unsalted butter in a skillet over medium-high heat until melted. Add the crumbs and season with coarse salt and freshly ground black pepper. Cook, stirring occasionally, until golden and crispy, about 5 minutes. Remove with a slotted spoon. Makes about 1¹/2 cups. Sprinkle the porcini crumbs over the salad and serve immediately.

Celery Ribbons with Tarragon Vinaigrette

SERVES 4 TO 6

Meme loved celery, but I find it sometimes gets the short end of the stick, or stalk, as the case may be. It's used as a flavoring agent in stocks and soup, but other than being stuffed with pimento cheese or served as an obligatory accompaniment for hot wings, it's seldom featured in the kitchen. Its flavor is assertively herbaceous and can be overpowering, but in this recipe, I celebrate celery (pictured on page 44).

Celery and its more sophisticated cousin, celery root, also known as celeriac, are cultivars of the same plant species, but not the same plant. In other words, the bunch of the celery we eat does not grow atop the root celeriac. They are more like kissin' cousins.

1 bunch celery

1 English cucumber

Juice of 1 lemon

1 tablespoon white wine vinegar

1 teaspoon Dijon mustard

Coarse salt and freshly ground black pepper

¼ cup extra-virgin olive oil

3 sprigs tarragon

Remove all the leaves from the celery; set aside for the garnish. Remove the outer stalks of the celery to use in the salad, reserving the heart for another use. Trim the tough white root ends from the stalks. Using a paring knife, pull and remove the tough strings. Hold the celery stalk flat against a clean work surface and use a vegetable peeler to make long ribbons from top to bottom. (Toward the end of peeling the stalks, it can become a bit more difficult to use the flimsy pieces; discard or save for another use, such as stock.)

Place the ribbons in a bowl. Peel the cucumber and discard the outer peel. Then, keep peeling ribbons from the outer fleshy part of the cucumber, turning as you go, stopping at and discarding the remaining seedy core. Add the cucumber ribbons to the bowl with the celery. Add the lemon juice. Toss to coat and set aside.

To make the dressing, whisk together the vinegar, mustard, and salt and pepper to taste in a large salad bowl. Add the olive oil in a slow, steady stream,

whisking constantly, until creamy and emulsified. Strip the leaves from 2 of the tarragon sprigs and chop to make about 1 tablespoon. Add the tarragon to the salad and season with salt and pepper. Pour the dressing over the ribbons and toss to coat. Taste and adjust for seasoning with salt and pepper.

Strip the leaves from the remaining sprig of tarragon. Serve the salad on chilled plates, garnished with the reserved celery leaves and whole tarragon leaves.

Brilliant: Short Recipe
Celery Duo

Using similar flavors to play one off another is a very chef-inspired way to coax flavor from a dish, so we're going to marry our kissin' cousins.

To heighten the flavors of this salad to Brilliant, peel and grate 1 small celery root (about 1 pound), preferably using the large holes of a box grater. Place in a small bowl and squeeze over the juice of 1 lemon to prevent it from turning brown. Toss to coat, then add to the prepared celery ribbons. Taste and adjust for seasoning with finishing salt and freshly ground black pepper. Serve immediately on chilled plates. This duo may be served solo or as a base for crab, poached shrimp, or even steamed lobster. The sweetness of seafood is an elegant counterpoint to the crisp, grassy salad.

Arugula with Country Ham and Pecans

SERVES 4 TO 6

This salad is a great example of sour, salty, bitter, sweet, and savory. Right out of the gate, we're hitting all our marks. The essential element that makes this basic recipe shine is country ham. Since ancient times, humans have cured pork, and people have loved the pig. Dry-curing the hind legs of pigs is one of the oldest ways of preserving meat. Ham pairs beautifully with sweet, spicy, and creamy foods; those flavors and textures counteract the meat's saltiness, which can range from mild to assertive. In my opinion, anything with country ham has a leg up on the competition.

8 cups arugula, dandelion, or frisée (about 6 ounces)

3 tablespoons apple cider vinegar

1/2 teaspoon firmly packed light brown sugar

Coarse salt and freshly ground black pepper

2 tablespoons canola oil

3 thin slices country ham, cut into lardons (see sidebar)

1/2 onion, preferably Vidalia, thinly sliced

1 small clove garlic, finely chopped

1/2 cup crumbled aged white Cheddar cheese (about 2 ounces)

1/4 cup chopped pecans

Place the greens in large bowl. Set aside. Stir together the vinegar, brown sugar, salt, and pepper in small bowl until the sugar dissolves. Set aside.

Heat the oil in a skillet over medium-high heat. Add the ham and cook, stirring occasionally, until crisp, 5 to 7 minutes. Using a slotted spoon, transfer the ham to a plate lined with paper towels.

Add the onion to the skillet and cook over medium heat, stirring frequently, until translucent, 3 to 5 minutes; add the garlic and cook until fragrant, 45 to 60 seconds. Add the vinegar mixture, then remove from the heat. Working quickly, scrape the bottom of the skillet with a wooden spoon to loosen any yummy browned bits. Set aside to cool just slightly.

Pour the warm dressing over the reserved greens, add the ham, and toss gently with tongs until the arugula is slightly wilted. Taste and adjust for seasoning with salt and pepper. Divide among chilled serving plates. Sprinkle over the cheese and pecans. Season with freshly ground black pepper and serve immediately.

Brilliant: Short Recipe
Crispy Deep-Fried Eggs

Green eggs and ham? How about Greens with Egg and Ham to take this Basic salad to Brilliant?

Bring 4 large eggs to room temperature. Line a plate with paper towels and set aside. In a small, heavy saucepan, pour in about 1 1/2 cups peanut oil to fill half full. Heat over medium heat until it reads 350°F on a deep-fry thermometer. Working with 1 egg at a time, break the egg into a small ramekin, and then slowly and carefully slide it into the hot oil. It will spit and sizzle. Cook until the egg is crunchy on the outside and the yolk is still runny, about 1 1/2 minutes. Using a slotted spoon, lift the egg out of the oil and transfer to the prepared plate. Season with finishing salt (see page 50) and freshly ground black pepper. Repeat with the remaining eggs. Serve immediately atop the wilted salad.

Lardon

A matchstick-size piece of bacon is called a lardon. Strictly speaking, however, lardons are long strips of fat sewn into lean meat with a larding needle (*lardoire*) to keep the meat moist and flavorful during cooking. I find it easier to cut the meat into lardons before cooking, instead of cooking strips of bacon whole, then crumbling.

Mama's Macaroni Salad

SERVES 4 TO 6

One summer while living in France, I surprised my mother and came home to visit for a week. Meme and my friend Evan were in on the ruse, but Mama was completely surprised. I told her ahead of time that I would be traveling but would call her—we usually spoke a few times a week. (My phone bill has always been fairly significant.) I flew into Atlanta, Evan picked me up at the airport, and we drove home, arriving about midnight. Using Evan's cell phone, I called Mama as we were pulling into the driveway and told her to look outside. At first she thought I was being silly, but she walked outside. I got out of the car, and we hugged each other so hard, I thought we'd crack each other's ribs.

I've always considered calling home to be as necessary as paying the power or water bill; it's just part of life. When Meme passed away, Mama and I started calling every night to check on each other. Now more than ten years later, the habit remains the same. Sometimes schedules or traveling in distant time zones get in the way, but for the most part we speak at least four or five times a week, even if it's only to say, "Good night, I love you."

1 (16-ounce) box elbow macaroni

3 celery stalks, very finely chopped

3 carrots, shredded

1 onion, preferably Vidalia, very finely chopped

1/2 cup mayonnaise (page 15), or to taste

Coarse salt and freshly ground black pepper

1 cup shredded mild Cheddar cheese (4 ounces), for garnish

Bring a large pot of salted water to a rolling boil. Add the macaroni and cook until tender, about 10 minutes, or according to package instructions. Drain well and transfer to a large bowl to cool.

Once the macaroni is cooled, add the celery, carrots, onion, and mayonnaise. Season with salt and pepper. Cover with plastic wrap and chill in the refrigerator until cold, at least 2 hours. Taste and adjust for seasoning with salt and pepper. Sprinkle the cheese over just before serving.

Brilliant: Short Recipe
Served with Jumbo Lump Crabmeat

Jumbo lump crabmeat is the best and most expensive crabmeat, consisting of whole lumps of white meat from the body of the crab. It is best used in recipes where appearance is important.

Pick through 1 pound jumbo lump crabmeat for shells and cartilage without breaking apart the large hunks of crab. Once the macaroni salad is prepared, add the prepared crab. Taste and adjust for seasoning with coarse salt and freshly ground black pepper. Add the cheese. Serve immediately on chilled plates.

Endive and Roquefort Slaw

SERVES 4 TO 6

Several years ago I was able to take part in a taste test at a food laboratory. A scientist in a pristine white lab coat measured our sensations and determined I was "bitter deficient," meaning that my palate did not recognize bitter. I was appalled. Something was wrong with my palate? I was confused because I love bitter tastes, but it makes sense—I don't fully taste bitter. My head hung low and I questioned if my career was over. We moved on to the next series of tests, on our sense of smell. We were given a dozen or so clear vials of liquid and asked to identify the scent. Not only did I make my way through the test, I got the best score. In fact, I was only the third person in thousands of tests in the history of the lab to do so well. They were incredulous, and I was relieved I would still have a job.

This slaw is not for the faint of heart. The greens are strong and slightly bitter, the dressing is lemony tart with smelly blue cheese (the Brilliant version is pictured on page 102). My "faulty" palate thinks it's delicious.

Finely grated zest of 1 lemon

Juice of 1/2 lemon

1 tablespoon white wine vinegar

2 teaspoons Dijon mustard

1 teaspoon chopped fresh thyme leaves

1 clove garlic, very finely chopped

1/2 cup extra-virgin olive oil

4 ounces Roquefort or best-quality blue cheese, crumbled

Coarse salt and freshly ground black pepper

4 large heads Belgian endive, halved lengthwise, cored, and cut lengthwise

6 cups loosely packed watercress, tough stems removed

In a small bowl, whisk together the lemon zest, lemon juice, vinegar, mustard, thyme, and garlic. Whisk in the oil in a slow, steady stream until emulsified. Add the Roquefort and stir until smooth. Season with salt and pepper. Set aside.

Place the endive and watercress in a large bowl and pour over some of the dressing. Toss to coat and add more dressing, if needed; season with salt and pepper. Serve immediately on chilled plates.

Brilliant: Short Recipe
Candied Walnuts

Walnuts and blue cheese make a lovely pair. They argue a bit, kind of like sisters, just enough to make things interesting, but love each other in the end. The addition of these to the full-flavored endive slaw takes this to chef-inspired Brilliant.

Preheat the oven to 325°F. Line a rimmed baking sheet with a silicone baking liner or spray with nonstick cooking spray. Combine 1 cup walnuts with 1 tablespoon honey, 1 tablespoon sugar, and a pinch of cayenne in a bowl. Season with coarse salt and freshly ground black pepper and toss to coat. Spread the nut mixture on the prepared baking sheet (some nuts may clump together). Bake, stirring occasionally to break up clumps, until the nuts are deep golden and the sugar mixture is bubbling, about 15 minutes. Cool completely on the baking sheet. Makes 1 cup. The nuts can be made 3 days ahead. Store in an airtight container.

Oven-Roasted Sweet Potato and Green Bean Salad

SERVES 4 TO 6

I wasn't always that fond of sweet potatoes. Then I realized it wasn't the sweet potato I didn't like, it was the insane amounts of granulated sugar, brown sugar, marshmallows, maple syrup, and butter Southerners ingloriously and traditionally heap on top of them. With all that topping, it's impossible to taste the naturally sweet, and earthy flavor of the actual sweet potato. I grew to love the naturally creamy richness of a roasted sweet potato with just a bit of butter and maybe a mere drizzle of cane syrup or sorghum.

When I tasted them charred and roasted in a salad made by my friend and colleague Laurey Masterton, chef-owner of Laurey's in Asheville, North Carolina, I couldn't get enough. Roasted high and hot in a convection oven, they were almost burnt, but not quite. The flavors were incredible with bittersweet dark caramel flavors. The potatoes became what I call "roll around in good." Her salad inspired this one.

1/4 cup pure olive oil, plus more for the baking sheet

3 medium sweet potatoes, peeled and sliced 1/4 inch thick on the diagonal

1 red onion, thinly sliced

6 ounces haricots verts or young tender green beans, ends trimmed

Coarse salt and freshly ground black pepper

2 tablespoons honey

Juice of 1 lemon

1/4 cup coarsely chopped fresh flat-leaf parsley

Brush a rimmed baking sheet with olive oil and place in the oven. Preheat the oven to 400°F. (If you have convection, use it like Laurey does, just check the potatoes sooner.)

Combine the sweet potatoes, onion, and green beans in a bowl. Pour over the olive oil and season with salt and pepper Toss to coat. Transfer to the heated baking sheet. Roast, stirring occasionally, until the potatoes are a deep orange and brown, 35 to 45 minutes. Remove from the oven and while still warm, drizzle with the honey and lemon juice. Sprinkle with the parsley. Toss to coat. Taste and adjust for seasoning with salt and pepper.

Serve at room temperature or, preferably, refrigerate to chill. If you are serving the salad cold, taste and adjust for seasoning again since chilling dulls the flavor. Then divide among chilled serving plates.

Brilliant: Short Recipe
Toasted Hazelnuts

You can't really get much more Southern than green beans and sweet potatoes. But serving them cold is not very Southern. The only way those vegetables would have been served cold in Meme's kitchen would have been if someone was sneaking leftovers out of the fridge. My suggestion for transforming this Basic chilled salad is to add roasted, peeled hazelnuts. Still, not very Southern. In this salad, however, toasted hazelnuts bring a welcome sweet, intense nuttiness that is Brilliant.

To toast nuts, preheat the oven to 350°F. Place 1 cup hazelnuts on a rimmed baking sheet and toast in the oven until the skins crack and begin to peel, about 10 minutes. Transfer to a large kitchen towel, then rub vigorously to loosen the skins. (For all other nuts, proceed with recipe as directed without removing skin.) Transfer the cleaned hazelnuts to a cutting board and coarsely chop. Makes about 1/2 cup. Sprinkle the chopped nuts over the chilled plates of salad and serve immediately.

Alabama "West Indies" Crab Salad

SERVES 4

This salad is the quintessential regional dish of the Lower Alabama Gulf Coast area. "LA," not the one on the West Coast, the one on the "third" coast, is an area rich in food history and culture. This recipe came to me when I was testing recipes for the second edition of *Southern Belly* by John T. Edge. Somehow I'd never had it before, even though I grew up going to the beach along the Gulf. My goodness, what a revelation! It's about as simple as you can get. Frankly, it tastes just as good on a plain old Ritz cracker as on a leaf of handpicked, family-farmed, shade-grown, expensive, heirloom, organic butter lettuce.

1 pound jumbo lump crabmeat

1 onion, preferably Vidalia, chopped

1 teaspoon celery seeds

2 teaspoons nonpareil capers, rinsed

2 bay leaves, preferably fresh

Coarse salt and freshly ground white pepper

3/4 cup apple cider vinegar

6 tablespoons canola oil

1/2 cup ice water

Butter lettuce leaves or Ritz crackers, to serve

Pick through the crabmeat for shells and cartilage without breaking apart the large hunks of crab. In a glass or ceramic dish, layer the crab with the onion, celery seeds, capers, and bay leaves. Season each layer with white pepper. In a liquid measuring cup, whisk together the vinegar, oil, and ice water. Pour the dressing over the crabmeat mixture. Cover with plastic wrap and refrigerate overnight.

Taste and adjust for seasoning with salt and pepper. Serve on chilled plates with the aforementioned lettuce leaves or Ritz crackers.

Brilliant: Short Recipe
Stacked Crab Salad

Stacking the salad with avocados and peaches is a Brilliant twist—more "LA" as in California than "LA" as in Lower Alabama.

First, make the salad as above and refrigerate overnight. Chop an avocado and set aside. Then, chop a skin-on, well-washed peach and set aside. (If peaches aren't in season, you can use a peeled mango instead.) To make a stacked crab cake, place a 2 1/2-inch-wide, 2-inch-tall ring mold, cookie cutter, piece of PVC piping, or even a well-rinsed tuna can with the top and bottom removed on a chilled serving plate. Layer one-quarter of the avocado and then one-quarter of the chopped peaches in the mold, gently pressing each layer lightly with the back of the spoon before adding the next layer. Then, using a slotted spoon, layer one-quarter of the crabmeat on top, pressing firmly. Carefully remove the ring mold. Repeat to make four stacks. Drizzle some of the accumulated juices around the plate and garnish each plate with a wedge of lime. Serve immediately.

Warm Summer Shrimp Salad

SERVES 4 TO 6

I love this sort of dish. A few simple ingredients perfectly executed, building layers of flavor. The shrimp are brined, making them crisp, yet tender and juicy. The corn is cooked in a quick shrimp stock, bringing out its sweetness. Paired with the tartness of the tomato, the zip of a light, lemony mayonnaise, and a spot of mildly pungent basil, this salad is a great summer starter. I prefer using a slightly bitter green, such as arugula or even sliced Belgian endive, to balance the sour, salty, and sweet.

The key word here is "summer" salad. Make this in summer with wild American shrimp when the corn, tomatoes, and basil are ripe.

2 pounds large shrimp (21/25 count), peeled and deveined, shells reserved

2 tablespoons coarse salt, plus more to season

Freshly ground white pepper

4 cups water

Scraped kernels from 6 ears fresh sweet corn (about 3 cups)

1 tablespoon corn oil, preferably unrefined, or pure olive oil

2 to 3 medium to large tomatoes, preferably heirloom, cored and chopped

2 lemons (finely grated zest and juice of 1, and 1 quartered)

1/4 cup mayonnaise (page 15), or to taste

1 small bunch basil leaves, chopped

1/2 cup loosely packed microgreens or arugula

Place the shrimp in a bowl. Rub and toss with 1 tablespoon of the coarse salt. Wash under cold running water. Rub once again with the remaining 1 tablespoon salt, wash well under cold running water, then drain in a colander. Pat dry with paper towels. Season the shrimp generously with the white pepper. Set aside.

Combine the shrimp shells and water in a saucepan. Bring to a boil over medium-high heat. Decrease the heat to simmer and let cook until the shells are pink and the broth is fragrant, about 3 minutes. Strain, reserving the broth and discarding the shells. Wipe the saucepan clean.

Return the strained broth to the now-clean saucepan. Add the corn and season with salt and pepper. Bring to a boil over medium-high heat. Decrease the

heat to simmer and cook until the corn is tender, about 3 minutes. Drain in a fine-mesh sieve. Place the corn in a medium bowl. Set aside.

Heat the oil in a large skillet over high heat until shimmering. Add the reserved shrimp and cook until pink and opaque, 3 to 5 minutes.

Add the shrimp and chopped tomatoes to the corn. Add the lemon zest, lemon juice, mayonnaise, and basil. Stir to combine. Taste and adjust for seasoning with salt and pepper. Divide among chilled plates. Garnish each with microgreens and a wedge of lemon. Serve immediately.

Brilliant: Presentation
Served with Popcorn

This recipe is already about building layers of flavor—using shrimp stock to cook the corn, using corn oil to cook the shrimp. To elevate this simple and elegant, yet Basic recipe to Brilliant, add popcorn to take it a step further.

Prepare the recipe as for Basic and spoon onto room-temperature serving places. Scatter each plate with 1/4 cup freshly popped, lightly salted popcorn. This popcorn enhances the already present flavor of the corn as well as mixing up the textures and temperatures.

Lentil Salad with Shallot Vinaigrette

SERVES 4 TO 6

Both green beans and shell beans are tropical and require a long, hot growing season, perfect for the South. I grew up eating beans and rice in Louisiana and, once introduced, quickly fell in love with lentils. They are a great dried legume—technically they are not beans—because they are very flavorful, almost meaty, and cook quickly. The best-quality lentils are the French *lentilles du Puy*, petite, gray-black, caviar-like disks.

8 cups water

1 pound lentils (2 cups), preferably lentilles du Puy, rinsed
    and picked over

Bouquet garni (1 bay leaf, preferably fresh; 2 sprigs
    thyme; 2 sprigs flat-leaf parsley; and 6 whole black
    peppercorns, tied together in cheesecloth)

2 slices bacon, cut into lardons (see page 54), or
    1 tablespoon pure olive oil

1 clove garlic, very finely chopped

1 onion, preferably Vidalia, finely chopped

1 carrot, finely chopped

1 celery stalk, finely chopped

Coarse salt and freshly ground white pepper

1 recipe Shallot Vinaigrette (page 14)

Combine the water, lentils, and bouquet garni in a saucepan and bring to a boil over high heat. Decrease the heat and simmer uncovered, skimming frequently, until the lentils are tender, about 30 minutes. Remove from the heat and drain in a fine-mesh sieve. Remove and discard the bouquet garni. Transfer the lentils to a large bowl.

Meanwhile, line a plate with paper towels. In a saucepan, cook the bacon over medium heat until crisp, about 5 minutes. Using a slotted spoon, remove the bacon to the prepared plate to drain. Pour off all but 1 tablespoon of the drippings (reserve the excess fat for another use). Or, heat the oil in a large skillet over high heat until shimmering. Add the onion, carrot, and celery and season with salt and white pepper. Quickly toss to cook and sear, about 3 minutes. Scatter over the cooling lentils. Pour the dressing over the lentils and toss to coat. Taste and adjust for seasoning with salt and pepper. Divide among shallow bowls. Serve warm or at room temperature.

Brilliant: Short Recipe
Turkey Sausage Patties

Homemade and healthy turkey sausage will take this Basic salad to a Brilliant and filling meal

Combine 12 ounces ground turkey; 1 pear, cored and grated on a box grater; 1/4 cup chopped fresh flat-leaf parsley; 1 tablespoon chopped fresh sage; 1 tablespoon chopped fresh rosemary; 1/4 teaspoon ground allspice; and 1 large egg in a large bowl. Season with coarse salt and freshly ground black pepper and mix well. Line a rimmed baking sheet with parchment paper. Using hands moistened with water, form 8 patties, each about 3 inches in diameter. Place on the prepared baking sheet and refrigerate until firm, about 30 minutes. Heat 2 tablespoons canola oil in a large skillet over medium-high heat. Working in batches, cook the patties, until browned on each side and the juices run clear, about 3 minutes per side. Makes 8. Place 2 patties each on top of each serving of the lentil salad. Serve immediately.

4

Eggs and Dairy

More and more city dwellers are getting in touch with their inner farmer and putting a chicken coop in the backyard. A friend of mine has quite the brood and once gave me a trio of chickens. Since it's kind of country to have chickens in the city, I named them Patsy, Tammy, and Loretty—not Loretta, but Loretty, just like husband Doolittle called the Queen of Country Music in the biographical movie, *Coal Miner's Daughter*.

Having fresh eggs in the fridge was a pleasure. A few weeks later we had a security breach, and I found a trail of bloody feathers leading to the dog "playing" with her chicken. It was Tammy. Somehow in this tragic death, it seemed appropriate that it was Tammy since her namesake led such a hard life. A few months later, we were gifted with another chicken. There are laying hens and eating hens, and we indicated their intended use by their designated name. Although I had no intention of asking Mama for a lesson on how to wring a chicken's neck, the latest addition was meant to be an eating hen and had a big full chest. We named her Dolly.

When taping any segments involving eggs at Martha Stewart Living Television, we used eggs freshly gathered from Martha's hens. Among the various residents at her *palais de poulet* were Araucana chickens that produce the distinctive powder blue eggs. As kitchen director, I was responsible for ensuring we composted for the garden, recycled, and saved any bits appropriate for chicken feed, resulting in very little trash. (Martha, taking a cue from simple country living, has been defining green for decades.) Once a rubber band was found in the feed, and I held my breath for a few days, hoping none of the flock fell to foul, not fowl play.

Many of the same farmers that sell eggs at my local farmer's market also sell both unpasteurized and pasteurized milk as well as fresh and cured cheeses. I guess if you've got chickens running around, a cow or a goat or two won't hurt. In Georgia, unpasteurized milk is for "pet consumption only." There's a raging debate about the raw milk and folks use suberterfuge and tacit methods to secure their dairy demands.

Along with the renewed interest in locally grown foods, there's a desire to seek out locally produced dairy. We're going back to the foods of our ancestors. One of my favorite yogurt and cheese makers, Atlanta Fresh, receives their milk fresh daily from Johnston Family Farms in Newborn, Georgia. Within a few days of receiving the milk, they make yogurt and cheese. Once you taste dairy products made only a handful of days ago, you quickly understand the difference.

Choosing Eggs

While I was living and working as an assistant to Anne Willan in France at Château du Fëy, my list of chores did not include feeding chickens and gathering eggs, but I did buy them at the farmer's market.

At the farmer's markets across France, eggs are sold at room temperature and, indeed, we did not always store eggs in the refrigerator. In the United States, however, we are instructed to always store eggs in the refrigerator due to the possibility of contamination from salmonella. Salmonella is an anaerobic bacteria that may enter our digestive tracts via contaminated food, causing abdominal pain and violent diarrhea. The symptoms usually last only a day or two in healthy people, but can lead to serious complications for the very young, pregnant women, the elderly, the ill, and those with compromised immune systems.

Egg whites and yolks left runny or raw increase the chances of a person contracting salmonella, since the product has not sustained enough heat to kill the bacteria. The shells of eggs may also be contaminated with salmonella, and when you crack the shells, the bacteria can contaminate the egg inside. Unfortunately, you can't see or smell salmonella bacteria on eggshells, so it's important to always practice good food safety when handling raw eggs.

In recent years there have been massive egg recalls that suggest factory farming is the culprit. Many chefs and cooks prefer to buy their eggs directly from small local farms. However, the United States FDA egg safety requirements don't apply to farms with fewer than 3,000 hens. While it may be easier to keep smaller facilities disease free, salmonella contamination can happen at any farm, both conventional and organic, so if you buy eggs from the farm, be sure that the farmers refrigerate their eggs, keep their facilities pest controlled and clean, and care for the chickens properly.

The experience of gathering an egg still warm from the hen is certainly not available to all, but the egg is still imminently incredible, edible, and economical. Eggs and dairy come to mind for breakfast, but give a few of these recipes a try in the evening with "breakfast for dinner." Cheesy, eggy goodness is obligatory on lazy, delicious weekend mornings meant to indulge and delight, a welcome respite from the harried, hectic workweek. Basic to Brilliant, eggs and dairy are exactly what they are cracked up to be.

Hard-Cooked Vs. Hard-Boiled Eggs

If you actually hard boil an egg, you are fairly likely to have overcooked, sulfurous eggs with shattered shells, tough plumes of rubbery white, and a green ring around a chalky yolk.

Hard cooking, also known as coddling, is the best technique for cooking eggs in the shell. The process involves bringing the eggs to a boil, removing the pan from the heat, covering the pan, and setting a timer.

Soft eggs are barely set at 4 minutes.

Mollet eggs are allowed to set for 5 to 7 minutes; the white is set and the yolks are warm but runny. *Mollet* eggs are perfect with crisp fingers of buttered toast.

At 10 minutes of coddling, the whites are firm and set and the yolk is **firm** yet barely soft at the center, excellent for creamy egg salad.

For **deviled**, **Easter**, **hard cooked**, and **sieved** eggs for mimosa garnish, let them coddle for 12 minutes; any longer and the egg will begin to overcook.

Skillet-Baked Eggs with Mushrooms and Spinach

SERVES 4

As a professional cook, I have a wall of cookware: copper from France; enamel-coated French or Dutch ovens (the nationality depends on the manufacturer); high-tech, stainless-steel sauté pans; thin pots for boiling pasta. If I go into a fancy, tricked-out designer kitchen, and there's a rack with all the same kind of pots, I know that person doesn't actually cook. Different pots are needed for different reasons. And even with all my expensive professional cookware, the pan I reach for the most is, without hesitation, my grandmother's cast-iron skillet.

I am generally a fan of using frozen spinach in recipes that require a lot of spinach. It's always a good idea to have a bag or box in the freezer for a quick meal, and certainly on a weekend morning.

16 ounces fresh baby spinach or 1 (12-ounce) bag thawed frozen leaf spinach

2 tablespoons unsalted butter

1 onion, preferably Vidalia, finely chopped

6 ounces mixed mushrooms (such as cremini, chanterelle, morel, shiitake, and white button), thinly sliced

1 clove garlic, very finely chopped

1/3 cup heavy cream

1/8 teaspoon freshly grated nutmeg

Coarse salt and freshly ground black pepper

4 large eggs

2 tablespoons finely grated Parmigiano-Reggiano cheese (1/2 ounce)

Position the oven rack in the upper third of the oven and preheat to 450°F. Prepare an ice-water bath by filling a large bowl with ice and water.

To cook the fresh spinach, heat 1/2 inch water in a large skillet over high heat. Add half the spinach and cook until wilted, about 30 seconds. Add the remaining spinach cover, and cook, over medium-high heat until tender, about 60 seconds. Drain well in a colander, then set the colander with spinach in the ice-water bath to set the color and stop the cooking, making sure the spinach is submerged. Remove the colander with spinach to drain. Working with a handful at a time, squeeze the freshly cooked, or thawed frozen, spinach between two dinner plates or by hand to remove any excess liquid. Set aside.

In the same skillet, heat the butter over medium heat. Add the onion and cook until translucent, 3 to

5 minutes. Increase the heat to medium-high, add the mushrooms, and cook, stirring occasionally, until softened and any liquid is released, about 4 minutes. Add the garlic and cook until fragrant, 45 to 60 seconds. Add the cream, nutmeg, and spinach. Season with salt and pepper and bring to a simmer. Remove the pan from the heat.

Using the back of a spoon, make 4 nests in the spinach-cream mixture in the skillet. Break an egg into each indentation. Season the eggs with salt and pepper and sprinkle with the cheese. Bake until the whites are set and the yolks are still runny, about 8 minutes. Serve immediately.

Brilliant: Presentation
Oeufs en Cocotte

Oeufs en Cocotte is made by cooking an egg in a petite casserole or ramekin, nestled on top of other ingredients, including vegetables or meat, with an optional topping of grated cheese. *Cocotte* translates to "casserole," but also "hen"—as well as "love" or "darling." When I was working in France, my chef's father would affectionately call me *cocotte*. You can imagine my immediate concern that he was calling me a casserole. There is something absolutely "darling" about serving individual dishes of baked eggs.

To do so, simply divide the spinach-cream mixture among 4 small ramekins. Top each with an egg, then sprinkle with the cheese. Bake until the whites are set and the yolks are still runny, about 8 minutes.

Perfectly Soft Scrambled Eggs with Grilled Buttered Toast

SERVES 4

It makes me madder than anything when I burn something I'm cooking. It's absolutely the most idiotic thing to do in the kitchen, and it's usually a result of not being dedicated, of not paying attention, of not being focused. I have a confession: Occasionally (actually often), I burn toast.

Being dedicated means doing something the right way and following through. It is tempting to not be dedicated, to take a shortcut, but, in reality, it's much easier to do things right to begin with, rather than try to fix a mistake. Great ingredients aren't enough. Making a great base for a dish is not enough. Cooking a dish until it's right is not enough. It takes all these things; it takes real dedication to all these steps even for something as simple as scrambled eggs and toast. Having said that, don't be scared even when saddling up to the stovetop to prepare these Perfectly Soft Scrambled Eggs. At the end of the day, it's just eggs and toast.

4 slices brioche, challah, or best-quality sandwich bread

2 to 3 tablespoons unsalted butter, at room temperature

5 large eggs

2 tablespoons low-fat or whole milk

1 tablespoon finely snipped fresh chives

Coarse salt and freshly ground white pepper

Position an oven rack 4 inches below the broiler and preheat the broiler. To make the toast, arrange the brioche slices on a baking sheet and spread the top sides with 1 tablespoon of the butter. Broil until brown, 2 to 3 minutes. Turn the bread and broil the other side. Remove the toasts from the oven and slice into triangles. Place on a clean cutting board and cover with a paper towel to keep warm.

Meanwhile, fill the bottom of double boiler with water and bring to a simmer over medium heat. Melt 1 tablespoon of the butter in the top of the double boiler. Whisk together the eggs and milk in a bowl. Add the eggs to the butter in the double boiler and cook until small curds form and the eggs are creamy

and almost set, 5 to 7 minutes. Remove from the heat just before the eggs fully set, because the eggs will continue cooking a bit after being removed from the heat. Add the remaining 1 tablespoon butter and the chives. (The last bit of butter is decadent and optional, but it will stop the cooking and ensure the eggs don't overcook in the residual heat.) Taste and adjust for seasoning with salt and white pepper. Serve immediately with the toast.

Brilliant: Short Recipe
Ham Crisps

These Ham Crisps are just a little detail, something so simple, but just different enough not to be confused with fried ham, they lift these Basic eggs to Brilliant.

Preheat the oven to 400°F. Line a rimmed baking sheet with a silicone baking liner or parchment paper. Place 8 slices thinly sliced country ham, prosciutto, or Serrano ham on the prepared baking sheet without crowding. Bake until crisp, about 10 minutes. Serves 4. Serve alongside the scrambled eggs and toast.

Tarragon Egg Salad

SERVES 4

I usually wind up making egg salad when I have to abort making deviled eggs because my eggs are too fresh. Very fresh eggs are difficult to peel. For deviled eggs, the trick is to think ahead and buy and refrigerate eggs for about seven days in advance of cooking. This allows the eggs to take in air, which helps separate the membranes from the shells. Every time, without fail, it occurs to me how nice old-fashioned egg salad is and I wonder why I don't start this recipe with intent, rather than as a backup plan. Why don't we start now?

6 large eggs

2 tablespoons mayonnaise (page 15)

1/2 teaspoon Dijon mustard

1 teaspoon freshly squeezed lemon juice

2 teaspoons chopped fresh tarragon, chives, dill, or
    fennel fronds

Coarse salt and freshly ground white pepper

1 small bunch watercress, tough stems removed

8 slices white sandwich bread or brioche, cut 1/2 inch thick

To hard cook the eggs, place the eggs in a saucepan and add water to cover them by 1 inch. Bring to a boil over high heat (you will see bubbles around the sides of the pot). Remove from the heat, cover, and let stand for 10 minutes for slightly soft eggs for egg salad, or 12 minutes for firmer eggs for deviled eggs and such. Drain the eggs and rinse them under cold running water. Set aside to cool completely.

To peel the eggs, tap each egg gently on the counter or sink all over to crackle it. Roll the egg between your hands to loosen the shell. Peel, starting at the large end, while holding the egg under running cold water; this facilitates peeling and also removes any stray shell fragments.

Halve the eggs and place in a bowl. Using a pastry blender or a fork, mash the eggs until slightly coarse. (I like the pieces of white to be about the size of an almond so that they don't become too small when you fold in the dressing.) In a small bowl, combine the mayonnaise, mustard, lemon juice, and tarragon. Add to the mashed eggs and season with salt and white pepper. Stir to combine. Taste and adjust for seasoning with salt and white pepper.

Place 4 slices of the bread on a clean work surface. Divide the egg salad equally among the bread and top with the watercress. Top with the remaining 4 slices of bread. Using a serrated knife, halve on the diagonal. Serve immediately.

Brilliant: Short Recipe
Egg Salad and Smoked Salmon Canapés

The flavor of smoked salmon marries well with egg salad.

To prepare a Brilliant (and admittedly slightly prissy) canapé, place the slices of brioche on a clean work surface. Place 4 to 6 ounces very thinly sliced smoked salmon in a single layer on the bread. Top the salmon with a thin, even layer of egg salad. Then, using a round cutter and pressing straight down, cut out individual, bite-size open-face sandwiches. When you are ready to serve, garnish each canapé with a single tarragon leaf. Serve immediately. (To make ahead, prepare the canapés and arrange on a rimmed baking sheet without the final tarragon leaf garnish. Spray a sheet of plastic wrap with flavorless nonstick cooking spray. Press the wrap directly on the surface of the egg salad. Refrigerate for up to 24 hours.)

Poached Eggs in Red Wine Sauce *Oeufs en Meurette*

SERVES 4 AS A MAIN COURSE, 8 AS A FIRST COURSE

I first learned to make this dish while living in northern Burgundy, famous for centuries for the wine produced in the region. When I describe this dish and how our humble egg is prepared—runny poached eggs in red wine sauce with sautéed mushrooms—many people wrinkle their noses. Then they taste it and wipe their plates clean. This Burgundian recipe is one of the classics of French cooking and is absolutely delicious.

In a nod to the extravagance of the dish, I am suggesting here toasted bread instead of the traditional butter-fried croutons.

1 tablespoon unsalted butter

1 onion, preferably Vidalia, chopped

1 carrot, chopped

1 celery stalk, chopped

1 clove garlic, crushed

2 tablespoons all-purpose flour

1 (750-ml) bottle red wine (such as Pinot Noir)

2 cups homemade beef stock (page 10) or reduced-fat, low-sodium beef broth

2 sprigs thyme

2 flat-leaf parsley stems, plus leaves for garnish

1 bay leaf, preferably fresh

1/2 teaspoon whole black peppercorns

8 large eggs

1 tablespoon distilled white vinegar

4 thick slices bacon, cut into lardons (see page 54)

15 to 20 pearl onions, peeled (see opposite)

4 ounces white button mushrooms, sliced

Coarse salt and freshly ground black pepper

8 slices best-quality white bread, toasted

2 tablespoons all-purpose flour

To make the sauce, heat the butter in a large, heavy saucepan over medium heat. Add the onion, carrot, and celery and cook until tender, 3 to 5 minutes. Add the garlic and cook until fragrant, 45 to 60 seconds. Add the flour and cook, stirring constantly until the vegetables are coated. Add the wine, stock, thyme, parsley, bay leaf, and peppercorns. Bring to a boil, decrease the heat to a simmer, and cook until the sauce is concentrated and reduced by half, 20 to 25 minutes.

To make the poached eggs, fill a large bowl with water and set aside (use hot water if serving them immediately, cold if making the eggs ahead). Fill a large saucepan with 3 inches of water, add the white vinegar, and bring to a boil over medium-high heat. Break one of the eggs into a ramekin or teacup. Using the handle (not the bowl) of a wooden spoon, swirl the water to create a whirlpool, which will help the eggs hold their shape. Decrease the heat to medium-low so the water is at a gentle boil and slide the egg into the center. Adjust the heat, if necessary, to keep the water just at a bare simmer and poach the egg until the white is solid and the yolk is firm but still soft to the touch, 3 to 4 minutes. Using a slotted spoon, remove the egg and transfer to the bowl of water; set aside. Return the water to a very gentle boil, and repeat the process with the other eggs. The eggs can be poached up to 12 hours ahead and refrigerated in a sealed container. To serve them, reheat briefly in hot water.

Heat a large skillet (I know, I know, it's a lot, but stay with me) over medium heat. Add the bacon and cook until brown, about 5 minutes. Transfer to a plate lined with paper towels. Discard all but 1 tablespoon of the bacon drippings, reserving it for another use. Add the pearl onions and cook them until brown and just tender, shaking the pan often so they color evenly, about 10 minutes. Add the mushrooms and stir to combine. Cook until all the vegetables are tender, 2 to 3 minutes. Add the reserved bacon and stir to combine.

Strain the red wine sauce over the mushroom-onion mixture, pressing to extract all the liquid and flavor. Bring to a boil, then decrease the heat to simmer. Taste and adjust for seasoning with salt and pepper. Keep over low heat.

To serve, reheat the eggs by immersing them in hot water for 1 minute. Set the warm toasts on warmed serving plates Drain the eggs on paper towels. Place one on each piece of toast. Spoon the sauce over the eggs. Garnish with parsley and serve immediately.

Brilliant: Presentation
Using Quail Eggs

Personally, I think the original recipe is Brilliant on its own, although all components of the recipe are Basic, there are a lot of elements and steps. But, I didn't want to dumb down this classic dish just to make the Basic to Brilliant concept work. How then to elevate this dish to truly Brilliant other than shaving over piles of black truffles or using expensive wild mushrooms in the dish? Quail eggs.

Substitute 3 quail eggs for each chicken egg for a total of 24 quail eggs. Gently tap the narrow part of the quail egg on the side of a bowl. Use your fingers to break off the top or narrow part of the shell, taking care not to rupture the yolk inside. (Skip the swirling part of creating a vortex; these eggs are so small they poach easily without it.) Proceed with the Basic recipe. Serve 3 quail eggs per person for an appetizer. (I think 6 eggs lined up would be a bit much, regardless of size.) Alternatively, for a real chef-inspired touch, serve the eggs individually in soup spoons as hors d'oeuvres. Instead of toast, make small toasted cubes of bread. Place a poached quail egg in a spoon. Top with the red wine–mushroom mixture. Garnish with a toasted bread cube and chopped parsley.

Peeling Pearl Onions

Pearl onions can be a bear to peel. To peel pearl onions, bring a small pot of water to a vigorous boil. Add the onions and cook until the skin begins to loosen, 2 to 3 minutes. Transfer to a bowl of ice water, then drain immediately. Use a paring knife to remove the top papery layer of skin, leaving the root end intact but trimming away the roots. Alternatively, you can sometimes find frozen peeled pearl onions in the freezer section of your grocery store. If you are using frozen onions, add them to the mushrooms *after* the mushrooms have cooked, not before. The frozen onions only need a few minutes of cooking.

Kale Omelet

SERVES 6 TO 8

Bagged greens may have saved a Southern foodway. Meme would have never used them, and Mama thinks they have too many stems, but this generation? I love the prewashed bags of winter greens. Lazy? Well, of course it is. When I am able to purchase kale or collards from my local farmer's market, I do; but for convenience, bagged kale, turnip, collard, and mustard greens are a great time-saver. For this recipe, give them a quick rinse under cold running water to freshen them, pick out the larger tough stems, and give the leaves another few chops with a knife.

I am pretty adamant, however, about not using nonstick skillets—except with eggs and delicate creatures such as the Classic Crêpes (page 225) or Parmesan Tuile (page 201), or when trying to use less oil, as with the Panfried Shrimp Po-Boy (page 94). For cooking and searing of meats, nonstick doesn't allow the fond, the yummy browned bits, to develop. For egg cookery, however, I think nonstick is essential.

3 slices thick bacon, cut into lardons (see page 54),
    or 2 tablespoons canola oil

1 onion, preferably Vidalia, chopped

5 cups hearty greens (such as kale, chard, or mustard
    greens), cleaned, tough stems removed, and chopped

Coarse salt and freshly ground black pepper

2 tablespoons water

6 large eggs, lightly beaten

$1/2$ cup freshly grated Parmigiano-Reggiano cheese
    (2 ounces)

$1/4$ teaspoon red pepper flakes

$3/4$ cup ricotta cheese (6 ounces)

1 tablespoon canola oil

Preheat the oven to 350°F. Line a plate with paper towels.

Heat a large nonstick ovenproof skillet over medium heat. Add the bacon and cook until crisp and brown, 5 to 7 minutes. Using a slotted spoon, transfer the bacon to the prepared plate; set aside.

Pour off all but 1 tablespoon of the drippings (reserve the excess fat for another use or dispose). Alternately, heat 1 tablespoon of oil in the skillet over high heat until shimmering. Add the onion and cook over medium heat, stirring occasionally, until golden, 4 to 6 minutes. Decrease the heat to medium-low, add half the greens, and toss until they begin to wilt, about 1 minute. Add the remaining greens and season with salt and pepper. Add the water. Toss to coat. Decrease the heat to low. Cover and cook, stirring occasionally, until the greens are wilted and tender, about 15 minutes. Using a slotted spoon, transfer the greens to a large bowl, leaving any cooking liquid behind.

Rinse and dry the skillet. To the greens, add the eggs, $1/4$ cup of the grated cheese, the reserved bacon, and red pepper flakes. Stir to combine. Fold in the ricotta. Season with salt and pepper.

Return the now-clean skillet to the stovetop over medium-high heat. Add 1 tablespoon canola oil and rotate the skillet to coat the bottom of the pan. When the oil is shimmering, pour in the egg mixture and spread evenly with a rubber spatula. Cook over medium-low heat until the omelet is barely set at the edges, 5 to 7 minutes. Sprinkle the remaining $1/4$ cup grated cheese over the eggs.

Transfer the skillet to the oven and bake until set, 15 to 20 minutes. Remove from the oven and, using a butter knife or long spatula, loosen the omelet from the sides of the skillet. Give the skillet a shake and slide the omelet out onto a clean cutting board. (Don't use a knife in the nonstick skillet!) Using a serrated knife, slice into wedges and serve immediately.

CONTINUED

Kale Omelet, *continued*

Brilliant: Presentation
Baked in a Sourdough Boule

Your brunch guests will certainly think this is Brilliant.

Preheat the oven to 350°F. Line a rimmed baking sheet with a silicone baking liner or parchment paper. Slice off the top of an 8-inch round sourdough or firm white loaf; remove the bread in chunks, leaving a shell.

Reserve the bread for another use. Prepare the filling. Instead of returning the egg and kale mixture to the skillet, transfer the mixture to the prepared boule. Top with remaining $1/4$ cup grated cheese. Bake until the eggs are set, 45 to 50 minutes. Transfer to a rack to cool slightly. Present on a wooden cutting board with a serrated knife. Serve immediately or at room temperature.

Vidalia Onion and Sweet Pepper Strata

SERVES 8

Being from Georgia, I am a huge supporter of Vidalia onions. Much in the way that France regulates food and wine with *appellation d'origine contrôlée*, the Georgia state legislature got together in 1986 and decided that Vidalia onions had to be grown within a certain region of Vidalia, Georgia. This is an unusually sweet variety of onion, due to the low amount of sulfur in the soil. If Vidalia onions are unavailable, use another sweet onion, such as Walla Walla or Texas Sweet.

A strata, also known as a breakfast casserole, is a great dish that can be made, and indeed should be made, the day before. The flavors marry, the bread soaks up the savory custard, and the dish sets before baking. The next day, all you have to do is set it out at room temperature to take the chill off, then bake it. This dish is a favorite for family gatherings as well as morning tailgates during football season.

2 tablespoons pure olive oil, plus more for the pan

8 ounces pork, turkey, or chicken breakfast sausage, in bulk or removed from casing

1 onion, preferably Vidalia, thinly sliced

1 red bell pepper, cored, seeded, and thinly sliced

1 yellow bell pepper, cored, seeded, and thinly sliced

Coarse salt and freshly ground black pepper

2 cloves garlic, very finely chopped

12 slices firm white sandwich bread, cut into 1-inch squares

1/2 cup freshly grated Cheddar, Gruyère, or mozzarella cheese (about 2 ounces)

6 large eggs

2 1/2 cups low-fat or whole milk

Leaves from 2 sprigs thyme, chopped

Brush a large baking dish with oil; set aside.

Heat the oil in a large skillet over medium heat. Add the sausage and cook until it starts to brown, 3 to 5 minutes. Drain off most of the cooking fat, leaving about 1 tablespoon. Add the onion and cook, stirring occasionally, until a rich golden, 6 to 8 minutes. Add the bell peppers and season with salt and pepper. Cook until the peppers are tender, about 5 minutes. Add garlic and cook until fragrant, 45 to 60 seconds.

Place half of the bread squares in the baking dish, and top with half of the sausage-vegetable mixture.

Sprinkle half of the cheese over the vegetables and top with the remaining bread and sausage-vegetable mixture. In a bowl, whisk together the eggs, milk, and thyme. Season with salt and pepper. Pour over the bread and vegetables. Cover and chill the strata for at least 3 hours, and up to 12 hours.

Preheat the oven to 350°F. Let the strata stand at room temperature for 20 minutes.

Sprinkle the remaining 1/4 cup cheese over the strata. Bake until puffed and golden brown around the edges, 30 to 45 minutes. Remove to a rack to cool slightly before serving.

Brilliant: Presentation
Individual Muffins

Basic strata is made Brilliant for serving to brunch guests when baked as individual portions. In a large sealable plastic container, combine the bread, sausage-vegetable mixture, egg mixture, and half the cheese. Seal and refrigerate for 3 to 12 hours. When you are ready to finish, preheat the oven to 350°F. Brush a standard 12-cup muffin tin with oil. Spoon the mixture into the tins, filling each cup no more than two-thirds full. Bake for about 30 minutes, until golden brown and set. Remove to a rack to cool slightly. Serve warm or room temperature.

Omelet with Herbs *Omelette aux Fines Herbes*

SERVES 1

While I was living and working in France for Anne Willan, we had a photo shoot for her cookbook, *Cook it Right*, an exhaustive tome that documents the various states of "doneness" (and over- and underdoneness) of everything from whipped cream to braised pheasant. When it was time to shoot the proper folding of an omelet, our "hand model," the talented writer and editor Marah Stets, was not able to execute the business-letter fold at the angle needed by the photographer. In her defense, (and yours, if you struggle), it can be tricky, which is why most omelets you see are simply in folded half. I am not even sure when the last time was that Anne had made an omelet, but she simply grabbed the skillet and spatula and, like a pro, quickly produced a perfect fold on demand.

3 large eggs

Coarse salt and freshly ground black pepper

2 tablespoons chopped fresh mixed herbs (such as flat-leaf parsley, chervil, tarragon, and chives)

1 teaspoon unsalted butter

In a bowl, beat the eggs, salt, pepper, and herbs with a fork. Melt the butter in an 8-inch nonstick skillet. When the butter foams, add the eggs. Holding your fork flat, stir the eggs quickly while shaking the pan back and forth. Continue so the eggs set uniformly.

When the eggs are lightly set but still moist, incline your pan forward so most of the egg gathers at the far end of the pan. Stop stirring. The mass of eggs should thin out around the edges at the near end. Using your fork, fold this thin edge toward the center of the omelet, enclosing the thick, moist center.

Press the fold into place, creating a rounded edge. Run your fork between the edge of the pan and the far edge of the omelet to loosen. Using the palm of one hand, tap the handle gently where it joins the pan to shake the omelet and make it twist and lift onto itself, so the lip rises above the edge of the pan. Fold this lip back toward the center of the omelet, meeting and over-lapping the edge of the other lip. Press with the flat of the fork to shape the omelet into a point at each end.

Holding a warmed serving plate, tap the under-side of the pan against the counter at the omelet end, so the omelet moves against the edge of the pan. Invert the omelet onto a plate. Press with the flat of the fork to shape the omelet into a point at each end. Smile and serve immediately.

Brilliant: Technique
Gratinée

Sometimes simple and Basic are best, but most things, eggs included, are made better and therefore Brilliant with the addition of warm melted cheese. This technique is particularly handy when you are serving omelets for brunch—unless you have your own per-sonally staffed omelet station. Position an oven rack 4 inches below the broiler and preheat the broiler. Slide the omelet into an oval gratin dish brushed with 1 tablespoon room-temperature butter. Repeat the process with additional omelets, if desired. Sprinkle 1 tablespoon grated Gruyère cheese over each omelet. Place under the broiler and cook until bubbly and lightly toasted, 3 to 5 minutes. Serve immediately.

Marinated Feta

SERVES 4 TO 6

There's lots of feta cheese out there, but true feta is made in Greece, and according to the European Union, you can't call it feta unless it was produced there. Like Georgia's own Vidalia onions or French Champagne, it isn't technically feta unless it's made where it's supposed to be made—in Greece. Having said that, many of the local dairies that are popping up across the United States raise sheep and goats and are producing delicious award-winning local feta, or fetalike, cheese. One of my favorites in the Atlanta area is Decimal Place Farms. Seek out your local cheeses at your farmer's market, Whole Foods Market, or specialty food store.

16 ounces feta cheese, cut into 1/4-inch squares

1 tablespoon whole cumin seeds

2 teaspoons whole coriander seeds

1 teaspoon red pepper flakes

Finely grated zest of 1 orange

1 1/2 cups best-quality extra-virgin olive oil

Leaves from 1/2 small bunch basil, chopped

2 sprigs rosemary

2 bay leaves

Place the feta in a sealable airtight container or glass jar. Set aside. Combine the cumin, coriander, and red pepper in a small skillet over medium-high heat. Shake the skillet gently until the spices are fragrant, about 1 minute. Place in a piece of cheesecloth and add to the feta along with the orange zest and olive oil. Add the basil, rosemary, and bay leaves and mix gently.

Cover and refrigerate for at least 1 day and up to 1 week. Bring to room temperature before serving.

Brilliant: Short Recipe
Grilled Zucchini Roulades

The cheese is phenomenal on its own, but wrap it in smoky, sweet grilled zucchini and it's a Brilliant summer snack or side dish.

Prepare a charcoal fire using about 6 pounds charcoal and burn until the coals are completely covered with a thin coating of light gray ash, 20 to 30 minutes. Spread the coals evenly over the grill bottom, position the grill rack above the coals, and heat until medium-hot (when you can hold your hand 5 inches above the grill surface for no longer than 3 or 4 seconds). Or, for a gas grill, turn on all burners to high, close the lid, and heat until very hot, 10 to 15 minutes. Meanwhile, slice 4 small zucchini lengthwise into even strips about 1/2 inch thick. Brush both sides of each strip with some of the seasoned feta oil. Season with coarse salt and freshly ground black pepper.

Place on the grill and cook until just tender and lightly charred, about 3 minutes. Turn the zucchini over and cook until the strips start to soften, about 2 minutes more. Remove to a rack to cool slightly. When cool enough to touch, roll up 1 feta square inside each strip of zucchini. Secure with a toothpick or skewer. Return to the grill to heat through, about 2 minutes. Remove to a warmed serving place. Season with freshly ground black pepper and serve immediately. Serves 4 to 6.

Oven-Roasted Camembert with Garlic Toasts

SERVES 4 TO 6

Similar to its better-known cousin, Brie, true Camembert is a creamy cow's milk cheese from Normandy, France. This is an astonishingly good, simple, little Basic recipe. A "little black dress" so to speak, perfect to whip out at the last minute for a delicious nibble as an aperitif or autumn snack.

Look for local Camembert-style cheeses and give them a try, too. (If your cheese doesn't come in a box, you can use aluminum foil to enclose it during the baking step.) I like to use Green Hill, made by my friends at Sweet Grass Dairy in Thomasville, Georgia.

1 (8-ounce) round Camembert, in a wooden box
1 baguette, diagonally sliced 1/4 inch thick
2 tablespoons pure olive oil
1 clove garlic, halved

Preheat the oven to 375°F.

Remove and discard the paper labels and any plastic from the Camembert. Return the cheese to its box and place on a rimmed baking sheet. Bake until soft and heated through, 20 to 30 minutes.

Position an oven rack 4 inches below the broiler and preheat the broiler.

To make the toasts, arrange the baguette slices on a baking sheet and brush the top side with some of the olive oil. Broil until brown, 2 to 3 minutes. Turn the toasts and broil the other side. Remove the toasts from the oven. While warm, rub the oiled side of each toast with a cut surface of the garlic clove. Transfer to a rack to cool. (The toasts may be made up to 2 days ahead and kept in a sealable plastic bag at room temperature.)

Once the Camembert is warmed, use a serrated knife to remove the top rind. Serve the warm cheese with the garlic toasts.

Brilliant: Short Recipe
Served with Boiled New Potatoes

Garnishes, the little something-something added at the end of cooking or just before serving, can quickly and quietly elevate a simple and delicious basic dish to something Brilliant. For our cheater's fondue, instead of serving with garlic toasts, serve boiled new potatoes for dipping, along with cornichons and Dijon mustard.

Scrub 1 pound of red new potatoes about the size of Ping-Pong balls under cold running water. Using a vegetable peeler or paring knife, remove a narrow strip around the equator of each potato. Then, using a paring knife, halve the potatoes vertically so that each half has a "racing stripe." Place the potatoes in a saucepan and add water to cover. Season with salt and pepper. Bring to a boil over high heat, then decrease the heat to simmer. Cook until tender and easily pierced with a knife, about 20 minutes. Drain well in a colander. Pat dry with paper towels. Season with coarse salt and freshly ground black pepper. Serve with the Camembert and with small bowls of cornichons and Dijon mustard.

5

Fish and Shellfish

When I went to the beach as a little girl, I couldn't wait to get in the water. Couldn't wait. We would vacation all along the coast in North Carolina, South Carolina, Alabama, Florida, and Georgia. Dede always packed fishing poles, and we'd fish off the dock and catch crabs off the jetty. Now that I am older I still love the beach, but I am absolutely mesmerized by the haunting beauty of the marsh. Little in this world is more satisfying to me than "wetting a hook," as Dede used to say—just standing on a dock enjoying nature.

The Georgia coastline, more than one hundred miles long and fringed with barrier islands, is part of the largest saltwater marsh in the world. Men and women have made their livelihoods for centuries harvesting fish and shellfish from the Low Country estuaries, where the tide flows in and the freshwater and saltwater mix. The islands are separated from the mainland by tidal marshes, some as long as six miles. From above, the coast looks like intricate lace, with the long, black curving lines of the rivers and creeks running through the green wire grass marsh.

With the Atlantic to the east and the Gulf of Mexico to the south, the seafood industry has both a large cultural and economic effect on the southeastern United States. It's a way of life from Virginia to Texas, and more than 250,000 people are employed in the seafood industry. The impact of the 2010 catastrophic oil spill off the Louisiana coast has been enormous and unimaginable, but the best thing we can do is support the seafood of the Gulf.

However, caution is necessary. We've been eating out of the ocean like it's a bottom-less bucket—and it's not. Overfishing—catching fish faster than they can reproduce—may be the single biggest threat to ocean ecosystems. There are simply too many boats chasing a dwindling number of fish. Aquaculture, or fish farming, sounds like a great solution to the ever-increasing pressures on our ocean resources. But, it's not that simple. The eco-logical impact of fish farming depends on the species chosen, where the farm is located, and how they are raised. It's important to know how and what it takes to get the food on your plate.

I was once able to go out on the *Dora F* out of Brunswick, Georgia, captained by Johnny Bennett with his first mate and daughter, Brande, and grandson, Jonathan. Jonathan was thirteen at the time, had been driving the boat since he was six, and was the fifth generation of Bennett shrimpers. The Bennetts generally leave in the early morning between 3:30 and 5:00 am, depending on which shrimp is in season, the moon, and the tides. The hours are long, the conditions can be breathtakingly hot, or cold and wet, and the work is very dangerous.

The day I was there, we had just docked after eight hours of hard work on the water. I had just finished interviewing the captain. In conversation, he explained that his brother had broken his leg. The packinghouse owner had lost a brother who had drowned. I related meeting a man who had lost his leg in the cables that hoist the large nets. Meanwhile, the crew was sorting the shrimp, preparing it for sale to the packinghouse.

I disembarked, and while walking on the dock adjacent to the *Dora F*'s sister ship, I was startled by the screeching sound of metal bending, warping, and twisting. I glanced up to see the nets swaying toward me; in fact, it seemed the entire boat was listing side-ways toward the dock. Terrified and trapped between the outrigger and heavy nets, I pulled my arms over my head and dropped to the ground. A cable snapped and one of the pair of outriggers—a thirty-foot-long length of steel scaffolding—violently collapsed. I scrambled to my feet, less than three feet from where the outrigger had crashed.

That memory and fear linger with me when I am considering what to cook for dinner. Someone literally risked life and limb to fill that seafood case at your local grocery store.

But, there's no doubt that fish and shellfish are part of a nutritionally sound diet. Seafood is high in protein, low in saturated fat, and contains heart-healthy omega-3s, which help boost immunity and reduce the risk of heart disease, stroke, cancer and other ailments. Omega-3s are especially important for pregnant and nursing women and young children.

Programs such as the Monterey Bay Aquarium's Seafood Watch or the Marine Stewardship Council offer information to help you choose seafood that's good for you and good for the oceans. They recommend which seafood to buy or avoid, helping consumers and businesses become advocates for ocean-friendly seafood. Their recommendations are available online, in printed pocket guides, or even downloadable on mobile devices.

Many cooks are easily overwhelmed with questions about cooking fish and shellfish. Mainly, how can you tell when fish is cooked, but not overcooked? The last thing that any cook wants to do is to overcook fish until it's dry. This chapter explains simple yet chef-driven techniques, such as coating with a flavorful crumb topping to protect the delicate flesh, oven poaching, and finishing fish in the oven. Once you're familiar with some of the Basic recipes, you may want to stretch your culinary chops on some of the Brilliant variations, such as the Salt-Crusted Whole Roast Fish (page 89) or Salmon fillets gently poached in olive oil (page 88). Whether you wet your own hook or visit the seafood case, these recipes fish and shellfish are sure to "catch on."

Sizing Up

Small, medium, and large are arbitrary designations for shrimp. Professional chefs buy shrimp according to industry designation: the count per pound. There's some wiggle room with the corresponding terms due to heads on versus heads off. The most important thing to remember is the smaller the number per pound, the bigger the shrimp.

- 10 shrimp or less per pound = Colossal
- 11 to 15 shrimp per pound = Jumbo
- 16 to 20 shrimp per pound = Extra-large
- 21 to 25 shrimp per pound = Large
- 26 to 30 shrimp per pound = Medium
- 31 to 35 shrimp per pound = Small

Pan-Seared Georgia Trout

SERVES 4

The North Georgia mountains are laced with rivulets and cold streams filled with mountain trout. Trout is a very forgiving fish to cook and very user friendly for people who don't like overly fishy fish, a concept that doesn't really make a whole lot of sense to me. The butter is a bit of glorious excess. Fresh trout would taste equally magnificent simply topped with toasted pecans.

1/4 cup canola oil, plus more for the baking sheet

1 cup pecans, finely chopped

1 cup plain or whole-wheat fresh or panko (Japanese) breadcrumbs

1/4 cup chopped fresh flat-leaf parsley

Coarse salt and freshly ground black pepper

4 (6- to 8-ounce) skin-on trout fillets

Lemon wedges, for garnish

Preheat the oven to 200°F. Brush a rimmed baking sheet with canola oil and place in the oven to warm.

Combine the pecans, breadcrumbs, and parsley in a shallow bowl or pie plate. Season with salt and pepper. Press the flesh side of each fillet into the pecan mixture.

Heat 2 tablespoons of the oil in a large skillet over medium heat. Place 2 trout in the pan, crust side down, and cook until golden brown, 2 to 3 minutes. Turn and cook until fish is opaque in the center and just cooked through, 2 to 3 minutes. Transfer the trout to the prepared baking sheet, crust side up. Place the baking sheet in the oven. Repeat the process with the remaining 2 tablespoons of oil and the remaining 2 trout fillets. Transfer to warmed serving plates and serve immediately, garnished with the lemon.

Brilliant: Short Recipe

Pecan Brown Butter

Basic panfried trout is elevated to Brilliant when dressed with Pecan Brown Butter. Wipe the skillet clean with paper towels. Add 1/4 cup (1/2 stick) unsalted butter and melt over medium heat. Allow the butter to foam and turn medium brown, swirling the pan occasionally. Remove the pan from the heat, add the finely grated zest and juice of 1 lemon, 1/4 cup chopped pecans, and 1/4 cup fresh flat-leaf parsley; season with coarse salt and freshly ground black pepper. Place the trout, crust side up, on warmed serving plates. Drizzle with the pecan butter. Serve immediately.

Poached Salmon with Herb Mustard Sauce

SERVES 4

My grandparents drove their motor home all the way from Georgia to Alaska three or four times. Dede loved Alaska, mostly because he liked salmon fishing. They would fish and then visit a local canning plant, returning with cases and cases of salmon preserved in mason jars. The processing renders the salmon bones soft. My sister and I would fight over what we referred to as the "buttons," which I now know to be the softened vertebrae.

Poaching is a classic French technique and the result, if executed properly, showcases the fish.

3 cups water

2 cups dry white wine

2 to 4 sprigs tarragon, leaves coarsely chopped and stems reserved

2 bay leaves, preferably fresh

1/2 teaspoon whole black peppercorns

1 carrot, sliced

Coarse salt and freshly ground white pepper

4 (5-ounce) skinless salmon fillets

1/2 cup Dijon mustard

1/2 cup extra-virgin olive oil, plus more for the greens

4 to 6 cups mixed greens (such as Belgian endive, mâche, and Bibb lettuce)

To poach the salmon, combine the water, wine, tarragon stems (leaves reserved), bay leaves, peppercorns, and carrot. Bring to a boil over high heat, then decrease the heat to low. Simmer gently for 15 to 20 minutes to make a flavorful court-bouillon. Season with salt and pepper.

Have ready a large, heavy-duty sealable plastic bag filled with ice cubes. Make an ice bath to cool the salmon by transfering several cups (or more, if needed) of the broth to a large heatproof bowl. Place the ice pack in the bowl of broth; move the pack around until the broth is well chilled (drain the bag and add more ice to it as needed). Return the heat to high and bring the remaining mixture to a rolling boil. Add the salmon fillets. Cover and simmer for 7 minutes.

Remove from the heat and remove the salmon from the poaching liquid. Transfer to the cooled broth and allow the salmon to cool in the bouillon. Cover the fish and broth with plastic wrap and chill in the refrigerator for 1 to 2 hours, or until you are ready to serve.

Meanwhile, put the mustard in a small bowl. Whisk the olive oil into the mustard in a slow, steady stream. Stir in the reserved chopped tarragon leaves. Taste and adjust for seasoning with salt and pepper.

When you are ready to serve, put the greens in a bowl. Drizzle with olive oil and season with salt and pepper. Toss to combine. Arrange the greens on 4 plates. Remove the salmon from the broth and pat dry with paper towels. Top each plate of greens with a piece of salmon. Spoon the mustard sauce over the fish to coat. (In French, this is known as *napper*, meaning to coat evenly with sauce, coming from the *nappe*, or "table-cloth.") Garnish with leaves from the remaining 2 sprigs tarragon. Serve, passing the remaining mustard sauce separately.

Brilliant: Short Recipe
Salmon Poached in Oil

Poaching salmon in olive oil makes it even richer. This technique works especially well with white-fleshed fish, such as halibut or barramundi. For a real flavor infusion, use the oil from Garlic Confit (page 14) and top it off with pure olive oil. Season the salmon with coarse salt and freshly ground white pepper. In a large, deep skillet, heat 2 cups pure (not extra-virgin) olive oil over medium heat until shimmering. Add the salmon fillets, without crowding, and cook over medium heat for 3 minutes. (They don't have to be completely submerged; just spoon the oil over them, bathing them while they cook.) Using a spatula, carefully turn the fillets and simmer until just cooked through, about 3 minutes longer. Repeat with remaining fillets, if necessary. Serve on top of greens. Brilliant.

Whole Roasted Fish with Herbs

SERVES 4

Cooking whole large fish is scary, but it doesn't have to be the culinary equivalent of summons to the principal's office or a call from the IRS. Both for cooking in the oven and on the grill, I often wrap the fish in foil to make it easier to flip and handle. No yummy charring, but no fish-crusted grill grates, either. Fear, like lemon for serving, is optional.

In the summer I like to serve the fish chilled. Fillet the fish and place it in a single layer on a shallow, rimmed plate. Pour the accumulated juices captured in the foil over and cover with plastic wrap. Refrigerate until cold and the juices have set due to the natural gelatin, an hour or so or overnight. It's refreshing and delicious.

1 tablespoon best-quality extra-virgin olive oil, plus more
 for serving

2- to 3-pound whole striped bass, arctic char, or croaker, gills
 removed, scaled, and gutted, leaving head and tail intact

Coarse salt and freshly ground black pepper

Bouquet garni (2 bay leaves, preferably fresh, 5 sprigs
 thyme, 4 sprigs flat-leaf parsley, 10 black peppercorns,
 tied together in cheesecloth)

2 bay leaves, preferably fresh

1 lemon, sliced, plus more for garnish

Preheat the oven to 450°F. Place a piece of aluminum foil large enough to hold the fish on a clean work surface. Brush the foil with the olive oil and season with salt and pepper. (Yes, the foil, so it will season the outside of the fish.)

Place the prepared fish at the center of the foil and season with salt and pepper. Stuff with the herbs and lemon slices. Fold the foil to seal. Place on a rimmed baking sheet. Roast in the oven for 8 to 10 minutes per inch of thickness, until an instant-read thermometer inserted into the center of the meat registers 135°F to 140°F and the flesh is opaque, about 20 minutes. Use an offset spatula to remove the top fillet from the bones. Transfer the fillet to a warmed serving plate. Break off the tail and pull away the central bone. Lift away the bottom fillet and place on the plate. Drizzle over the olive oil and garnish with lemon. Serve immediately.

Brilliant: Technique
Salt-Crusted
Whole Roast Fish

A salt crust seals in the juices, but amazingly doesn't overwhelm the fish with a salty taste! Present the fish whole at the table, then return to the kitchen for "surgery."

Preheat the oven to 450°F. Line a rimmed baking sheet with aluminum foil for easy cleanup. Combine 2 pounds kosher salt and 1 tablespoon dried herbes de Provence in a bowl. Mix until well combined. Pour over 1 cup water and mix together until the salt has the consistency of wet sand. (It's like building sandcastles, only deliciously edible.) Spread half of salt mixture in a rectangle on the foil just larger than the fish. Place the stuffed fish on top. Pat the remaining salt mixture over the fish to cover completely. (If the tail sticks out, it's okay.) Transfer to the oven and bake for 30 minutes. Remove from the oven and let rest for 2 to 3 minutes so the salt will cool just slightly. Using the back of a chef's knife or large spoon, rap all around the edge of the salt crust to loosen it. Remove the salt top and carefully remove the skin. Use an offset spatula to remove the top fillet from the bones. Keep a few paper towels handy to wipe away any stray salt. Transfer the fillet to a serving plate. Break off the tail and pull away the central bone. Lift away the bottom fillet, leaving the skin attached to the bottom salt crust, and place on the plate. Drizzle over the olive oil and garnish with lemon. Serve immediately.

Oven-Roasted Crusted Fish Fillets

SERVES 4

My Fish 101 classes consistently sell out and have a waiting list. People are scared to cook fish. Salmon is a great fish to start with because it's firm, flavorful, readily available, and just oily enough not to dry out unless you really overcook it. Think of it as cooking fish with training wheels. After you've graduated from salmon, try this technique with a fillet, such as catfish, tilapia, trout, or barramundi—all fish farmed sustainably in a closed system above ground.

The fish is protected from the direct heat of the oven by a flavorful topping of breadcrumbs and olive oil. Once you've tried this simple technique, you'll never be scared to cook fish again.

1/4 cup extra-virgin olive oil

1/2 cup plain or whole-wheat fresh or panko (Japanese) breadcrumbs

1/4 bunch fresh flat-leaf parsley, chopped

8 sprigs tarragon, chopped

4 small cloves garlic, very finely chopped

1 teaspoon red pepper flakes, or to taste

Coarse salt and freshly ground black pepper

4 (8-ounce) catfish, tilapia, trout, or barramundi skinless fillets

Preheat the oven to 450°F. Oil a rimmed baking sheet with some of the olive oil.

Combine the breadcrumbs, parsley, tarragon, garlic, and red pepper in a small bowl. Brush each fish with olive oil, then add the remaining oil to the breadcrumb mixture. Season the breadcrumb mixture with salt and pepper and stir to combine. Dust the top side of each fillet with the breadcrumb mixture. Place the fish on the prepared baking sheet and roast until the breadcrumbs are browned and the fish is opaque, 5 to 7 minutes. Serve immediately on warmed serving plates.

Brilliant: Short Recipe
Creamy Garlic Sauce

This creamy sauce is a delicate mayonnaise. Don't skip the garlic blanching process. The result is Brilliant.

Combine the peeled cloves from 1 head of garlic in a small saucepan with 1 cup cold water. Bring to a boil over medium-high heat, then drain. Repeat the process four times, always starting with cold water. Drain well. Combine the softened garlic, 1 large egg yolk, 6 sprigs flat-leaf parsley, juice of 1/2 lemon, and 1/2 cup pure olive oil in a blender; blend until creamy. Season with coarse salt and freshly ground white pepper. Makes about 1/2 cup. To serve, spoon some of the garlic sauce onto warmed serving plates and top with the fish fillets.

Catfish

Wild catfish can have a strong flavor because, as bottom feeders, the fish burrow in the mud of lakes and ponds. Sustainable farm-raised catfish are fed a diet of grain pellets, resulting in a clean, mild-flavored fish.

Fried Benne Shrimp

SERVES 4 TO 6

Mama and I both love fried shrimp—we can't go to the beach without enjoying a meal of fried shrimp. It's sad how many of those beach restaurants are serving imported shrimp. I like to put my money where my mouth is and try to patronize restaurants that are supporting the local fishing industry.

Slaves brought benne to the Carolina Sea Islands directly from Africa. Benne seeds are more widely known as sesame seeds. Modern sesame is grown mainly for oil production. During the colonial and antebellum eras, benne was grown not only for its extraordinary oil, but also for the seeds, which are very nutritious and can be used whole, ground into a paste, or milled to a flour.

4 cups peanut or canola oil, for frying

24 large white shrimp (21/25 count), peeled and deveined, tails on

1 cup all-purpose flour

1 cup cornstarch

1 (12-ounce) bottle beer, chilled

2 tablespoons white sesame seeds

1/2 cup black sesame seeds

2 tablespoons chopped or snipped fresh chives

1 tablespoon chopped fresh flat-leaf parsley

Coarse salt and freshly ground black pepper

Tartar or cocktail sauce, for serving

Pour the oil into a heavy-bottomed saucepan, deep fryer, or Dutch oven, filling it no more than one-third full. Heat the oil over medium heat until it reaches 350°F. Meanwhile, put the shrimp on a plate lined with paper towels and pat dry with additional paper towels to eliminate all moisture. Line another plate with paper towels and set aside.

In a large bowl, mix the flour and cornstarch. Slowly whisk in the beer until a smooth, thick batter forms. Stir in the sesame seeds, chives, and parsley. Holding 4 shrimp by the tail at a time, dip them into the batter. Gently shake off the excess batter and slip the shrimp into the hot oil. Remove the shrimp when crispy and brown, about 3 minutes. Drain on the second plate lined with paper towels. While the shrimp are still hot, season with salt and pepper. Let cool slightly before serving.

Brilliant: Short Recipe
Celery Slaw

This Brilliant side dish is somewhere between a salad and traditional tartar sauce. It's an excellent accompaniment to the fried shrimp.

Remove the strings from 4 celery stalks, then thinly slice on the diagonal. Combine with 1/2 cup mayonnaise (page 15); 1 tablespoon Dijon mustard; 1 tablespoon capers, rinsed and chopped; 1 tablespoon chopped fresh tarragon; 1 tablespoon chopped fresh flat-leaf parsley; and the finely grated zest and juice of 1 lemon in a bowl. Stir to mix. Season to taste with coarse salt and freshly ground black pepper. Cover and chill until you are ready to serve. Makes about 1 cup.

Frozen Vs. Fresh

The vast majority of shrimp and a lot of fish are processed and frozen on the boat or at the farm before they ever get anywhere near your fishmonger or supermarket. This means that the "fresh" seafood you're seeing at the fish counter may be frozen seafood that has been defrosted and put on display. Buy from a reputable market that tells the truth and ask if it has been frozen. If you have to buy frozen seafood, look for IQF, or Individually Quick Frozen. The more rapidly something is frozen, the better the texture. IQF means each piece is individually frozen before being packaged, as opposed to being frozen in a block.

Grilled Shrimp "Gumbo"

SERVES 6

Leave the soup pot in the cupboard! Succulent shrimp and spicy andouille sausage team up with sweet onion, tomatoes, and okra for a delicious dish that tastes like gumbo but doesn't take hours to cook. This dish is going to knock your socks off.

1 pound large shrimp (21/25 count), peeled and deveined

12 ounces fully cooked andouille sausage, halved lengthwise

1 pint grape tomatoes

12 ounces finger-size okra, stems trimmed

1 onion, preferably Vidalia, sliced into 1/4-inch rings

1 red bell pepper, cored, seeded, and cut into strips

1 poblano or green bell pepper, cored, seeded, and cut into strips

1/4 cup pure olive oil

2 teaspoons Creole or Cajun seasoning, plus more to taste

1/4 cup ketchup, warmed

4 green onions, white and pale green parts only, chopped

Coarse salt and freshly ground black pepper

Hot cooked rice, for serving

Prepare a charcoal fire using about 6 pounds of charcoal and burn until the coals are completely covered with a thin coating of light gray ash, 20 to 30 minutes. Spread the coals evenly over the grill bottom, position the grill rack above the coals, and heat until medium-hot (when you can hold your hand 5 inches above the grill surface for no longer than 3 or 4 seconds). Or, for a gas grill, turn on all burners to high, close the lid, and heat until very hot, 10 to 15 minutes.

Combine the shrimp, sausage, tomatoes, okra, onion, and bell peppers in a large bowl. Add the oil and Creole seasoning, and toss to coat the ingredients. Thread the shrimp, tomatoes, okra, and pepper onto separate skewers. (The onions can go directly on the grill.) Or, use a grilling basket instead of skewers for the vegetables.

Place the vegetables on the hottest part of the grill. Arrange the sausage over slightly cooler heat and the shrimp at the edges of the grill. Cook, turning once or twice, until the shrimp is opaque, the sausage is heated through, and the vegetables are tender and slightly charred, 8 to 10 minutes (the shrimp will take less time to cook). Slice the sausage, onion, and bell peppers into bite-size pieces, then transfer them, along with the other ingredients, to a large bowl.

Toss the meat and vegetable mixture with the ketchup and green onions. Cover the mixture tightly with plastic wrap and let the vegetables steam and wilt slightly, about 5 minutes. Remove the plastic wrap from the bowl. Taste and adjust the seasoning with salt, pepper, and Creole seasoning to your liking. Ladle over cooked rice in warmed serving bowls. Serve immediately.

Brilliant: Short Recipe
Grilled Creole Oysters

This is just a little lagniappe to elevate our Basic "gumbo" to Brilliant.

While the gumbo is steaming and the grill is still hot, place 12 whole oysters on the hottest part of the grill. Cook until they open, about 5 minutes. Remove the oysters from the grill. Holding each with a hot pad and using an oyster knife or a clean flathead screwdriver, pry off the top shell and discard. Slide the knife between the oyster and shell to disconnect. Squeeze the juice of 1 lemon over the oysters and drizzle a dash of hot sauce on each. Season with freshly ground black pepper. To serve, ladle the "gumbo" over the rice as directed. Top each portion with 2 oysters on the half shell. Serve immediately.

N'awlins-Style BBQ Shrimp

New Orleans, aka N'awlins, is in mind and spirit quite separate from the rest of Louisiana. It's deep, deep South, flavored with a heavy dose of the Caribbean. The food of New Orleans is incredibly rich. I often tease my Cajun colleagues that the only green you'll find on your plate is the tarragon in the cream sauce. Situated on the Gulf, shrimp is a mainstay of Cajun and Creole cuisine. BBQ Shrimp may seem to be a funny name—there's no grilling or barbecuing involved—but that's the traditional name for this Louisiana favorite.

The biggest mistake with cooking shrimp is cooking them too long. Most people overcook them, and the shrimp bounces in your mouth like a rubber ball. Shrimp should only take two to three minutes to cook. Normally, this Big Easy classic uses dried herbs, but I prefer fresh. Try this as a first course with crusty baguette to sop up all the delicious juices.

1 cup (2 sticks) unsalted butter

1/2 cup pure olive oil

4 cloves garlic, finely chopped

4 bay leaves, preferably fresh

4 to 6 large sprigs rosemary, leaves chopped to make
2 teaspoons and whole stems reserved

1 teaspoon chopped fresh basil

1 teaspoon chopped fresh oregano

1 teaspoon chopped fresh thyme

1/2 teaspoon red pepper flakes

1 tablespoon paprika

Coarse salt

2 teaspoons freshly squeezed lemon juice

2 pounds large shrimp (21/25 count), in the shell

Freshly ground black pepper

Crusty baguette, for serving

Combine the butter and oil in a heavy ovenproof saucepan over medium heat. Add the garlic, bay leaves, rosemary, basil, oregano, thyme, red pepper, paprika, salt, and lemon juice. Cook, stirring constantly, until the sauce begins to boil. Decrease the heat to low and simmer, stirring frequently, until the flavors have infused, 7 to 8 minutes.

Meanwhile, skewer the shrimp on the rosemary branches so the bodies and tails are oriented in the same direction; do not arrange tightly pressed together, or the parts touching one another will not cook. Season with salt and pepper.

Add the shrimp to the sauce. Cook the shrimp over medium heat just until they turn pink, 2 to 3 minutes per side. Transfer the shrimp to warmed serving plates. Taste and adjust for seasoning with salt and pepper. Serve immediately, leaving the shrimp on the skewers, and give each diner a bowl of the herbed butter and slices of crusty baguette for dipping.

Brilliant: Technique
Beurre Monté

Instead of using Basic butter to cook the shrimp, prepare a Brilliant *beurre monté*, a suspended butter-water emulsion, and the liquid culinary equivalent of fine silk.

Bring 2 tablespoons water to a simmer in a heavy saucepan over medium heat. Decrease the heat to medium-low and gradually whisk in 1 pound unsalted butter, 1 tablespoon at a time, until the water and butter have emulsified. Keep the temperature between 180°F to 190°F. (If the mixture boils, it will separate.) Add the garlic, paprika, red pepper, lemon juice, and herbs. Add the shrimp (not skewered) and stir to combine. Cook the shrimp over medium heat until they just turn pink, 2 to 3 minutes per side. Taste and adjust for seasoning with salt and pepper. Remove the shrimp with a slotted spoon and transfer to warmed serving plates. Serve immediately. Give each diner a bowl of the herbed butter and slices of crusty baguette for dipping.

Panfried Shrimp Po-Boy

SERVES 4

Po-boys are iconic in coastal cuisine, especially in Louisiana. It's a New Orleans classic said to have originated in the early twentieth century, the name deriving from the plea, "Give a po' boy (poor boy) a sandwich?" According to food and travel writer and general NOLA (a friendly nickname acronym for New Orleans, LA) bon vivant and raconteur Pableaux Johnson, the original po-boys were hollowed out loaves of bread layered with fried potatoes and brown gravy. Seafood po-boys include fried shrimp, fried oysters, fried catfish, and fried soft-shell crab. See a trend?

This version is lighter and healthier than the deep-fried versions. The shrimp are breaded in egg whites and coated in panko, or Japanese breadcrumbs. Panko gives food a lighter and crunchier texture than any other breadcrumb.

1 baguette, quartered crosswise and split

2 egg whites

1 tablespoon water

Coarse salt and freshly ground black pepper

$1/2$ cup plain or whole-wheat fresh or panko (Japanese) breadcrumbs

16 large shrimp, (21/25 count) peeled, deveined, and butterflied

$1/4$ cup canola oil, plus more as needed

2 cups shredded romaine lettuce

2 tablespoons tartar sauce

1 teaspoon hot sauce, or to taste

1 large tomato, cored and very thinly sliced

1 lemon, quartered

Preheat the oven to 350°F.

Place the bread on a rimmed baking sheet in the oven to warm and crisp while you prepare the shrimp. Line a baking sheet with paper towels and set aside.

Combine the egg whites and water in a small bowl and whisk until light and frothy. Season with salt and pepper. Put the breadcrumbs in another shallow dish. Dredge the shrimp in the egg white mixture, then dredge in the breadcrumbs.

Heat the oil in a large nonstick skillet over medium-high heat. Add the breaded shrimp without overcrowding the skillet; cook until golden brown on each side, 2 to 3 minutes per side. (If your skillet is not large enough, you may need to cook the shrimp in two batches, and may need to add a little more oil.) Transfer to the prepared baking sheet to drain.

Combine the lettuce, tartar sauce, and hot sauce in a bowl. Season with salt and pepper.

Remove the bread from the oven. Arrange 3 tomato slices over the bottom half of each quarter. Top each with 4 shrimp, $1/2$ cup of the lettuce mixture, and the top halves. Garnish with lemon wedges and serve immediately.

Brilliant: Short Recipe
Fried Capers

I know. This is a case of me lightening up the Basic to have a decadent Brilliant. Taste them. You'll be convinced. Fried capers are a flavorful explosion of vinegar and salt. Indulge with a little Brilliance.

Rinse $1/4$ cup salted capers in a fine-mesh sieve. Transfer to a small bowl. Add enough water to cover the capers by 2 inches, then soak for 30 minutes. Drain and rinse capers, then pat very dry between paper towels. Heat $1^1/2$ cups canola oil in a heavy saucepan over medium-high heat until it registers 375°F on a deep-frying thermometer. Fry the capers a tablespoon at a time until golden, 30 to 45 seconds per batch. Transfer with a slotted spoon to paper towels to drain. Season with freshly ground black pepper. Return the oil to 375°F between batches. Makes about $1/2$ cup. Serve scattered over the po-boys.

Steamed Herbed Mussels *Moules Marinière*

SERVES 4

Mussels are incredibly inexpensive and perhaps the original fast food. It takes no time whatsoever to make a savory, satisfying meal with a bag of mussels. Mussel farming is a shining example of how nutritious and delicious food can be raised in a sustainable way. France and Belgium are well-known for *moules frites*, or steamed mussels and French fries, served with a side of mayonnaise.

5 pounds mussels

3 tablespoons pure olive oil

1 onion, preferably Vidalia, finely chopped

1 fennel bulb, halved, cored, and thinly sliced

1 tablespoon finely chopped garlic

2 large ripe tomatoes, preferably heirloom, cored, seeded, and chopped

1/8 teaspoon red pepper flakes, or to taste

1/2 cup dry white wine

4 sprigs thyme

1 bay leaf, preferably fresh

Freshly ground black pepper

1/4 cup fresh basil leaves, cut in chiffonade (see page 193)

Coarse salt

Crusty baguette, for serving

Scrub the mussels and remove the beards. Wash them under cold running water, agitating them with your hand. Discard any mussels that do not close to the touch.

Heat the oil in a large Dutch oven over medium-high heat. Add the onion and fennel. Cook until the onions are translucent, 3 to 5 minutes. Add the garlic and cook until fragrant, 45 to 60 seconds. Add the tomatoes, red pepper, wine, thyme, and bay leaf. Season with pepper. (Do not season with salt, as the mussels may be salty.) Bring to a boil and simmer for 2 minutes.

Add the mussels and basil. Cover tightly and cook over high heat until all the mussels have opened, 5 to 6 minutes. Discard any that fail to open. Taste and adjust for seasoning with salt and pepper. Serve immediately with a crusty baguette.

Mussel Bound

Cultivated blue mussels often come with a tag that tells you when the mussels were harvested and a "best by" date. The tag will be attached to the mesh bag, or you can ask for it at the seafood counter if you are buying them loose. An easy way to tell if they are fresh is to use your nose—they should smell like the ocean. It's an added bonus that you don't have to eat them as soon as you get home. Depending on the date, you usually can buy and store them in your fridge at home for a few days before eating. Take the mussels out of the mesh bag and place them in a bowl or tray. Cover with a damp cloth or paper towel to keep them moist. Do not store them in fresh water or in a sealed container. Once you're ready to cook, just take them out of the refrigerator and discard any with closed shells; give them one last sniff to check on the freshness. Just before cooking, rinse the mussels in fresh water in a pot or colander. Seafood should smell like the sea.

Brilliant: Short Recipe
Moules Mouclade

I prefer to serve mussels as in the Basic recipe, with crusty bread for sopping. But the same way that blue jeans are comfortable, sometimes it's nice to dress up a bit, as here with Brilliant Moules Mouclade, a stew in which the mussels are removed from their shells and bathed in a decadent, creamy sauce.

CONTINUED

Take the cooked mussels out of their shells and place in a large baking dish; set aside. To make the sauce, melt 2 tablespoons unsalted butter in a medium saucepan over medium heat until foaming. Add 3 shallots, chopped, and cook until translucent, 3 to 5 minutes. Stir in 2 tablespoons all-purpose flour and, while it is bubbling, add 1 cup of the strained mussel broth, stirring continuously. (This is a form of a velouté; see page 11.) Add 1 cup heavy cream and strain in the remaining broth; simmer until it thickens and coats the back of a spoon, 5 to 10 minutes. Add 1 tablespoon chopped fresh flat-leaf parsley. Season with salt and freshly ground white pepper. Spoon the sauce over the mussels and put under a heated broiler until browned and bubbling, about 5 minutes. Once again, serve with crusty bread for sopping. Serves 4.

Seafood Jambalaya

SERVES 4 TO 6

Jamba-lye, crawfish pie, filé gumbo . . . I spent my summers in Georgia, but my entire elementary school-age experience was in Rapides Parish, Louisiana. This set me on a path to understanding and learning different foods. Since Mama liked to cook, and we were adventurous eaters, we all had a good time in the kitchen. I encourage parents to get their kids into the kitchen; when children help produce what goes on the table, they are more likely to try it. Growing up in Louisiana exposed my sister and me to all sorts of things we would have never had in Georgia, such as this jambalaya. Instead of shrimp, you can use pieces of catfish. Simple, basic, and delicious—and on the table in less than 45 minutes.

1 tablespoon canola oil

1 tablespoon unsalted butter

6 ounces andouille sausage, sliced

1 tablespoon Cajun or Creole Seasoning

1 onion, preferably Vidalia, chopped

1 celery stalk, chopped

1/2 poblano or green bell pepper, cored, seeded, and chopped

1 clove garlic, very finely chopped

1 1/2 cups long-grain rice

1 (4-ounce) can tomato sauce

2 1/2 cups seafood stock (page 13), chicken stock (page 9), or water

1 pound large shrimp (21/25 count), peeled and deveined

Coarse salt and freshly ground black pepper

Preheat the oven to 350°F. In a large ovenproof skillet, heat the oil and butter over high heat until shimmering. Add the andouille and cook until the meat starts to brown and render fat, about 3 minutes. Sprinkle over the seasoning. Add the onion, celery, and poblano pepper; cook, stirring occasionally, until the vegetables start to color, 5 to 7 minutes. Add the garlic and cook until fragrant, 45 to 60 seconds. Add the rice and stir to coat. Stir in the tomato sauce and seafood stock and bring to a boil.

Transfer to the oven and bake, uncovered, for 30 minutes. Add the shrimp and stir to combine. Continue baking until the rice is tender and the shrimp are opaque, about 10 minutes. Remove from the oven to a rack to cool slightly. Taste and adjust for seasoning with salt and pepper. Spoon the jambalaya into warmed serving bowls. Serve immediately.

Brilliant: Short Recipe
Cracklin' Powder

I can hear the gasps now. What? Cracklin' Powder? Yep. Do it. It's Brilliant. It's an idea I got from my friend and colleague, cookbook author Sandra Guitterez, the Culinary Latinista. Restaurants all over the South are making homemade cracklings, which are fried pig skin. The process is very labor intensive, so just run on out to the Jiffy Mart and buy a bag instead.

Empty a (1.75-ounce) bag of fried pork skins into a food processor fitted with a metal blade. Pulse until finely ground to a powder. Keeps in an airtight container for up to 1 month. Makes 1/2 cup. To use, sprinkle over the jambalaya and serve immediately.

Creole Country Bouillabaisse

SERVES 6 TO 8

This is a marriage made in heaven. I grew up in Louisiana enjoying crawfish boils. The Low Country, the area of the Atlantic coast between Savannah, Georgia, and Charleston, South Carolina, is famous for its Low Country boil, also known as Frogmore Stew. The south of France is famous for bouillabaisse. All are simple country seafood stews. I've combined the three, taking the best from each. Crawfish are available by mail order, online, and are sold live in better seafood markets in the spring.

2 tablespoons pure olive oil

1 onion, preferably Vidalia, chopped

Coarse salt and freshly ground black pepper

12 to 16 red new potatoes, about the size of golf balls

4 quarts homemade seafood stock (page 13) or water

1 head garlic, cloves separated and peeled

1/2 cup (3-ounce bag) Old Bay Seasoning

Bouquet garni (2 bay leaves, preferably fresh, 5 sprigs thyme, 4 sprigs flat-leaf parsley, 10 black peppercorns, tied together in cheesecloth)

1/4 cup tomato paste

2 (28-ounce) cans crushed tomatoes

1/4 teaspoon cayenne pepper, or to taste

2 pounds fresh kielbasa, cut into pieces

6 ears fresh sweet corn, shucked and silk removed, broken in half

12 live crawfish

1 1/2 pounds skinless halibut fillet, cut into large chunks

12 large shrimp (21/25 count), in the shell

12 mussels, scrubbed and debearded

12 cherrystone clams, scrubbed

Jalapeño Cornbread Muffins (page 230) or crusty bread, for serving

Heat the oil in a large, heavy stockpot over medium-high heat until shimmering. Add the onion and cook until translucent, 3 to 5 minutes. Season with salt and pepper. Add the potatoes, seafood stock, garlic, Old Bay, bouquet garni, tomato paste, tomatoes, and cayenne pepper. Cover the pot and heat to a rolling boil. Decrease the heat to simmer and cook until fragrant and flavorful, about 15 minutes. Add the sausage, corn, and live crawfish and return to a boil. Cook until the potatoes are tender, about 10 minutes.

Add the fish and cook gently until just opaque, 3 to 4 minutes. Add the shrimp, mussels, and clams and cook until the shrimp shells are pink and the meat is white and opaque and the mussels and clams have opened, an additional 3 to 4 minutes. Taste the broth and adjust for seasoning with salt and pepper.

To serve, transfer portions of the seafood to warmed shallow soup bowls. Spoon the broth over the seafood and serve immediately with the muffins.

Brilliant: Short Recipe
Sautéed Fennel

Fennel is a traditional ingredient in the French version of this stew. To elevate our tasty Basic stew to Brilliant, try making a caramelized Sautéed Fennel garnish. Heat 1 tablespoon olive oil (or bacon fat if you are feeling really decadent) in a large skillet over medium-high heat. Add 1 fennel bulb, cored and chopped, and 1 clove garlic, mashed into a paste. Decrease the heat to medium. Season with coarse salt and freshly ground black pepper. As the fennel starts to brown and caramelize, after about 15 minutes, add 1/4 cup homemade seafood stock (page 13), homemade chicken stock (page 9), or reduced-fat, low-sodium chicken broth. Cover with a tight fitting lid to steam until tender, about 3 minutes. Remove from the heat. Taste and adjust for seasoning with salt and freshly ground black pepper. Makes about 1/2 cup. To serve, fill the warmed bowls with the seafood and broth. Garnish with the fennel and serve immediately.

Grilled Soft-Shell Crabs with Lemon Gremolata

SERVES 4 TO 6

I learned to make this from my friend chef Penn Lehman. We were like peas and carrots in culinary school. As an avid fisherwoman seafood is her specialty—even in Park City, Utah, home of her award-winning restaurant, The Blind Dog Grill, where the the fish is flown in daily from all over the world. Gremolata is an Italian condiment made from finely minced parsley, garlic, and lemon zest. It is traditionally served with osso buco, but it is also an excellent accompaniment for fish and shellfish dishes.

1/4 cup chopped fresh flat-leaf parsley

1 tablespoon chopped fresh thyme

2 cloves garlic, very finely chopped

Grated zest and juice of 1 lemon

1/3 cup pure olive oil

Coarse salt and freshly ground black pepper

4 to 6 soft-shell crabs

1/4 cup (1/2 stick) unsalted butter, melted, or 1/4 cup clarified butter (see sidebar)

To make the gremolata, combine the parsley, thyme, garlic, lemon zest, and olive oil in a small bowl. Season with salt and pepper. Set aside.

Prepare a charcoal fire using about 6 pounds of charcoal and burn until the coals are completely covered with a thin coating of light gray ash, 20 to 30 minutes. Spread the coals evenly over the grill bottom, position the grill rack above the coals, and heat until medium-hot (when you can hold your hand 5 inches above the grill surface for no longer than 3 or 4 seconds). Or, for a gas grill, turn on all burners to high, close the lid, and heat until very hot, 10 to 15 minutes.

Meanwhile, clean and prepare the crabs. Hold a crab in one hand and bend back the pointed ends of the shell. Using your fingers, remove the cottony pale gray gills on the sides. Turn the crab over and snip off the small flap (the apron) and the head with a pair of kitchen scissors. Tomalley is the soft green liver and is considered a delicacy. It is very rich; however, if you don't like the taste of the tomalley, gently squeeze the crab to remove it. Rinse the entire crab well, pat dry, and set aside.

Brush the surface of the crabs with melted butter and season with salt and pepper.

To cook the crabs, grill over direct heat until bright red and slightly charred, 3 to 5 minutes per side. Serve immediately, topped with gremolata.

Brilliant: Short Recipe
Soft-Shell Crabs with Shrimp Stuffing

I did a little happy dance when I first tasted this dish. Brilliant almost doesn't express how good this is. Combine 2 lightly beaten egg whites, 2 teaspoons dry mustard, 1/3 cup mayonnaise (page 15), and the juice of 1/2 lemon in a bowl. Fold in 1 pound peeled small shrimp, very finely chopped. Season with salt and pepper. To stuff the crabs, insert just enough of the shrimp mixture to fill the opening between the top shell and the body of each crab; don't overstuff. If any of the shrimp mixture remains, reserve for another use such as shrimp cakes or a decadent omelet filling. Proceed as directed for the Basic recipe.

Clarified and Browned Butter

Cut 1 1/2 cups (3 sticks) of unsalted butter into 1-inch pieces and melt over low heat in a heavy saucepan. When the butter stops sizzling, remove the pan from the heat and let stand for 3 minutes. With a spoon, skim the froth off the top; discard. Slowly pour the rest into a jar or crock, leaving the milky solids in the bottom of the pan; discard. Store the clarified butter in an airtight container in the refrigerator for up to 1 month. Makes 1 cup. Browned Butter or *Beurre Noisette* is prepared in the same way, but the butter is heated a bit longer, until the milk solids turn into rich, golden brown flecks.

6

Gospel Birds and Game Birds

"Boy, you got a good scald on that chicken," said Ed to Evelyn in the movie *Fried Green Tomatoes.* Okay, so not everyone can quote dialogue about fried chicken like I can. It's my own "special gift" because fried chicken is the absolute quintessence of cooking in the South. And, to translate this bizarre nugget of cinematic commentary, Ed is referring to the high, but controlled heat that scalds the skin into crispy goodness and creates moist, juicy meat. The title of this chapter may seem equally puzzling. What's a gospel bird? Gospel bird is an old-fashioned term for fried chicken, traditionally a special treat reserved for Sundays. When I lived far away from home and flew home to visit, it didn't matter what time of the day or night I arrived, my grandmother Meme would be at the stove frying chicken to welcome me home. And now, my mother does the same. Even though it is part of my mission to convince people the South is more than fried chicken, fried chicken would still be my hands-down choice for my last supper if I were "on the way to the chair." The smell of biscuits baking and chicken frying reaches into my soul.

Long, squatty chicken houses dot the landscape of North Georgia. The gentle sloping foothills of the Appalachian Mountains provide the perfect cool climate for raising chickens. Increasingly, chicken producers have moved farther south in the state for cheaper

103

land with the advent of better cooling systems to adjust for the searing hot weather. On an average day, Georgia produces 24.6 million pounds of chicken and 14 million eggs. That's a whole lot of bird.

It hasn't always been that way. Before World War II, small flocks, tended to by the farmers' wives, scratched and pecked their way around the yards and barnyards, producing the majority of eggs. The profits received from the sale of the eggs, often called "egg money," were kept by the wives.

The rural South has always been very poor, and the 1920s and 1930s were economically disastrous. Then, according to the *Georgia Encyclopedia*, in the 1930s, an enterprising feed and seed salesman from Gainesville named Jesse Jewell offered farmers a deal: He would sell them baby chicks and feed on credit. When the chicks were grown, Jewell would buy back the adult chickens at a fair price that would guarantee the farmers a profit. Once he had recruited enough farmers to produce broilers for him, Jewell took his business venture to the next level by investing in his own processing plant and hatchery.

With World War II, the War Food Administration, an agency created during World War I to manage food stock, reserved all the chicken in North Georgia. Georgia farmers had a sure bet, a guaranteed buyer. These developments brought enormous changes in production: more facilities, as well as packaging fully dressed birds, with no head, feet, or entrails, better for freezing and transport, similar to what we have today.

Jewell added a feed mill and rendering plant in the postwar boom of the 1950s, triggering a change in the business model of the modern poultry farm. After the war, poultry farming steadily increased, then soared in the 1970s and 1980s, as Americans decreased their consumption of red meat.

The same rural women who once raised the eggs, along with African Americans, became the labor force for these growing chicken-production facilities. Although it is now far better, working in a chicken plant was, and still is, dangerous work. Poor working conditions in some plants have led to attempts at unionization. However, union presence in the South in all fields of industry has always been vehemently resisted, and the chicken industry has been no different. There are some plants that have unionized, but more are not. Currently, the overwhelming majority of production workers in Georgia's processing plants are Latin American immigrants, mainly from Mexico.

I was able to visit a chicken-processing plant in North Georgia several years ago. I saw *everything*, from incubated eggs to chicken fingers flash frozen in a freezer the size of my house. Frankly, it was a lot cleaner than I expected, and quite a bit of the work is now done by machine. The breasts are scanned by laser, configured by computer to allow the maximum number of cutlets per breast, automatically adjusted on the belt by the machine, and cut with high-pressure water, the same technology used to cut steel. It was astonishing. The robot was impressive, but one of the most amazing things I saw was a Hispanic man boning out thighs by hand. His knife was moving so fast it was an absolute blur. He was paid not by the hour, but by the pound.

There are literally tens of thousands of chickens moving through these plants every day. Not surprisingly, increased scrutiny of the poultry industry, the political implications of 200 to 300 percent increases in the immigrant population to meet the labor needs in North Georgia and across the South, and growing concerns about the negative effects of agribusiness have created a slow-foods movement toward smaller farms and smaller production facilities. It's the beginning of some people wanting to unravel what the enterprising Jesse Jewell started decades ago.

Choosing Poultry

Antibiotic-free and hormone-free stickers appear on packages throughout the meat case at local markets. It can be a bit confusing. Actually, *all* chicken is hormone free. USDA regulations prohibit poultry growers from giving hormones or steroids to their birds. So, this label, while truthful, is also potentially misleading. It would be similar to putting a "cholesterol-free" label on an apple—sounds great until you realize that all apples are cholesterol free.

The use of antibiotics is necessary to control illness in massive chicken houses that can hold up to 25,000 chickens. It's common sense. Too many animals in an enclosed environment can become sickly and harbor disease; yet folks are concerned about ingesting too many antibiotics. Trouble is, some poultry that is labeled antibiotic free only means the chickens themselves haven't been given antibiotics, it doesn't mean the chicken feed doesn't contain antibiotics, or that they were administered to eggs before the chicks hatched.

Consumer response to the massive poultry farms and production facilities is the increased desire for what are known as free-range chickens. It is to a large extent a marketing term. Producers of free-range chickens must simply be able to demonstrate to the USDA that the poultry has been allowed access to the outside. This does not necessarily mean the chickens are pecking away in a bucolic farmyard. They may simply have a door open in one of these large houses. And, although many people are convinced that free-range birds are healthier, according to the USDA, there is no discernible difference in salmonella levels between free-range, organically produced poultry and conventionally produced birds.

Speaking of salmonella, according to the USDA, washing chicken is not necessary. Washing the chicken actually increases the chance of cross contamination; water that has touched raw chicken and splashed into the sink can potentially contaminate other food. Nothing is getting washed off with cold water, that's for sure; and if the chicken is slimy, well, you don't want to be eating it anyway.

Another word cropping up in poultry production is heritage, sometimes heirloom. "Heritage" is usually used to describe animals, while "heirloom" refers generally to plants. Heritage describes varieties of animals that have unique genetic traits and were grown or raised many years ago, before the drastic reduction of breed variety caused by the rise of industrial agriculture. Typically heritage breeds are produced in a sustainable manner. The main criteria for sustainability, for example, applied most often to turkeys are that they are able to mate naturally, be able to withstand life outdoors, and have a slow growth rate.

Another fairly common set of buzzwords is "certified organic." The USDA's National Organic Program regulates the standards for any farm, wild-crop harvesting operation, or handling operation that wants to sell an agricultural product as organically produced. Livestock must be fed a diet of 100 percent organic feed, raised free of antibiotics and hormones, and have access to the outdoors and sunlight.

In the vocabulary of poultry production, foods labeled "natural" are not subject to the same set of strict USDA standards as those that are labeled organic. In essence, the meat must be minimally processed; contain no added food colorings, preservatives, or flavoring agents; and the producers must define what they mean by natural (such as "no added colorings or artificial ingredients" or "minimally processed").

Organic, natural, heritage—whatever your choice may be, in this chapter you'll find old-fashioned recipes for perfect for Sunday dinner as well as a selection of what are sure to become weeknight family favorites. Basic to Brilliant, gospel to game bird, there's a little something for everyone.

Chicken Breasts with Tarragon Velouté

SERVES 4

A velouté is one of the five French mother sauces (see page 11). It starts with a roux, which in classic French cooking is made by melting butter and adding all-purpose flour. The mixture is cooked until foamy, then white stock is added to make the sauce. Now, in Georgia we'd call that sauce gravy. In this recipe we poach the chicken in stock, then use that cooking liquid to make the velouté.

Large bunch of tarragon

4 cups homemade chicken stock (page 9) or reduced-fat, low-sodium chicken broth

4 boneless, skinless chicken breasts (about 2 1/2 pounds)

Coarse salt and freshly ground white pepper

2 tablespoons unsalted butter

2 tablespoons all-purpose flour

Juice of 1/2 lemon

Preheat the oven to 350°F.

Remove the leaves from the tarragon stems. Place the stems and half of the leaves in a saucepan with the chicken stock. (Reserve the other half of the leaves for the sauce.) Bring to a boil and decrease the heat to simmer. Cook until the stock is very flavorful, about 5 minutes.

Season both sides of the chicken breasts with salt and white pepper. Place the chicken breasts in a shallow baking dish. Strain over the tarragon-flavored stock. Cover and seal with aluminum foil or a tight-fitting lid. Bake until the chicken juices run clear when pierced with a knife, 15 to 20 minutes.

Remove the chicken breasts from the stock to a warmed plate and cover to keep warm and let rest. (See Crystal Clear on page 108. It's here you strain the stock, if you choose.)

Melt the butter in a saucepan. Whisk in the flour and cook until foaming but not browned, 45 to 60 seconds. Whisk in the 2 cups of the cooking liquid and bring to a boil. Decrease the heat to a simmer and cook until the sauce is reduced and thickened, 15 to 20 minutes.

Meanwhile, finely chop the reserved tarragon. Add the chopped leaves and lemon juice to the sauce. Taste and adjust for seasoning with salt and white pepper.

Slice the breasts on the diagonal and spoon the sauce over the breasts to lightly coat. Serve immediately.

Brilliant Technique
Vol-au-Vent

When I was growing up, Mama would sometimes make "patty shells." I didn't know they were puff pastry, and I sure didn't know what that was or how to make it. I want to emphasize the technique here. It's easy to get lost and bewildered in rulers and measurements. We basically want a little pastry boat, a solid base of dough with a ring of dough placed on top that makes a wall to contain a saucy filling. So don't think recipe, think technique.

To prepare vol-au-vent, on a lightly floured surface, roll out 1 pound Quick Puff Pastry (page 19) or 1 (14-ounce) box store-bought puff pastry about 1/4 inch thick, if needed. Cut out 8 vol-au-vent circles using a 3-inch round cookie cutter. Set aside half of the pastry circles. Then with the other half of the circles, using a smaller round cutter, remove the center of the circles to form a ring. Brush the reserved full circles with an egg wash made from 1 large egg and 2 tablespoons of cold water. Place the rings on the reserved whole circles and gently press so they will stick. (Remember, we're making a boat, so the ring of dough on top forms the sides of the boat.) Brush the ring with egg wash and prick the center of the bottom circle with the tines of a fork. (You can decorate the ring by marking in the egg wash with the back of a knife or the tines of the fork.) Refrigerate until well chilled, at

CONTINUED

Chicken Breasts with Tarragon Velouté, *continued*

least 15 minutes. Bake at 375°F until the sides are firm and the pastry is deep golden brown, about 25 minutes. Transfer to a rack to cool. With a fork, gently scrape out the unbaked dough in the center. There you are. Vol-au-vent. Wasn't that easy? Makes 4. To serve, place a vol-au-vent on each warmed serving plate. Fill with sliced chicken breasts and spoon sauce into the "boat." Serve immediately.

Crystal Clear

When the chicken is cooking in the stock, it begins to clarify the stock as if for consommé. Consommé is made by whisking a mixture of egg whites, vegetables, and sometimes ground meat into stock. The protein in the egg whites and meat brings the impurities to the surface of the stock, forming a "raft." Once the raft begins to form, the heat is decreased and the consommé is simmered until the raft is solid. The resulting liquid is very clear, perhaps not colorless, but very clear. Finally, a hole is made in the raft and the crystal clear broth is carefully ladled into a fine-mesh sieve lined with cheesecloth. When the chicken breasts are cooking in the stock, a similar process occurs. The stock sometimes becomes quite clear, and there are some bits that coagulate. Don't worry. There's nothing wrong with it. You can choose to strain out the bits, or not.

Ruby's Peanut-Crusted Chicken Fingers

SERVES 4 TO 6

One of my best recipe-testing assistants is also my friend, a young girl named Ruby. Whenever I develop recipes with young adults and children in mind, I try to pass them by Ruby. She's already starting her own recipe book and is meticulous about writing the ingredients in order and documenting her technique. Granted, her palate is a bit more advanced than that of some of her schoolmates because she is the daughter of two chefs.

One of the great tragedies in the United States is what we feed schoolchildren. I was invited to the White House to help launch Let's Move, the initiative started by First Lady Michelle Obama with an ambitious but important goal, to solve the epidemic of childhood obesity within a generation. Some chefs insist on not mimicking junk food and staying away from the chicken fingers, pizza, and hot pockets. Me? I just want them to eat healthful, not processed food. This one fits the bill and passes muster with Ruby.

1/4 cup coarse salt

1 tablespoon sugar

2 teaspoons dry mustard

1 teaspoon paprika

1/2 teaspoon freshly ground white pepper, plus more to season

4 boneless, skinless chicken breasts (about 2 1/2 pounds)

4 cups buttermilk

2 cups plain or whole-wheat fresh or panko (Japanese) breadcrumbs

1 cup finely chopped unsalted dry-roasted peanuts

2 large eggs

Preheat the oven to 350°F. Line a rimmed baking sheet with aluminum foil, then set a large wire rack on the foil.

To make the brine, combine the salt, sugar, mustard, paprika, and 1/2 teaspoon white pepper in a large plastic or glass container. Add the buttermilk and stir until the salt is completely dissolved. Immerse the chicken breasts in the brine and marinate at room temperature for 30 minutes. (Do not brine any longer or the chicken will be too salty.)

Meanwhile, combine the breadcrumbs and peanuts in a shallow dish. Season with white pepper. In a second shallow dish, whisk the eggs until they are loose, not ropey.

Working with 1 breast at a time, remove the chicken from the brine and shake off any excess liquid.

Transfer to a plastic cutting board and, using a chef's knife, cut the breasts on the diagonal into strips or fingers. (Yes, there is a reason I don't cut them before I brine them; it makes them too salty.)

Dip the chicken into the egg mixture, coating both sides. Place the fingers in the breadcrumb mixture, sprinkle with crumbs to cover, and press so the coating adheres; turn the chicken over and repeat the process. Gently shake off any excess crumbs. Place the coated fingers on the rack set on the baking sheet.

Bake until the chicken is golden brown and the juices run clear, 20 to 25 minutes. Remove from the rack and serve immediately.

Brilliant Technique
Pounding Breast for Paillard

Perhaps one of the most outlandish paillards I have ever seen was in the backwoods of southern Indiana near the Kentucky border. An entire pork tenderloin was pounded into a cutlet, breaded, deep fried, and sandwiched into a bun. The result was comical to say the least. It resembled a pork airplane with the large wings of the paillard hanging off the edges of the plate. But, I will say this, it was nicely and evenly pounded.

CONTINUED

Ruby's Peanut-Crusted Chicken Fingers, *continued*

When pounding meat, instead of using thin plastic wrap or paper, I protect it with a heavy-duty freezer bag that I've separated into two thick sheets. I place the meat between the sheets and pound it with a flat meat pounder or the bottom of a heavy skillet. The meat is pounded and pulled simultaneously, practically stretching the meat into an evenly thin piece of meat about 1/4 inch thick. Each pounded breast should measure roughly 6 inches wide and 8½ inches long. This technique works equally well with chicken, turkey, pork, or veal. For this recipe, once the meat is pounded, proceed with the recipe as with the fingers. Bake until golden brown, about 20 minutes. Remove from the rack and serve immediately.

Salty Stats

I can see hands being frantically waved about the 1/4 cup salt in the brine. Let's do the math. Our brine is 32 ounces buttermilk + 1 1/4 ounces of salt + less than 1/2 ounce sugar. Therefore, the salt content is about 4 percent of the solution. With me so far? Brined meats can soak up about 10 percent of *their* weight in brine, which is to say that if you have 1 pound (16 ounces) of meat in your brine, it will absorb 1.6 ounces of the solution. With the chicken fingers, 2 1/2 pounds chicken breasts will absorb 4 ounces of the solution. So, 4 ounces x 4 percent salt results in .16 ounce or 4.72 grams salt. That's a lot, you say! But salt is not pure sodium, and sodium is the health culprit. Salt is sodium chloride, which is only about 40 percent sodium. So, 4.72 grams salt is about 1.9 grams or 1,900 milligrams of sodium. Divide that total by the 4 breasts and you have about 475 milligrams per breast, well below the U.S. recommended daily sodium intake of less than 2,400 milligrams.

Oven-Fried Chicken Stuffed with Goat Cheese and Spinach

SERVES 4

It often occurs to me when buying chicken breasts that the chicken breast consortium is in league with the buttermilk mafia. Have you ever noticed how hard it is to buy four boneless, skinless chicken breasts? They always come in packs of three. It's the same with buttermilk, every now and then a pint jumps the wall, but mainly it's a deluge of a half a gallon when you really only need a cup. This recipe is a bit fussy with the various steps and technique, but they are necessary, and the result is delicious and well worth the effort. Warm goat cheese and spinach stuffed inside a tender, golden brown chicken breast. Save this recipe when you have some time on a weekend to savor your time in the kitchen.

1 tablespoon unsalted butter

1 onion, preferably Vidalia, finely chopped

1 clove garlic, finely chopped

1 pound fresh baby spinach or 1 (12-ounce) bag thawed frozen leaf spinach

4 ounces fresh goat cheese

1 teaspoon chopped fresh thyme leaves

Coarse salt and freshly ground black pepper

4 boneless, skinless chicken breasts (about 2 1/2 pounds), pounded into paillards (see page 109)

1 cup all-purpose flour

4 large eggs

3/4 cup canola oil

1 tablespoon water

1 1/2 cups plain or whole-wheat fresh or panko (Japanese) breadcrumbs

Prepare the spinach as for the Skillet-Baked Eggs with Mushrooms and Spinach (page 68). Heat the butter in a skillet over low heat until melted. Add the onion and sauté, stirring occasionally, until soft and translucent, 3 to 5 minutes. Add the garlic and cook until fragrant, 45 to 60 seconds. Add the prepared spinach and stir to combine. Cook until dry and all of the moisture is removed, 3 to 5 minutes. Transfer to a bowl and set aside to cool.

Add the goat cheese and thyme to the cooled spinach mixture and stir to combine. Season with salt and pepper.

Place each breast, smooth side outward, on a clean work surface. Top with filling and roll to seal. Wrap each stuffed breast tightly in plastic wrap, twisting the ends in opposite directions so that the breast becomes tightly compact. (It looks like chicken twisted in a hard-candy wrapper.) Refrigerate until the filling is firm, at least 45 minutes.

Position the oven rack in the lower middle of the oven and preheat to 400°F.

Place the flour in a shallow baking dish and lightly season with salt and pepper. Crack the eggs in another shallow dish and beat with 1 tablespoon of the oil and the water. Season with salt and pepper. Put the bread-crumbs in another shallow baking dish. Season with salt and pepper.

Unwrap the chicken breasts and roll in the flour; shake off any excess. Using tongs, roll the breasts in the egg mixture; let the excess drip off. Transfer the breasts to the breadcrumbs; shake the pan to roll the breasts in the crumbs, then press with your fingers to help the crumbs adhere.

Heat the remaining oil in a skillet over medium-high heat until shimmering but not smoking, about 4 minutes. Add the chicken, seam side down, and cook until medium golden brown, about 2 minutes. Turn each roll and cook until medium golden brown on all sides, 2 to 3 minutes longer. Transfer the chicken rolls to a baking sheet.

Bake until the breasts are deep golden-brown and an instant-read thermometer inserted into center of each roll registers 165°F, about 15 minutes. Let stand for 5 minutes before slicing each roll crosswise on the diagonal into medallions. Transfer to a warmed plate, fanning the medallions just slightly, and serve immediately.

Brilliant: Short Recipe
Cauliflower Purée

Creamy goodness in the form of Cauliflower Purée plays off the creamy, cheesy stuffing and makes a Brilliant bed for the oven-fried chicken. Cut 1 head cauliflower into 1-inch florets. Place in a microwave-safe bowl. Add 1 tablespoon water and a pinch of freshly grated nutmeg; season with coarse salt and freshly ground white pepper. Cover tightly with plastic wrap or seal with a microwave-safe lid. Microwave on high until the cauliflower is very tender, about 10 minutes. Transfer the cauliflower and some of the liquid to a food processor fitted with a metal blade. Purée until smooth, about 5 minutes, adding more of the liquid, if necessary. Add 2 tablespoons heavy cream, if desired, and purée until very smooth. Taste and adjust for seasoning with coarse salt and freshly ground white pepper. Serves 4. To serve, place a spoonful of the purée on a warmed plate and fan the medallions of stuffed breast at an angle on the top. Serve immediately.

Grandmother's Chicken *Poulet au Grand-Mère*

SERVES 4 TO 6

The concept of laissez-faire may be something that most of us remember from seventh-grade social studies and the Louisiana Purchase. Laissez-faire means "leave it alone." Well, sometimes cooking is as much about knowing when to stir the pot as not. Try to flip that fish fillet before it's ready, and it will simply tear. Leaving something alone to cook will allow it to develop and grow. The key is to pay attention, but let it be.

To achieve a rich dark flavor, it's important to leave the chicken alone and let it become nicely seared. And, this concept seemed particularly appropriate to mention for grandma's chicken. It seems that grandmothers hold the wisdom of the world in their hands and hearts.

1 tablespoon canola oil

1 tablespoon unsalted butter

1 (4-pound) chicken, cut into 8 pieces, or 6 bone-in, skin-on breasts or thighs

Coarse salt and freshly ground black pepper

4 slices bacon, cut into lardons (see page 54)

6 shallots, peeled and trimmed

2 heads garlic (about 20 cloves), separated, peeled, and tough ends removed

3 sprigs thyme

2 bay leaves, preferably fresh

18 bite-size fingerling potatoes, or 6 Yukon gold potatoes, cut into 1-inch chunks

12 white button or cremini mushrooms, stems trimmed

1/2 cup dry white wine

1 1/2 cups homemade chicken stock (page 9) or reduced-fat, low-sodium chicken broth

Heat the oil and butter in a large, heavy pot over medium-high heat. Season the chicken with salt and pepper. Cook without moving the pieces or crowding the pan, in batches if necessary, until well browned on all sides, 5 to 7 minutes. (Take your time; you want a nice, rich brown.) Transfer the chicken to a platter and keep warm while you cook the vegetables.

Pour off all but 1 tablespoon of the fat from the pan. Decrease the heat to medium. Add the bacon, shallots, garlic, thyme, and bay leaves. Cook, stirring occasionally, until the bacon starts to render and the vegetables start to take on a little color, 3 to 5 minutes. Add the potatoes and mushrooms, season with salt and pepper, and return the chicken to the pan. Pour over the white wine and stock. Cook until the vegetables are tender and the juices of the chicken run clear when pierced with a knife, 20 to 25 minutes. Taste and adjust for seasoning with salt and pepper. Serve immediately.

Variation You can make this recipe with boneless, skinless breasts instead of bone-in pieces. Simmer the breasts as directed on top of the stove along with the other ingredients, but just until the juices run clear, 8 to 10 minutes. Remove the breasts to a warmed plate and cover with aluminum foil. Let the sauce continue to simmer until the vegetables are tender and the sauce is thick enough to coat a spoon. Return the breasts to the sauce and finish as directed.

Brilliant Technique
Monter au Beurre

Monter au beurre is a term used to mean whisking cold butter into a sauce to add richness and gloss. Using a slotted spoon, remove the vegetables and chicken to a warmed serving platter. Tent it with aluminum foil to keep warm. Increase the heat to medium-high and boil until the sauce is reduced by half. Remove the pan from the heat. Using a whisk, swirl in 1 tablespoon cold unsalted butter. Taste and adjust for seasoning with coarse salt and freshly ground black pepper Pour the sauce over the chicken and vegetables, and serve immediately with a crusty baguette to sop up the sauce.

Deviled Chicken Thighs *Poulet Grillé à la Diable*

SERVES 6

In French cooking, any meat or poultry seasoned with mustard and hot pepper and then coated with breadcrumbs is called *à la diable,* since the devil, or *diable,* is associated with anything hot and fiery. The French, however, aren't known for a whole lot of heat in their cooking.

There are a couple of variations you can try if you want it hotter. You can obviously increase the amount of red pepper, but I also like using powdered chiles—not chili powder, or at least not the blend that often includes cumin, oregano, garlic powder, and salt. I use a powdered chile, such as ground Hatch or Dixon chile peppers from New Mexico.

2 tablespoons smooth Dijon mustard

1 tablespoon coarse-grain Dijon mustard

1/4 teaspoon red pepper flakes or powdered chile,
    or to taste

2 large eggs

Coarse salt and freshly ground black pepper

6 bone-in, skin-on leg quarters or chicken breasts,
    or 12 bone-in, skin-on thighs

1/2 cup plain or whole-wheat fresh or panko (Japanese)
    breadcrumbs

2 tablespoons unsalted butter (optional)

Preheat the oven to 375°F. Line a rimmed baking sheet with a silicone baking liner or piece of aluminum foil (this will help with cleanup).

Combine the two mustards and red pepper in a small bowl. Crack the eggs into a shallow bowl or pie plate and whisk lightly with a fork to blend; season with salt and pepper.

Using a pastry brush, brush the mustard mixture all over the chicken. Dip each piece in the eggs, coating evenly on all sides. Sprinkle with the breadcrumbs, coating as evenly as possible. Place the chicken pieces on the prepared baking sheet.

Dot with the butter and and bake until the juices run clear, 45 to 60 minutes for leg quarters, 30 to 35 minutes for thighs, and 35 to 40 minutes for breasts. Remove the chicken from the oven and transfer the pieces to a rack to cool slightly before removing from the baking sheet. Tent with foil and let rest for 3 to 5 minutes. Serve immediately.

Brilliant: Short Recipe
Ham and Cheese–Stuffed Deviled Thighs

The simple addition of two ingredients and the use of boned chicken thighs takes this Basic recipe to Brilliant without a whole lot of effort.

Cut 1 ounce Gruyère into batons approximately 2 inches long (each baton needs to be about the same size as the bone that was removed, because you are going to snuggle that cheese into that place). Set aside. Have 6 paper-thin slices (about 3 ounces) country ham, prosciutto, or Serrano ham ready for use. Season 6 boneless, skinless thighs on both sides with salt and pepper. Place the batons of cheese in the thigh bone cavity. Fold the thigh to close. Place a piece of ham on the work surface, place the filled thigh, seam side up, on the ham, and roll to wrap the chicken in the ham. Repeat with remaining ingredients. Proceed as directed in the Basic recipe, first brushing with the seasoned mustard, then dipping in egg, and finally coating in breadcrumbs. Bake until the juices run clear when pierced with a knife and the topping is a rich golden brown, about 35 minutes. Serve immediately.

Stewed Chicken in Peanut Gravy

SERVES 4

I like using chicken quarters in this spicy West African–influenced stew. The dish is somewhat unusual because peanuts did not permeate the cuisine like okra or other African foodways, even though many of the slaves brought to the United States were from the peanut-growing countries of Senegal, Congo, and Angola. Also, goober, from the African nguba, is another common name for peanut in the South.

I grew up in the country about thirty miles from Plains, home of former president and peanut farmer Jimmy Carter. In fact, my grandfather called him Goober Carter. Peanuts are harvested by uprooting the whole plant and then drying the plants in the field for a few days. Driving through the countryside, the air is perfumed with the heady aroma of iron and earth. Every year in early November, a local farmer would unload a pickup truck of peanut plants at the top of the driveway. We'd separate the nuts from the plants and shake off most of the dirt. Mama would then wash the nuts without soap in the washing machine to remove every last bit of dirt before boiling and canning them.

4 to 6 chicken leg quarters (about 4 pounds)

Coarse salt and freshly ground black pepper

1 tablespoon canola oil

2 onions, preferably Vidalia, thinly sliced

2-inch piece fresh ginger, peeled and grated

1 tablespoon red pepper flakes, or to taste

1 teaspoon ground coriander

1 teaspoon ground cumin

4 ripe tomatoes, preferably heirloom, cored and
  quartered

3 cups homemade chicken stock (page 9) or reduced-fat,
  low-sodium chicken broth

1/3 cup crunchy peanut butter

2 sweet potatoes, peeled and sliced 1/4 inch thick

4 green onions, white and green parts, chopped, for garnish

1/2 cup chopped chopped unsalted dry-roasted peanuts,
  for garnish

2 tablespoons chopped fresh mint, for garnish

Hot cooked rice, for serving

Season the chicken with salt and pepper. Heat the oil in large, heavy pot over medium-high heat. Add the chicken, skin side down first, and cook until nicely browned on all sides, 5 to 7 minutes. Transfer the chicken to a plate.

Add the onions, ginger, red pepper flakes, coriander, and cumin; cook until the onions are translucent,

3 to 5 minutes. Return the chicken to the pot. Add the tomatoes.

Combine the chicken stock and peanut butter in a measuring cup and mix until smooth. Pour over the chicken. (You may need a little less or a little more depending on the size of your pot; you want the chicken mostly, but not completely, covered.) Increase the heat to high and bring to a boil. Cover and decrease the heat to simmer. Cook for 15 minutes.

Add the sweet potatoes and spoon some of the cooking liquid over to moisten. Return the lid and continue to cook until the juices run clear when pierced with a knife, 30 to 45 minutes more. Taste and adjust for seasoning with salt and pepper. Serve immediately with rice and garnished with the green onions, peanuts, and mint.

Brilliant: Short Recipe
Savory Calas

Calas are Creole rice fritters traditional to New Orleans. They marry Brilliantly with this West African–influenced stewed chicken.

In a bowl, whisk together 6 tablespoons all-purpose flour, 2 teaspoons baking powder, and 1/4 teaspoon

CONTINUED

coarse salt. Add 2 cups cooked rice, 2 beaten eggs, and 1/4 cup chopped ham. Season with freshly ground black pepper. Stir well to combine. Pour 4 cups peanut oil into a heavy saucepan, deep fryer, or Dutch oven, filling it no more than one-third full. Heat the oil over medium heat until it reaches 350°F. Line a plate with paper towels and set by the stovetop. To fry the calas, scoop up the batter with a medium ice cream scoop and drop it into the hot oil without crowding. Fry, stirring occasionally with a slotted spoon, until golden, 2 to 3 minutes. Remove with a slotted spoon to the prepared plate. Adjust the heat to maintain the proper temperature and repeat with the remaining batter. Makes 10. Serve immediately with the garnished stewed chicken and rice.

Mama's BBQ Chicken

SERVES 4 TO 6

You know how it is when you are itching for summer to start. You are ready for it. It buzzes in your brain like a hungry mosquito zeroing in for a feast on a naked expanse of skin. Warm weather, sunshine, and swimming. Porches, fishing, and lying on the grass by the river. I love summer food. Okra. Lady peas and butter beans. Tomatoes. Summer squash. Corn. Garrison Keillor is rumored to have said, "Sex is good, but not as good as fresh sweet corn." Well, fresh sweet corn *is* really good. Simple. Uncomplicated. Satisfying.

Regardless of your opinion of sex and corn, I am sure you can agree summer does mean grilling. I love to grill throughout the year, but in the summer, it's just practical to keep the heat out of the kitchen. Burgers and brats are brilliant, steaks and seafood are stupendous, but perhaps my absolute fave? The cheap and cheerful pedestrian chicken. Chicken can be absolutely sublime on the grill: smoky and charred, yet tender and juicy (pictured on page 102). It can also be drier than chalk and just about as tasty, too. The trick is if you pierce the meat with the tip of a knife and the juices run clear, it's done. If the juices run pink? It's underdone. If there are no juices? Ahem.

4 quarts tepid water

3/4 cup coarse kosher salt

1/3 cup firmly packed light brown sugar

2 cups ice cubes

1 (4-pound) chicken, cut into 8 pieces, or 6 bone-in skin-on breasts or thighs

Coarse salt and freshly ground black pepper

Mama's Barbecue Sauce (see page 120), warmed

Combine the water, salt, and brown sugar in a large plastic container and stir to dissolve. Add ice to chill, then add the chicken; cover and marinate in the refrigerator for 4 to 6 hours.

Prepare a charcoal fire using about 6 pounds of charcoal and burn until the coals are completely covered with a thin coating of light gray ash, 20 to 30 minutes. Spread the coals evenly over the grill bottom, position the grill rack above the coals, and heat until medium-hot (when you can hold your hand 5 inches above the grill surface for no longer than 3 or 4 seconds). Or, for a gas grill, turn on all burners to high, close the lid, and heat until very hot, 10 to 15 minutes.

Meanwhile, remove the chicken from the marinade and rinse under cool running water. Pat dry with paper towels, season with pepper, and set aside.

Using a wad of paper towels or an old cloth and a pair of tongs, apply some canola oil to the grill grate. Place the chicken on the grill, leaving plenty of space between each piece. Grill until seared, 1 to 2 minutes per side for legs and thighs, and 3 or so minutes for breasts. Move the chicken to where the heat is medium-low or lower the heat in a gas grill to medium. Continue to grill, turning occasionally, until the juices run clear when pierced, 12 to 18 minutes. During the last 5 to 7 minutes of cooking, brush the chicken with the barbecue sauce. (Any sooner and the sauce will burn.)

Remove the chicken pieces from the grill as soon as they are done and transfer to a warmed platter. Give them a final brush of sauce for flavor and serve immediately with additional sauce on the side.

CONTINUED

Mama's Barbecue Sauce

Make a batch, then separate out a cup or so for brushing on the chicken. Don't dip your brush in the big pot, then dab it on half-cooked chicken and then serve that same sauce on the side. Eew. That's just bad food safety and asking for a tummy ache.

1 cup (2 sticks) unsalted butter

1 onion, preferably Vidalia, very finely chopped

2 1/2 cups ketchup

2 cups apple cider or distilled white vinegar

1/2 cup Worcestershire sauce

1/4 cup Dijon mustard

2 tablespoons firmly packed dark brown sugar

Juice of 2 lemons

2 tablespoons freshly ground black pepper, or to taste

Coarse salt

In a saucepan, melt the butter over medium heat; add the onion and simmer until soft and melted, 5 to 7 minutes. Add the ketchup, vinegar, Worcestershire sauce, mustard, brown sugar, lemon juice, and pepper.

Bring to a boil, decrease the heat to low, and simmer until the flavors have smoothed and mellowed, at least 10 and up to 30 minutes. Taste and adjust for seasoning with salt and pepper. Store in an airtight container in the refrigerator. It will last for months.

Brilliant: Presentation
Chicken Barbecue Salad

The first time I saw "barbecue salad" listed on a menu, I was in Alabama on the way to the Southern Foodways Alliance conference in Oxford, Mississippi. It made me chuckle. Only a Southerner would heap a mountain of barbecue on a bed of lettuce and consider that a salad. Dubious, I ordered one, and it was really, really good. The warm meat slightly wilted the greens and yet still there was a lovely crunch. The way to transform this Basic recipe into Brilliant is to transform it into a salad. Remove all the bones and skin from the chicken and pull, not chop, into bite-size pieces. Toss with just enough warmed barbecue sauce to make it wet, but not sopping. For the salad greens, thinly slice 1 head romaine lettuce and place in a bowl. Work with what's in season such as green onions, thinly sliced raw okra, tomato wedges, shredded carrot, or radishes. Top with the chicken and serve immediately.

Brined Roast Turkey Breast with Herb Pan Gravy

SERVES 6 TO 8

Several years ago I was asked to style the food for a commercial with Paula Deen. They called me during the ten-day photo shoot for my first cookbook, *Bon Appétit, Y'all.* I was exhausted, but it was good work, and I have an attitude that you can do anything for two days. I drove south and, with toothpicks holding my eyes open, did my work. On the afternoon of the second day, her assistant told me *Ladies Home Journal* was coming to shoot the Thanksgiving cover story, a big deal in the magazine world. He said, "We thought they were bringing a stylist; they thought we had a stylist. Will you stay two more days?" Well, I can do anything for two days so I pushed through and stayed, creating an iconic roast Thanksgiving turkey cover shot and all.

The experience turned out to be a life lesson. Six months later, *Ladies Home Journal* posted that my first cookbook was one of their favorite books of the year, and Paula soon thereafter had me as a guest on her show. I believe sometimes you have to put it all out there for good to happen. That, and you can do anything for two days.

1 cup kosher salt

1 cup sugar

1¹/2 gallons water

1 whole bone-in, skin-on turkey breast (6 to 7 pounds)

¹/4 cup (¹/2 stick) unsalted butter, room temperature

1 teaspoon very finely chopped fresh sage

1 teaspoon very finely chopped fresh thyme

Freshly ground black pepper

3 celery stalks, chopped

3 carrots, cut into chunks

3 onions, preferably Vidalia, quartered

2¹/2 cups homemade chicken stock (page 9) or reduced-fat, low-sodium chicken broth, plus more if needed

2 tablespoons all-purpose flour

Coarse salt

Dissolve the kosher salt and sugar in the water in large, clean bucket or stockpot. Set the turkey breast in the brine, making sure it is submerged. Cover and refrigerate for at least 8 hours or up to overnight.

Remove the turkey breast from the brine. Pat dry and set aside. Place the butter in a bowl; add the sage and thyme. Season the butter well with pepper and stir to combine. Set aside.

Twenty minutes before roasting, preheat the oven to 450°F.

Place the turkey on a clean work surface. Using a chef's knife, remove the remaining portion of the neck and reserve it for the stock and gravy. Remove the wishbone to make carving easier; set it aside with the neck for the gravy. With your hand, carefully release the skin on both breasts to form two pockets. Rub the seasoned butter under the released skin. If there is any extra butter, massage it on the outside of the skin.

Put the celery, carrots, and onions in a large roasting pan. Pour ¹/2 cup of the chicken stock into the pan bottom to prevent the drippings from burning. Place the prepared turkey, skin side up, on top of the vegetables. Place the pan in the oven with the wide neck end toward the rear of the oven. Roast for 15 minutes, then rotate the pan back to front. Roast for 15 minutes more, until skin turns golden. Decrease the oven temperature to 325°F and continue to roast, rotating the pan once more about halfway through the cooking, until the internal temperature in the thickest part of the breast registers 160°F to 165°F, 30 to 45 minutes.

Remove the pan from the oven and transfer the turkey breast to a cutting board, preferably with a

CONTINUED

moat. Cover the turkey loosely with aluminum foil. Pour the remaining 2 cups chicken stock into a saucepan. Add the reserved neck and wishbone and bring to a boil. Decrease the heat to simmer.

Place the roasting pan over medium-high heat. Add the flour to the pan drippings and stir until well combined. Strain the warmed stock over the flour-vegetable combination and bring to a boil. Decrease the heat to simmer and cook until thickened, 5 to 7 minutes. Strain the mixture into a saucepan (the saucepan that held the stock is fine to use), pressing on the vegetables to get every drop and all the flavor. Check and make sure the sauce is thick enough to coat a spoon; if not, continue simmering the sauce until the correct consistency is achieved. (If it's too thick, add a little water or additional stock.)

Carve the turkey breast and plate on a warm platter. Add any juices that run into the moat to the gravy. Taste and adjust for seasoning with salt and pepper and serve with the gravy on the side.

Brilliant: Short Recipe
Pear and Cranberry Chutney

I have a love-hate relationship with canned cranberry sauce. It is so evocative of the holidays, with its familiar ridges produced from being packed in the can. But I struggle with not making something fresh when making homemade is so easy. Transform this Basic Turkey recipe into Brilliant with Pear and Cranberry Chutney.

Combine 3 cups cranberries and 3/4 cup sugar in a saucepan over medium heat. Cook, stirring occasionally, until the berries release their juices, about 8 minutes. Add the juice of 2 oranges (about 1/2 cup), 1/2 cup golden raisins, 1 cinnamon stick, and 1 star anise. Season with salt and freshly ground black pepper. Increase the heat to medium-high and bring to a boil, stirring occasionally. Peel 3 firm pears, then core and cut into 1/2-inch dice and add to the chutney with the finely grated zest and juice of 1 lemon. Decrease the heat to medium-low and cook until the mixture thickens and the pears are tender, about 10 minutes. Transfer to a bowl and cool completely. Store in an airtight container in the refrigerator for up to 2 weeks. Serves 8.

Roasted Lemon Cornish Hens with Thyme Jus

SERVES 4 TO 6

My grandparents used to drive their motor home south and spend the winter in Florida. Hilariously, Meme once told Mama that she wasn't certain she liked it, that Florida was "full of nothing but old people." She was in her eighties. They would return with bushels of fruit, and occasionally Meyer lemons. Sunshine yellow Meyer lemons are native to China and a happy marriage of a lemon and a mandarin orange. If it is Meyer lemon season, late November through April, seek them out. I really fell in love with them while working for Martha. They are amazingly fragrant and perfumed.

Mama would serve Cornish hens for "company supper" when we were growing up. Cornish hens are young, immature chickens (usually five to six weeks of age), weighing not more than two pounds. I find one bird perfect to serve two guests.

2 cups water

2 or 3 Cornish hens (about 1¾ pounds each), halved (see opposite) and wing tips, neck bone, and giblets reserved

1 bunch thyme, plus more for garnish

3 tablespoons unsalted butter, at room temperarature

3 lemons, preferably Meyer (1 thinly sliced; 1 halved, for squeezing; and 1 cut into wedges, for serving)

¼ cup loosely packed fresh flat-leaf parsley leaves

Coarse salt and freshly ground black pepper

Preheat the oven to 400°F. Line a rimmed baking sheet with a silicone baking liner or parchment paper.

In a small saucepan, combine the water, wing tips, and the neck bone. (Keep the giblets for the Brilliant, or, if not preparing, save for another use or discard.) Add a sprig of thyme. Bring to a boil, then decrease the heat to a low simmer, and cook to make stock while the birds are in the oven.

Loosen the skin from each breast without tearing by running your fingers between the skin and the flesh of the bird. Rub a little bit of butter under the skin and all over the halves. On the prepared baking sheet, scatter a couple of thyme sprigs and then arrange 4 to 6 beds of sliced lemon large enough to accommodate each half. Place the hen halves skin side up on each lemon "bed." Squeeze the lemon halves over the hens. Season on both sides with salt and pepper.

Roast, rotating the pan halfway through, until the skin turns golden brown and an instant-read thermometer inserted into the thickest part of the thigh registers 165°F, about 30 minutes. Let stand for 10 minutes. Transfer the hens to warmed plates or a warmed serving platter. (I like to transfer the browned and leathery lemon slices, too; otherwise, simply remove and discard both the lemon and the now-dried thyme sprigs.) Garnish the platter with flat-leaf parsley, fresh thyme sprigs, and lemon wedges. Tent with foil while you make the jus.

Place the roasting pan over medium-high heat. Strain the neck bone and wing tip stock into the roasting pan, loosening the brown bits with a wooden spoon. Bring to a boil, then decrease the heat to simmer. Cook until reduced by half, about 10 minutes. Tip any accumulated juices from the platter into the roasting pan. Strain the jus into a warmed serving bowl; add 1 teaspoon fresh thyme leaves. Taste and adjust for seasoning with salt and pepper. Serve the Cornish hens with the thyme jus on the side.

Brilliant: Short Recipe
Giblet Jus

Each bird contains only a few organs. Don't be alarmed if your bird has more than one liver or is missing a heart. The bag doesn't always match the bird. Sometimes I treat these little bits as a *benefice de cuisine*, or a chef snack to cook and enjoy while preparing the meal. You can, however, be a little less greedy and really impress your dining companions with a French-inspired version of giblet gravy.

If you are not using them immediately, keep the giblets refrigerated while the hens are cooking. When you are ready to cook, pat the giblets dry with paper towels. Season with salt and pepper. Heat 1 tablespoon canola oil in a skillet over medium-high heat. Add the heart and gizzard and cook until browned on both sides, 3 to 5 minutes. Remove to a cutting board and let cool slightly. Chop into 1/4-inch pieces. Once the hens are cooked and the jus is prepared, add to the jus and stir to combine. Taste and adjust for seasoning with coarse salt and freshly ground black pepper and serve immediately.

Halving Hens

To halve a Cornish game hen, chicken, or other bird, place the bird on a clean cutting board, breast side down. Using poultry shears or a chef's knife, first remove the wing tips. Set aside for stock. Then, make a lengthwise cut on both sides of the backbone from neck to tail. (You can use shears or a knife for this.) Remove the backbone and save it for stock. Open the bird like a book. Return it the cutting board, skin side down and sternum facing up. At the tip of the breast, there is a pointed bit of cartilage that is easy to cut through. Cut the cartilage in half so that only the sternum remains uncut. Place the tip of your knife on the board, lined up with the cut in the cartilage. Align the blade on the sternum and forcefully bring down the handle, using the heft of the knife to cut through the bone. The two halves of the bird are now separated.

Crisp Roasted Duck with Peach Barbecue Sauce

SERVES 2 TO 4

There is no doubt a well-prepared, well-executed roast duck can be a bit of trouble for not a whole lot of meat. You will notice this recipe serves two to four, not the normal four to six. But, oh my, the flavor is worth every bit of effort.

Duck possesses a rich, red-meat flavor. Much in the way that pork has a natural affinity for sweet-tart barbecue sauce, so has duck. When peaches are not in season, you can substitute frozen peaches for the barbecue sauce.

1 (4- to 5-pound) whole duck

2 bay leaves, preferably fresh

Coarse salt and freshly ground black pepper

2 tablespoons canola oil or rendered duck fat

1 onion, preferably Vidalia, finely chopped

1 clove garlic, finely chopped

1-inch piece fresh ginger, peeled and grated

1 1/2 cups ketchup

1/2 cup peach jam

2 ripe peaches, cut into 3/4-inch chunks

2 tablespoons apple cider vinegar

Pull any loose fat from the duck. Using the tip of a paring knife, make 1/4-inch incisions all over the body of the duck. (This will allow for the fat to render during cooking.) Place the duck on a wire rack set over a baking sheet, and refrigerate, uncovered, until dry, at least overnight or up to 3 days.

Place the bay leaves in the cavity of the duck. Set aside to come to room temperature, about 20 minutes. Fill a roasting pan with 1/4 inch water and place on the lowest oven rack. (This will create steam and catch fat as it is released from the duck during roasting.) Pat the duck completely dry with paper towels. Season the duck inside and out with salt and pepper.

Position a second rack in the center of the oven and preheat to 400°F.

Place the duck, breast side up, directly on the oven rack and roast for about 15 minutes, until it starts to sizzle. Turn the duck onto one side, baste it with any accumulated fat, and roast for 15 minutes more. Turn the bird onto the other side, baste it with accumulated fat, and roast for 15 minutes more. Finally, return the

duck to its back and continue roasting, basting often, until dark brown and slightly puffed, about 45 minutes. Total roasting time is about 1 1/2 hours. (I know, cooking directly on the rack is a little dramatic. It is a technique I learned from the chef at Four Seasons in New York, once famous for its crisp roast duck. You can also place the duck on a rack in a roasting pan.)

Meanwhile, heat the oil in a saucepan over medium-high heat. Add the onion and cook until translucent, about 3 minutes. Add the garlic and ginger and cook until fragrant, 45 to 60 seconds. Add the ketchup, peach jam, peaches, and vinegar. Season with salt and pepper; decrease the heat to low and simmer, stirring occasionally, until the sauce thickens, about 30 minutes.

When the duck is cooked, transfer it to a warmed platter. Cover with foil and let it rest for 10 to 15 minutes before carving. (Turn off the oven and allow the roasting pan of water to cool before removing it. Remember the magic fat? Pour the cooled water into a fat separator. Pour off and discard the water, but save the fat.)

Carve the duck (see opposite) and transfer to a warmed serving platter. Serve immediately with the warm barbecue sauce on the side.

Brilliant: Short Recipe
Quick Cucumber Pickle

Old-school barbecue joints almost always serve barbecue with pickles. Change this Basic, but somewhat fancy-pants roast duck to Brilliant by humbling it with a simple quick pickle. Slice 1 English cucumber into 1/4-inch-thick slices. Place the slices in a colander set in the sink. Sprinkle with 1/2 teaspoon kosher salt; stir to combine. Let stand for 20 minutes. Rinse, drain, and transfer to a large heatproof bowl. Meanwhile, combine $1/2$ cup apple cider vinegar; $1/4$ cup firmly packed light brown sugar $1/2$ Vidalia onion, thinly sliced; 1 clove garlic, thinly sliced; and $1/4$ teaspoon mustard seeds in a small saucepan. Bring to a boil. Decrease the heat and simmer for 10 minutes. Pour the hot liquid over the cucumbers; stir to combine. Store in an airtight container in the refrigerator for up to 2 days before serving alongside the duck. Makes about $1 1/2$ cups.

How to Carve a Cooked Bird

When carving a chicken, turkey, or duck, let the bird guide the way. This may sound funny, but the parts should separate at the joints with little or no effort. I often tell my students that if the bird is fighting you, the knife is not in the right place.

Set the bird breast side up on a cutting board. If the bird is hot, I use a clean kitchen towel instead of a carving fork to protect my hand, but you can use a fork. I prefer to use the towel because it doesn't tear the skin, and I have those asbestos fingers chefs often have. Do what feels comfortable to you.

Pull the leg and thigh back to expose the joint that attaches it to the body.

Somewhat forcefully bend a leg away from the body until the joint pops apart. Use a sharp knife to sever the leg from the body, cutting through the separated joint. As you separate the leg, using the tip of the knife, be sure to get the "oyster," a yummy nugget of delicious dark meat toward the back of the chicken just above the thigh. Repeat the process with the other leg and thigh.

Place each leg quarter on the cutting board, skin side down. Use a chef's knife to cut through the joint that connects the leg to the thigh. (It should be fairly easy to cut through the joint.) Look for a line of fat, and if the knife meets resistance, your knife is hitting bone and is not placed at the joint, which is easy to carve through. So, reposition the blade slightly and try again.

Place the bird, breast side up, on the cutting board. Feel for the breastbone, which runs along the top center of the chicken carcass. Begin separating one side of the breast from the body by cutting immediately alongside the breastbone with the tip of your knife. Work from the tail end of the bird toward the neck end. When you hit the wishbone, angle the knife and cut down along the wishbone toward the wing, then make a cut between the breast and the wing.

Finish separating the breast by simultaneously pulling back on the meat and using little short strokes of the knife tip to cut the meat away from the carcass. Do the same to remove the breast meat on the other side.

Find the joint where the wings connect to the body and bend until the joint pops apart. Use a sharp knife to sever the wing from the body, cutting through the separated joint.

Using a chef's knife or your hands, remove whatever meat remains on the carcass. (Reserve the carcass for stock.) Arrange the legs, thighs, wings, and meat on a platter, pour over any accumulated juices to moisten the meat, or use in pan sauce, and serve.

Roasted Quail with Muscadines

SERVES 4

Muscadines and scuppernongs are wild grapes indigenous to the Southeast. More than forty years ago, Dede planted an arbor of muscadines, and the thick, twisted, and gnarled vines are still producing fruit over forty years later.

Store-bought quail are available whole, split, and semiboneless in better grocery stores and gourmet markets. This recipe calls for semiboneless quail. If you have access to wild quail, and if boning out a bony little bird is too much, simply halve the bird right down the backbone (see page 125).

8 semiboneless quail

Coarse salt and freshly ground black pepper

2 tablespoons unsalted butter

1 tablespoon canola oil

8 sprigs thyme

2 tablespoons bourbon, brandy, or Cognac

1 cup dry white wine

1 cup homemade chicken stock (page 9) or reduced-fat
    low-sodium chicken broth

4 ounces muscadines or scuppernongs, halved, seeded, and
    peeled, or large seedless grapes (see sidebar)

Preheat the oven to 400°F. Pat the quail dry and season with salt and pepper. Heat a roasting pan over medium-high heat. Add the butter and oil and heat until shimmering. Add the quail and sear on both sides until deep brown, about 3 minutes per side. Sprinkle the thyme over the birds and transfer the pan to the oven.

Roast until cooked through but still pink, 8 to 10 minutes. Transfer the quail to a warmed platter; cover with aluminum foil to keep warm.

Off the heat, add the bourbon to deglaze the pan. Stand back, as it may flame up. Return the pan to the heat, add the wine, and bring to a boil. Stir with a wooden spoon to loosen any browned bits from the pan. Decrease the heat to medium and simmer, stirring occasionally, until the liquid is well reduced, 8 to 10 minutes. Add the stock and continue to simmer until reduced by half, about 5 minutes. Add the grapes and stir over low heat to warm, for 1 to 2 minutes. Taste and adjust for seasoning with salt and pepper. Garnish with the thyme and serve the quail immediately with the sauce on the side.

Brilliant: Short Recipe
Savory Chestnut Purée

Earthy chestnuts and quail are a traditional combination in France and will heighten the flavors in this autumnal dish to Brilliant.

Combine 1 (14.8-ounce) jar roasted chestnuts 1 cup homemade chicken stock (page 9) or reduced-fat, low-sodium chicken broth, 1 sprig thyme, and a large pinch of coarse salt in a saucepan. Bring to a simmer and cook, partially covered, until the chestnuts are hot, about 20 minutes. Remove the thyme. Transfer to a food processor fitted with a metal blade. Process until the mixture is very smooth and has the consistency of a thick spread. Taste and adjust for seasoning with coarse salt and freshly ground black pepper. Place a dollop in the center of each warmed serving plate. Top with 2 quail and the sauce. Serve immediately. Serves 4.

Peel Me a Grape

Muscadines and scuppernongs have tough, sour skins concealing their sweet, juicy flesh. To peel and seed, halve the grapes through the stem end with a sharp chef's knife. Using the tip of the knife, remove the seeds. Squeeze each half over a bowl. The flesh will separate from the skin. Use immediately.

Mama's Fried Quail with Cream Gravy

SERVES 4 TO 6

One of my dearest friends despises what she calls "little bony birds," but I absolutely love them. I grew up eating the quail, doves, and ducks my father, uncle, and grandfather shot in the fall. One of the best places to hunt these birds is in corn, millet, or wheat fields that have recently been harvested. Unethical hunters will reseed an area with store-bought feed, but that's not fair and would be more like shooting a fish in a barrel.

10 whole quail

Coarse salt and freshly ground black pepper

1 cup all-purpose flour

2 tablespoons unsalted butter

2 tablespoons canola oil

8 sprigs thyme, plus more for garnish

1 cup homemade chicken stock (page 9) or reduced-fat, low-sodium chicken broth

1 cup heavy cream, half-and-half, or whole milk

1 tablespoon Dijon mustard

Preheat the oven to 350°F. Pat the quail dry; tie the legs together with kitchen twine. Season with salt and pepper. Place the flour in a shallow bowl and season with salt and pepper. One at a time, dredge the quail in the flour, then shake to remove any excess flour.

Meanwhile, heat 1 tablespooon each of the butter and oil in a large skillet over medium-high heat until shimmering. Without crowding and working in batches with the remaining butter and oil, add the quail and sear on both sides until deep brown, about 3 minutes per side. Sprinkle the thyme over the birds and transfer the skillet with all the quail to the oven.

Roast until cooked through but still pink, 8 to 10 minutes. Transfer the quail to a warmed platter; cover with aluminum foil to keep warm.

Place the skillet on the stovetop over high heat. Add the stock and cream. Stir with a wooden spoon to loosen any browned bits from the skillet. Bring to a boil. Decrease the heat to medium and simmer, stirring occasionally, until thick enough to coat the back of a spoon, about 10 minutes. Whisk in the mustard. Taste and adjust for seasoning with salt and pepper.

Pour the gravy over the quail. Garnish with thyme; serve immediately.

Brilliant: Short Recipe
Warm Mustard Relish

Heat 1 tablespoon canola oil in a skillet over medium heat. Add 1 teaspoon each yellow and brown mustard seeds. When they start to pop and release their aroma, after about 5 seconds, add 3 onions, preferably Vidalia, sliced, and season with coarse salt and freshly ground black pepper. Cook, stirring occasionally, until the onions are soft, 15 to 20 minutes. Increase the heat to medium-high. Add 2 tablespoons red wine vinegar and cook, stirring occasionally, until the vinegar is reduced and the onions are a deep golden brown, about 15 minutes more. Taste and adjust for seasoning with salt and pepper. Makes 1 cup. Serve a dollop of the warm mustard relish with the quail and gravy.

To Truss or Not to Truss a Bird

Trussing refers to tying up the whole bird before it is roasted, to ensure it holds its shape during cooking so it cooks more evenly, carves more easily, and is more attractive upon presentation. The trouble is, it's a pretty complicated process that sometimes involves a needle and twine and winds up looking like a bird in bondage. So, I use the cheater's method: I just cross the drumsticks and tie the ends of the legs together, resulting in a more ladylike bird. If you want the bird to cook faster, skip trussing.

7

Beef, Pork, and Lamb

I have been known to say, "A day without pork is a day without sunshine." However, occasionally eating meatless is a choice I have made for years with my own diet. It may seem shocking with my Southern heritage and French training, especially at the beginning of a thick, juicy chapter on meat. Until major developments in meat production after World War II, we as a nation, especially the people of the impoverished South, did not consume massive amounts of meat. Meat was not part of every meal or even consumed every day. Meat was not a choice; it was a luxury. Today, many people feel meat eating is a luxury in terms of both health and environmental consequences.

One family who has seen the ebb and flow of meat, especially beef, consumption is the Harris family of Bluffton, Georgia. Will Harris III is a fifth-generation cattleman. Will's ancestor founded White Oak Pastures in the late 1800s, after returning home from the Civil War. Will is a cowboy straight out of central casting. He's tall and rugged with a rich, deep voice—and a legendary drawl that makes the ladies swoon. He is a Deep South cattleman from the top of his Stetson hat to the tip of his well-worn leather boots.

Until the years following World War II, the Harris family raised cattle as they always had, as free-range beef. After the war, "improvements" were made in production, pastures were fertilized for year-round green grass, herd size was increased, and antibiotics and hormones were developed to keep the animals healthy. It was science; it was progress.

Dispensing antibiotics to healthy animals has become routine on the large, concentrated farms that now dominate American agriculture. Grain-fed cattle spend most of their lives eating grass in pastures, and then move on to a feedlot where they eat an inexpensive, high-calorie grain diet for three to six months.

Will raised his cattle in pastures his family had been farming for decades, but then had to send them to the Midwest for corn finishing. He grew to despise sending his cattle off in double-decker trucks on a journey that would take them across the country, without food and water for several days, the cattle on the upper level soiling the animals below.

Will says it just wasn't right. Actually, I think one of his more salty quotes was, "It was like raising your daughter to be a princess and then hauling her off to the whorehouse." So, he stopped. He made a choice to buck the system and return to the methods his forebears used: traditional, sustainable, and humane. His beef now meets the Humane Farm Animal Care standards, which include "a nutritious diet without antibiotics or hormones, animals raised with shelter, resting areas, sufficient space, and the ability to engage in natural behaviors."

According to Will, these standards are not just better for the cattle; it's better for the consumer and the environment, too. Grass-fed beef is higher in beta-carotene, vitamin E, and omega-3 fatty acids than traditionally raised beef. The diet of grass-fed cattle creates a naturally alkaline stomach, minimizing the possibility of E. coli contamination. His and other grass-fed cattle consume a purely vegetarian diet that contains no animal by-products, thereby virtually eliminating the opportunity for bovine spongiform encephalopathy, or mad cow disease. In terms of environmental impact, when cattle are raised outdoors on pasture, their manure is spread over a wide area of land, making it a welcome source of organic fertilizer, not a waste-management problem.

The trouble with all those benefits is that they come at a cost. Grass-fed meat is more expensive, generally three times as much. There's just not that much grass-fed beef, as well. Large-scale meat plants slaughter more cows at one plant in one hour than Will does in two weeks. It's simple supply and demand.

Another interesting consequence is flavor. Grass-fed beef is more intense, full flavored, and meaty—just exactly what most Americans don't want. Grain finishing increases the intramuscular fat in cattle. The result is rich marbling, which makes the meat tender and moist. (Humans are hardwired to like the flavor of fat. Fat is like a drug, and like addicts, we are overdoing it.) Even riding the wave of local and sustainable, chefs are struggling to serve grass-fed meat. A restaurant can't keep its doors open selling customers what they perceive as "tough" steaks that cost three times as much.

Fatty, tender, and moist meat? Sounds like pork, the hands-down Southern favorite. The Spanish introduced pigs to Florida in the mid-1500s. The animals later made their way north to Georgia, where they came to be appreciated for their ability to forage for food, while pastoral cattle proved to be more expensive to feed.

The same issues exist with factory farming in pork production as with beef. In fact, it's a larger problem in the South because of the long relationship the South has had with the pig and general absence of large-operation cattle farming. Communities are split in this hard economy over the economic potential of allowing large farms in— or more likely, choosing not to sue to keep them out—versus waste runoff from raising thousands and thousands of pigs at once.

There's a reason ham is so cheap. Massive-scale farming and government subsidies lower the price. To complicate the issue even further, the problems aren't exclusive to "factory farms." The "Giant Meat Company" doesn't always actually own the farm itself. Often the farmers are contracted to sell to the "Giant Meat Company," and the sellers, the farmers, are forced to accept the prices and growing conditions dictated by the meat giants. It gets worse. Not only do behemoths overwhelm farmers with their sheer size, they also directly compete with farmers, further giving the conglomerates leverage on price. Plenty of honest, good, hardworking men and women labor long hours to put that ham on your plate. Their livelihoods are wrapped up in the system. It's not always a factory; it's a family.

Some farmers have responded by converting to raising heirloom or heritage breeds that are more suitable to free-range outdoor systems. However, this is being done on a very small scale. Outdoor systems are usually less economically productive, and the meat is more expensive. Once again, it's all about supply and demand.

Sheep have been raised in the South for centuries. Historical evidence from the 1700s and 1800s suggest that lamb and wool production were important. However, the production of lamb and sheep has been declining both nationally and in the South since World War II, coinciding with the growth of large-scale farming. Sheep do better in pastoral environments. Growing up, my personal exposure to lamb was very limited. Neither Meme nor Mama cooked it, and I didn't learn how to prepare it until I worked with my French-trained mentor, Nathalie Dupree. The lamb recipes in this chapter are reflective of my time in France.

Eating meat is a choice, whether beef, pork, or lamb. I love to eat meat and as a chef, I love to cook meat. As often as possible, I purchase from my local farmer, but I am not going to lie and tell you that's all I ever eat. It's simply not realistic for most people to eat local, sustainable meat. For many the cost is too high, and the resources are too limited. My suggestion is, when you can choose, do.

Here I offer you a selection of delicious Basic recipes with their stunning Brilliant counterparts, so that when you do make the choice to eat meat, you are able to really enjoy it.

Steak Your Claim: Steak Temperatures

Blue/*Bleu*

The steak is seared on both sides and when cut, it is very red, almost blue, with a cool center. When inserted into the thickest part of a steak at an angle and avoiding the bones and pan surfaces, an instant-read thermometer reads 115°F.

Rare/*Saignant*

The steak is seared on both sides, yet the center is red and just slightly warmed. When inserted into the thickest part of a steak at an angle and avoiding the bones and pan surfaces, an instant-read thermometer reads 120°F to 130°F.

Medium/*À Point*

The steak is seared on both sides and the center is firm, pink, and hot. When inserted into the thickest part of a steak at an angle and avoiding the bones and pan surfaces, an instant-read thermometer reads 140°F to 155°F.

Well Done/*Bien Cuit*

The meat is firm to the touch without a trace of pink. In my opinion, it's a waste of money for steak. When inserted into the thickest part of a steak at an angle and avoiding the bones and pan surfaces, an instant-read thermometer reads 155°F to 165°F.

Spiced Skirt Steak with Shallot Marmalade

SERVES 4

Skirt steak is an interior muscle, the diaphragm, of the cow. It is prized for its meaty, intense flavor, rather than for its tenderness. *Faja* translates as "belt" in Spanish and is the origin of the word *fajitas*. The French term for the cut is *bavette*, which means "ribbon." The muscle is long and thin, like a belt or ribbon. Skirt steak is a relatively inexpensive cut; it was traditionally one of the cuts the butcher would take home to his family. It has become increasingly available in recent years as stores try to satisfy customer demand for more affordable beef. If you are unable to find it in your local grocery store, look to an Hispanic *carniceria,* or "meat market."

Shallot Marmalade

2 tablespoons unsalted butter

1 tablespoon firmly packed dark brown sugar

4 shallots, sliced

1/2 cup red wine vinegar

1 cup dry red wine

1 tablespoon chopped fresh thyme

Coarse salt and freshly ground black pepper

Steak

2 pounds skirt steak

Coarse salt and freshly ground black pepper

2 teaspoons quatre épices or Chinese five spice powder
(see page 36)

1 tablespoon canola oil

To make the marmalade, melt the butter in a heavy saucepan over medium heat. Add the shallots and brown sugar and cook until the shallots are a rich brown and caramelized, about 10 minutes. Add the vinegar and wine. Bring to a boil, then decrease the heat to low and cook until well reduced and thick, about 20 minutes. Add the thyme, then taste and adjust for seasoning with salt and pepper. Keep warm.

Meanwhile, remove the steaks from the refrigerator and allow to come to room temperature, about 20 minutes. Pat dry with paper towels and season with salt and pepper. Sprinkle over the quatre épices.

Heat the oil in a large skillet over medium-high heat until shimmering. Add the steaks and cook, turning once, for about 3 minutes per side for medium-rare. (Skirt needs to be cooked to medium-rare; it's too tough to be cooked blue or rare.) Transfer the steaks to a cutting board, preferably with a moat to catch the meaty juices. Tent with foil to rest and let the juices redistribute, about 2 minutes. Slice on the diagonal against the grain. Tip any accumulated juices into the marmalade and stir to combine. Serve the steak on warmed plates with the marmalade on the side.

Brilliant: Presentation
Skirt Steak Roulade

The skirt steak is a Brilliant piece of meat for a roulade. It is long, thin, and flat. This means that when the skirt steak is rolled, cooked, and sliced, the meat fibers are going to be short and thus easy to chew.

Preheat the oven to 350°F. Prepare the Shallot Marmalade and let cool slightly. Meanwhile, cut the steaks crosswise at 4-inch intervals. Cut a sealable freezer bag into two sheets and put a steak between the two. Pound it with a flat meat pounder or the bottom of a heavy skillet until it is 1/4 inch thick. (The idea is to create an evenly thin piece of meat, not beat it senseless.) Repeat with the remaining pieces of meat. Season both sides of the steaks with coarse salt and freshly ground black pepper. Spread the marmalade over one side of the steak. Roll the steak from the short side into a pinwheel and then tie to secure with kitchen twine. Heat the oil in a large skillet over medium-high heat until it is shimmering. Cook the rolls on all sides until browned and medium-rare, about 8 minutes. Remove the twine and slice into 1/2-inch pinwheels with a sharp knife.

NY Strip Steaks with Sautéed Mushrooms

SERVES 4

My grandfather raised grass-fed cattle when I was growing up. He put a salt lick, a block of salt provided as a nutritional supplement, out in the pasture for them, but the only corn they ever saw was the cobs tossed out after one of Meme's mammoth corn "puttin' up" sessions.

Steaks from grass-fed cattle aren't as marbled with fat as the rib-eye and strip steaks from corn-feed cattle. Rib-eye steaks are one of the more popular—and expensive—steaks. NY strip steaks are also known as Texas, Kansas City, or just plain old strip steaks. They are still more pricey than the skirt steak in the previous recipe, but not as expensive as rib-eye steaks. They are cut from the loin after the tenderloin is removed. The remaining muscle, known as the shell, is cut into strip steaks. The meaty flavor of mushrooms is a natural partnership with a flavorful, meaty steak.

4 (6- to 8-ounce) boneless NY strip steaks (about 1 inch thick)

Coarse salt and freshly ground black pepper

2 tablespoons canola oil

1 pound mixed mushrooms (such as cremini, chanterelle, morel, shiitake, and white button), sliced

1/4 cup dry red wine

1/4 cup homemade beef stock (page 10) or reduced-fat, low-sodium beef broth

1 tablespoon unsalted butter (optional)

Remove the steaks from the refrigerator and allow to come to room temperature, about 20 minutes. Pat dry with paper towels and season with salt and pepper.

Heat 1 tablespoon of the oil in a large skillet over high heat until it is shimmering. Add the steaks and cook for 3 to 4 to minutes per side for medium-rare. Transfer the steaks to a cutting board, preferably with a moat to catch the meaty juices. Tent with foil to rest and let the juices redistribute.

Heat the remaining 1 tablespoon oil in the same skillet over medium high heat. Add the mushrooms and season with salt and pepper. Cook, stirring occasionally, until just tender, 3 to 4 minutes. Add the wine and stock to the skillet. Cook until slightly reduced, about 3 minutes. Tip any accumulated juices from the resting meat into the skillet. Remove the skillet from the heat. Add the butter and swirl to combine. Taste and adjust for seasoning with salt and pepper. Serve the steaks topped with the mushroom wine sauce.

Brilliant: Short Recipe

Dried Mushroom Rosemary Rub

A heady dose of umami-rich dried mushrooms takes this cowboy steak to chef-worthy Brilliant. Put 1 ounce dried mushrooms (such as porcini, shiitake, chanterelle, or morel) and 1 sprig rosemary, coarsely chopped, in a food processor fitted with a metal blade. Purée until very finely ground. Transfer to a shallow plate. Makes about 1/4 cup. Coat both sides of the room-temperature steaks in the porcini-rosemary mixture. Cook as directed.

Feel the Heat

Checking a steak for doneness by touch and feel is an inexact science. My internship with Nora Pouillon was on the line, grilling steaks, and I learned it takes practice to get it right. Work with an instant-read thermometer to get an idea of the feel of the steak to the corresponding temperature. First, touch a raw steak with your forefinger. Then, feel the fleshy part of the top of your hand, between the thumb and forefinger, to approximate the soft, squishy feel of raw meat. Next, grasp a pencil in your hand. Touch the top of your hand again. The muscles will have tightened slightly. This is the feeling of rare meat. The tighter your fist, the more the feel corresponds to well-done meat.

Mama's Salisbury Steak with Mushroom Gravy

SERVES 6

Salisbury steak, known on French bistro menus as *bifteck haché*, is made by mixing ground beef with minced or grated onion, shaping it into a patty, and frying or broiling it. It is often served with a rich gravy made from pan drippings. The preparation was named after a nineteenth-century English physician, Dr. J. H. Salisbury, who recommended that his patients eat plenty of beef for all manner of ailments. Oddly enough, when my mother was pregnant with my sister and me, her doctor told her to eat very rare beef. Can you imagine hearing that advice today?

I remember having this meal often when I was young. Inexpensive, filling, quick, and easy, it's still a good meal for a family supper.

1 teaspoon canola oil, plus more for the broiler pan

1/2 onion, preferably Vidalia, grated

2 cloves garlic, very finely chopped

11/2 pounds ground round beef

8 ounces ground pork

1 tablespoon chopped fresh flat-leaf parsley

Coarse salt and freshly ground black pepper

3 tablespoons unsalted butter

1 pound mixed mushrooms (such as cremini, chanterelle, morel, shiitake, and white button), sliced

2 tablespoons all-purpose flour

2 cups pan drippings plus homemade beef stock (page 10) or reduced-fat, low-sodium beef broth, or as needed

Position an oven rack 4 inches below the broiler and preheat the broiler.

Heat the oil in a small skillet over medium heat. Add the onion and cook until translucent, 3 to 5 minutes. Add the garlic and cook until fragrant, 45 to 60 seconds. Remove from the heat to cool slightly.

With clean hands, combine the ground beef, pork, parsley, and cooled onion mixture in a bowl; season with salt and pepper. (Sauté a spoonful of the mixture in a bit of oil to taste for seasoning.) Shape the mixture into 6 oval patties, about 1/2 inch thick. Place the patties on a broiler pan.

Broil until the meat is no longer pink in the center and an instant-read thermometer inserted into the center of the meat registers 160°F, about 6 minutes per side. Remove to a warmed serving platter and tent with foil to keep warm. Reserve the pan drippings for the gravy.

Heat 1 tablespoon of the butter in a large skillet over medium heat. Add the mushrooms and season with salt and pepper. Cook until tender, about 5 minutes. Taste and adjust for seasoning with salt and pepper. Remove from the skillet and keep warm.

Heat the remaining 2 tablespoons butter over medium heat in the same skillet until bubbling. Add the flour and cook until foamy. Pour the pan drippings into a 2-cup measure or fat separator. Remove the fat, then add enough beef stock to the drippings to make 2 cups. Whisking constantly, add the stock mixture to the butter-flour mixture. Bring to a boil, stirring constantly, and cook until the sauce thickens, about 5 minutes. Decrease the heat to simmer. Add the reserved cooked mushrooms with any accumulated liquid. Taste and adjust for seasoning with salt and pepper. Serve immediately with the steaks.

Brilliant: Short Recipe
Stuffed with Roquefort

Melted cheesy goodness takes Basic *bifteck* to chef-inspired Brilliant. Crumble 13/4 ounces blue cheese, such as Roquefort, to make about 1/2 cup. Take one-quarter of the meat mixture and shape into a flat patty; repeat to make 4 patties. Make a depression in the center of each patty and place 2 tablespoons blue cheese in the center. Form the meat around the cheese to enclose it, then shape into an oval patty about 1/2 inch thick. Refrigerate for up to 15 minutes. Proceed with the recipe as above.

Mama's Spaghetti Bolognese with Venison

SERVES 6 TO 8

My family grew up eating spaghetti with a traditional meat sauce. Well, sort of. . . . The meat was ground venison from a deer Daddy shot, and Mama always added Dede's homemade scuppernong wine. She also used a McCormick's seasoning packet, still does. (In my version I add porcini mushrooms to bolster the flavor instead.) This was one of those rare meals mama didn't make completely from scratch. And, I am not sure why, but she always broke the spaghetti noodles in half and cooked them far, far past al dente, more like "all done."

I've enjoyed Bolognese in Rome, "gravy" in Jersey City, and even served marinara sauce to none other than Giuliano Hazan, but Mama's "Southern-style" sauce is still one of my favorite dishes in the world. Food memories are precious things. The sense of smell, more so than any other sense, is intimately linked to the parts of the brain that process emotion. One whiff of this and I am immediately transported to my childhood. Buon appetito, y'all!

1 tablespoon pure olive oil

1 onion, preferably Vidalia, chopped

8 ounces white button mushrooms, sliced

2 cloves garlic, very finely chopped

2 pounds ground venison, or 1 pound ground round beef
   and 1 pound ground turkey

2 (28-ounce) cans crushed tomatoes

Coarse salt and freshly ground black pepper

1/2 ounce dried porcini mushrooms

3/4 cup dry red wine

1 (16-ounce) package spaghetti

Heat the oil in a large saucepan or straight-sided skillet over medium-high heat. Add the onion and cook until translucent, 3 to 5 minutes. Add the mushrooms and sauté until the mushrooms are soft and all the liquid in the pan has evaporated, about 5 minutes. Add the garlic and cook until fragrant, 45 to 60 seconds. Add the ground meat and crushed tomatoes. Season with salt and pepper. Using a wooden spoon, break up the meat into small chunks. Increase the heat and bring the mixture to a boil. Add the dried porcini and wine. Stir to combine. Decrease the heat to simmer and cook until thick, about 30 minutes. Taste and adjust for seasoning with salt and pepper.

Meanwhile, bring a large pot of salted water to a boil. Add the pasta and cook until al dente, about 10 minutes or according to package instructions.

Drain the spaghetti through a colander placed in a large serving bowl (to heat the bowl). Drain the water from the bowl and pat dry. Put the cooked spaghetti in the now-warmed bowl. Spoon over 1 large spoonful of the sauce and toss to coat. Spoon over several additional spoonfuls, depending on how many are at the table. Serve immediately.

Brilliant: Short Recipe
Pasta Bolognese Bake

Honestly, the most Brilliant thing about this is that there will be leftovers.

My friend and colleague Carlin Breinig, who is a personal chef, explained to me that recipe titles are supremely important when presenting to clients. The term *casserole* is considered too pedestrian, but a gratin is considered far too fancy. She finds the "bake" to be the perfect solution. It's user friendly, not too snooty, and it doesn't scream, "can of cream of mushroom soup."

Preheat the oven to 350°F. Brush a casserole dish with oil. Set aside. For a half recipe, combine 4 cups sauce with 8 ounces cooked spaghetti or your preferred pasta shape in a large bowl. Add 2 lightly beaten eggs. Stir to combine. Transfer to the prepared dish and bake in the oven until heated through and set, about 30 minutes. No pretense, no fuss—just good.

Grilled Entrecôte with Red Wine Compound Butter

SERVES 4 TO 6

Literally meaning "between the ribs," *entrecôte* is the French term for a double cut, boneless rib eye. Hands down, no question, this is my favorite steak, although I often like a bone to gnaw on, too. Compound butter is a vehicle for flavor; here, it's red wine, shallot, and garlic, though we could also use herbs or spices. A pat of compound butter melting on the charred crust of a smoking hot steak, the rich juices mingling . . . it is enough to make you want to avert your eyes in modesty. This technique is excellent for grilled or broiled steaks when there is no opportunity to make a pan sauce, or if you want to be able to make the "sauce" ahead.

1 cup dry red wine

1 shallot, sliced

1 clove garlic, smashed

$1/2$ cup (1 stick) unsalted butter, at room temperature

1 tablespoon chopped fresh flat-leaf parsley

Coarse salt and freshly ground black pepper

2 ($1^3/4$-pound) boneless rib-eye steaks, each about
    2 inches thick

2 tablespoons canola oil

Combine the red wine, shallot, and garlic in a small saucepan; bring to a boil over high heat. Boil until the wine is reduced to about 1 tablespoon, 12 to 15 minutes. Remove from the heat and cool. Put the butter in a food processor fitted with a metal blade. Add the cooled wine mixture and chopped parsley; season with salt and pepper. Pulse until well combined.

For immediate use, transfer to a bowl and set aside. For later use, transfer to a sheet of plastic wrap, roll the butter in the sheet, and twist the ends in opposite directions (like the wrapping on hard candy) to shape the butter into a uniform cylinder about 5 inches long. To store, wrap tightly in plastic wrap and refrigerate for up to 1 week or freeze for up to 1 month.

Preheat the oven to 350°F. Meanwhile, remove the steaks from the refrigerator and let come to room temperature, about 20 minutes.

Pat the steaks dry with paper towels. Season on both sides with salt and pepper. Heat the oil in a large cast-iron skillet over high heat until shimmering. Add the steaks and sear on all sides until a rich brown crust forms, about 4 minutes per side, plus the thick edges.

Once seared on all sides, transfer to the oven and cook to desired doneness, 15 to 17 minutes for rare (120°F to 130°F on an instant-read thermometer), or 17 to 20 minutes for medium (140°F to 155°F).

Meanwhile, if the butter is chilled, remove it from the refrigerator to come just to room temperature. Remove the steaks from the oven to a cutting board, preferably with a moat to catch the juices. Tent the steaks loosely with aluminum foil. Let the steaks rest and the juices redistribute, about 5 minutes. Slice the steaks into strips $1/4$ inch thick and assemble on warmed serving plates. Top with the red wine compound butter. Drizzle over any collected juices. Serve immediately.

Brilliant Technique
Stuffing the Entrecôte with Compound Butter

The only thing that could be better than warm, buttery juices bathing the outside of a steak would be warm buttery juices gushing from the inside of a steak.

Slice the butter into tablespoon-size pats and freeze until firm. Place a raw steak on a clean work surface. Insert a thin slicing knife into the side of the steak. Rotate the tip of the knife to create an interior pocket *without* making the incision larger. Insert your index finger through the hole; push and press to separate the meat and balloon the interior. Insert 4 of the frozen pats of butter. Repeat with the remaining steak and butter. Insert one-quarter of a small sweet onion into the hole to seal the opening. Cook the steaks as directed above. Once the steaks have rested, cut them in half rather than in strips and serve on warmed plates. Scandalously Brilliant.

Garlic-Stuffed Prime Rib Roast with Crispy Potatoes

SERVES 8

For a steak, I love a bone-in rib eye with a crisp charred crust on the outside and rare tender meat on the inside. Although this prime rib roast is essentially four steaks bound together, I like to cook it to medium-rare. The reason for the difference is that a rib roast is marbled with fat and has a thick ribbon of fat running through the roast between the eye of the meat and the bone. When a steak is cooked quickly over high heat, it allows some of this fat to render. The larger roast doesn't have the opportunity and the cold fatty texture is unpleasant.

Don't add the potatoes at the beginning of cooking, otherwise they will be overcooked. Since the roast is going to rest for at least 15 minutes, and the potatoes only need about an hour to cook, add them when the roast has only 45 minutes to go. Then, when the roast is ready to come out of the oven, transfer the meat to a board to rest, but leave the potatoes in the oven, ensuring a well-rested roast with the juices redistributed, as well as crispy hot potatoes.

1 (8- to 9-pound) prime rib or standing rib roast (4 ribs)

4 to 5 cloves garlic, very thinly sliced and seasoned with salt and pepper

1 tablespoon canola oil

12 ounces fingerling potatoes, halved lengthwise

Coarse salt and freshly ground black pepper

Remove the roast from the refrigerator. Using a paring knife, make 1/2-inch deep slits every 2 inches on all of the meaty sides of the roast. Insert a sliver of garlic into each slit. Set aside and let the roast stand at room temperature for 1 hour.

Preheat the oven to 450°F.

Season the meat all over with salt and pepper. Heat a large roasting pan over medium-high heat. Add the canola oil and heat until shimmering. Add the prepared prime rib, fat side down. Cook until dark brown and crusted on all sides, about 5 minutes per side. Finish with the roast meat side up and rib side down.

Roast for 15 minutes, then decrease the heat to 350°F and roast the meat for 18 to 20 minutes per pound, adding the potatoes and tossing them to coat in the pan drippings about 1 hour before the roast is expected to be done. The roast is done when an instant-read thermometer inserted into a fleshy section registers 115°F to 120°F for blue, 120°F to 130°F for rare, or 130°F to 140°F for medium-rare.

Remove the roast to a meat carving board and cover it loosely with foil. Let it rest for at least 15 and up to 30 minutes. (The temperature will increase another 5°F to 10°F.) Return the potatoes to the pan to continue cooking while the roast rests.

To carve, lay the roast on its side. Using a chef's knife, remove the meat in one piece from the bone. Set aside the bones. Remove the potatoes from the oven. Taste and adjust for seasoning with salt and pepper. Transfer to a warmed serving platter. Slice the meat against the grain into 1/4-inch-thick slices. Serve immediately.

Brilliant: Short Recipe
Herb Horseradish Crust

Garlic-Stuffed Prime Rib is even better when each slice is capped with a crisp herb crust.

Position an oven rack 4 inches below the broiler and preheat the broiler. In a small bowl, combine 11/2 cups plain or whole-wheat fresh or panko (Japanese) breadcrumbs, 1/4 cup chopped fresh mixed herbs (such as flat-leaf parsley, thyme, basil, rosemary, and chives), 1/4 cup (1 ounce) freshly grated Parmigiano-Reggiano cheese, 2 tablespoons freshly grated horse-radish, and

2 tablespoons pure olive oil. Season with salt and pepper. Once the roast has rested, carve it into slices. Using a paring knife, remove the plug of fat between the meat and the bone. (It's one thing when you can see to cut around it; it's quite another to bite into because it's hidden by the crust.) Transfer the slices to a rimmed baking sheet. Divide the breadcrumb topping among the slices of prime rib. Transfer to the broiler and broil until golden brown, about 5 minutes. Serve hot with the potatoes.

Cook's Treat

Although my grandfather pretty much gave his country "yard dogs" leftover bones, I'd rather consider them a *benefice de cuisine*, or cook's treat. Prime rib bones are normally fatty, so they are best served with pungent mustard to cut the richness. Preheat the oven to broil. Brush the bones with Dijon mustard and season with coarse salt and freshly ground black pepper. Roast, turning once or twice, until heated through and deep brown. Serve with additional mustard and gnaw to your heart's content!

Beef Daube Provençal

SERVES 6 TO 8

Regardless of how fancy this dish may sound, this is simple, satisfying country cooking. I grew up eating beef stew quite similar to this that Mama prepared in her slow cooker. (Okay, no olives or orange zest, but very similar.) Sometimes, instead of beef, Mama prepared stew with deer meat shot by my father or given to us by an uncle or a neighbor. (I grew up calling it deer meat and never called it venison until I went to culinary school.) Venison is meaty, full flavored, and lower in fat than beef, so it responds well to long, slow cooking. She'd make a big batch, and we would enjoy it for several nights, each successive night providing a richer, fuller stew with the flavors increasingly mingled and married. One of my favorite lunch spots serves "yesterday's soup." This could be an argument for making this daube ahead and refrigerating it overnight before serving. Accompany this hearty dish with rice, potatoes, or buttery egg noodles.

4 pounds boneless lean rump roast, chuck pot roast, sirloin tip, top round, or bottom round, cut into 2-inch cubes

1 (750-ml) bottle dry red wine (such as Côtes du Rhône, Bandol, or Mourvèdre)

1 carrot, cut into 1-inch pieces

1 celery stalk, cut into 1-inch pieces

1 onion, preferably Vidalia, coarsely chopped

3 tablespoons pure olive oil, plus more if needed

Coarse salt and freshly ground black pepper

Bouquet garni (5 sprigs thyme; 4 sprigs flat-leaf parsley; 2 bay leaves, preferably fresh; and 10 whole black peppercorns, tied together in cheesecloth)

1 cup pitted green olives

Finely grated zest of 2 oranges

1 tablespoon anchovy paste

6 cloves garlic, coarsely chopped

1 cup homemade beef stock (page 10) or reduced-fat, low-sodium beef stock, if needed

To marinate the beef, place the meat cubes in a large nonreactive bowl. Add the wine, carrot, celery, and onion. Cover and refrigerate for at least 2 hours or up to overnight.

Preheat the oven to 350°F. Line a rimmed baking sheet with paper towels. Remove the beef from the marinade and transfer to the prepared baking sheet. Pat the meat dry with paper towels. Strain the marinade, reserving both the vegetables and the liquid separately.

To cook the beef, heat a large, heavy Dutch oven over medium-high heat. Add 2 tablespoons of the oil and heat until shimmering. Season the beef with salt and pepper. Working in two or three batches without crowding, sear the beef until nicely browned on all sides, about 5 minutes. Remove and discard the paper towels; transfer the beef to the prepared baking sheet when done. (In this case, it's okay to use the same baking sheet for the raw and cooked beef because the meat will be cooked further.) Return the beef to the Dutch oven.

Tie the vegetables from the marinade in cheesecloth with cotton twine. (This makes it easier to purée the sauce later.) Add the bundle of vegetables, bouquet garni, olives, orange zest, anchovy paste, and garlic to the pan. Bring to a boil over high heat. Cover and transfer to the oven. Cook until the meat is tender, 3 to 3 1/2 hours.

Remove the bouquet garni from the Dutch oven and discard. Transfer the beef and olives with a slotted spoon to a bowl. Open the bundle of vegetables and add to the sauce. In the Dutch oven, using an immersion blender, purée the sauce and vegetables until smooth. Or, once the beef and olives are removed, ladle the sauce and vegetables into a blender a little at a time and purée until smooth. Cook the puréed sauce over medium-high heat until it coats the back of a spoon;

CONTINUED

if needed, thin with beef stock to achieve this consistency. Taste and adjust for seasoning with salt and pepper. Return the beef and olives to the sauce and turn to coat. Taste and adjust for seasoning with salt and pepper. Serve immediately.

Brilliant: Technique
Preparing Dough
(Pâte à Luter) to Seal a Baking Pot

Traditional, dramatic, and perhaps a bit overzealous, this technique is Brilliant. The dough isn't edible— there's no salt or leavener—but it seals the casserole completely and prevents any moisture from escaping, therefore ensuring every last flavorful drop stays in the dish. For presentation, it's a technique most appreciated when you prepare the stew base and then ladle it into individual Dutch ovens or casseroles for cooking and serving.

In a large bowl, combine 4 cups all-purpose flour with 1 cup cold water until it forms a dough. Roll it on a lightly floured surface into a long snake. Put the cover on the Dutch oven and seal by pressing the dough where the pot and the lid meet. Cut the dough and repeat if making individual-size portions. If you are cooking a large casserole, loosen and break apart with the back of a knife, and remove the lid in front of your guests. If you are preparing individual portions, I suggest serving them still sealed and letting your guests break the seals.

Sweet Tea–Brined Pork Blade Steaks

SERVES 4

You can't get much more Southern than sweet tea. Well, maybe kudzu is more Southern than sweet tea, but you can't drink kudzu. Blade steaks are from the shoulder of the pig and are much more economical than pork chops. They're not as pretty, but are equally delicious and good. In my opinion, one of life's most perfect breakfasts is a leftover cold pork chop the next day.

Sometimes we get a little hung up on competition. I'm all about doing one's best and a healthy contest, but there's a lot to be said for sharing. The best way to explain this is The Pork Chop Theory, a valuable lesson I learned from my friend Nathalie Dupree. The Pork Chop Theory is based on the premise that if you put one pork chop in the skillet and turn the heat on high, the chop will burn. However, if you put two pork chops in the skillet and turn the heat on high, the chops will feed off the fat of each other. It's the ultimate in giving, sharing, and developing mutually beneficial relationships. And, you know what? The older I get, the more I know that's what life is all about.

1/4 cup kosher salt

3/4 cup sugar

2 family-size or 8 regular size black tea bags

2 cups boiling water

3 cups ice cubes

4 blade or center-cut pork chops on the bone, 3/4 inch thick

Freshly ground black pepper

Combine the salt, sugar, and tea bags in a heatproof bowl. Pour over the boiling water and stir to dissolve. Let steep for 10 minutes. Add the ice and stir to cool. Add the pork, cover the bowl, and refrigerate for about 30 minutes. Remove the meat from the brine, rinse well, and pat dry with paper towels. (Do not brine any longer, or the chops will be too salty.)

Prepare a medium-hot charcoal fire (see page 119). Or, for a gas grill, turn on all burners to high, close the lid, and heat until very hot, 10 to 15 minutes.

Season the chops with pepper. Place them on the grill and grill until the internal temperature reads 145°F, 3 to 5 minutes per side. Remove to a warmed serving platter. Tent with foil to rest and let the juices redistribute, about 5 minutes. Serve immediately.

Brilliant: Short Recipe
Grilled Onions and Sherry Vinegar

Grilled onions, sweet, smoky, and charred with yummy browned bits, are the best way to layer the flavors in our blade steaks and take this recipe to Brilliant. Plain old onions making something Brilliant? Yes. You don't need to use something fancy to make a home-style dish more like a chef-inspired one.

While the chops are marinating, slice 3 onions, preferably Vidalia, into 1/2-inch rings. Place on a rimmed baking sheet and brush on both sides with a couple of tablespoons of canola or grapeseed oil. Season with coarse salt and freshly ground black pepper. While the chops are cooking, place the onion rings on the cooler part of the grill and cook, turning once or twice, until tender, 3 or so minutes per side. Remove to a bowl and cover tightly with plastic wrap. (This will trap the heat and the onions will continue to wilt.) Let rest until you are ready to serve. Then add 2 tablespoons chopped fresh flat-leaf parsley and drizzle over 1 teaspoon sherry wine vinegar. Season with salt and pepper and toss to combine and coat. Serves 4. Serve a tangle of rings on top of each pork chop.

Pork Belly with French Market Red-Eye Gravy

SERVES 4 TO 6

Pork is a key ingredient in both French cuisine and down-home Southern cooking. The concept of using every last bit of the pig but the squeal is country cooking the world over and certainly not exclusive to the *petits villages* in the French countryside or the Deep South. Pork belly is one of the "low on the hog" cuts of meat. It's uncured bacon, with a high proportion of fat to meat. Pork belly has risen to prominence in recent years because it makes chefs as happy as a pig in slop. Although popular in restaurants, it can be difficult to find in traditional grocery stores. Look for pork belly at Asian or Hispanic markets.

The concept of lowly pork belly served with an equally low red-eye gravy made "uptown" is pretty comical. Red-eye gravy, a simple but essential component of the full-on Southern ham breakfast, gets its name from the eye, or bone, in the center of the slice of ham. Traditionally coffee is used to make the unthickened gravy. Once upon a time both those bellies and coffee were only for those who had to "make do." Funny thing is, this is one of the more restaurant-style dishes in this book.

3 to 4 pounds pork belly, cut into 3 x 2-inch portions

Coarse salt and freshly ground black pepper

2 tablespoons canola oil

2 onions, preferably Vidalia, coarsely chopped

2 carrots, coarsely chopped

2 celery stalks, coarsely chopped

4 cloves garlic, crushed

4 cups homemade chicken stock (page 9) or reduced-fat, low-sodium chicken broth

1/4 cup red wine vinegar

4 sprigs flat-leaf parsley

4 sprigs thyme

1 bay leaf, preferably fresh

10 whole black peppercorns

1 tablespoon ground Louisiana-style coffee with chicory (such as Café du Monde or Luzianne)

Remove the pork belly from the refrigerator and allow to come to room temperature, about 30 minutes. Pat the meat dry with paper towels and heartily season with salt and pepper on both sides. Preheat the oven to 350°F.

Heat the oil in a large Dutch oven over medium-high heat until shimmering. (It seems redundant to start with fat and then pour it off since the belly is so fatty, but it's necessary to get things going.) Add the pork, skin side down, and sear until browned on both sides, 8 to 10 minutes. Remove the pork to a plate. Pour off all but 1 tablespoon of the rendered fat.

Add the onions, carrots, and celery. Season with salt and pepper. Cook, stirring occasionally, until golden brown, 5 to 7 minutes. Add the garlic and cook until fragrant, 45 to 60 seconds. Add the stock, vinegar, parsley, thyme, bay leaf, and peppercorns. Bring to a boil. Decrease the heat to simmer. Place the pork on top of the vegetables, nestling the meat into the liquid, but not so deep that the top of the meat and skin is covered (think of it being "shoulder high").

Transfer to the oven and roast, uncovered, basting occasionally, until the pork is tender, 2 1/2 to 3 hours. Remove the pork from the liquid and place it on a warmed platter. Tent the pork with foil to keep warm while you finish the sauce.

While the meat is resting, remove the fat from the broth using a fat separator and transfer it to a clean saucepan, or tip off most of the fat with a spoon and leave the rest in the Dutch oven. You should have about 4 cups. Add the coffee to the skimmed stock and bring to a boil. Decrease the heat to simmer. Cook until flavorful and fragrant, about 10 minutes. Strain the liquid through a fine-mesh sieve into a saucepan,

CONTINUED

Pork Belly with French Market Red-Eye Gravy, *continued*

using a rubber spatula or spoon to press all the goodness out of the vegetables. Taste and adjust for seasoning with salt and pepper. Place the pork in warmed shallow serving bowls. Spoon the coffee-flavored jus around the meat. Serve immediately.

Brilliant: Short Recipe
Spicy Watermelon Pickle

The fatty pork belly and flavorful, bitter sauce need crisp, cold, and spice to cut through the richness. This juicy addition makes it Brilliantly lip-smacking good.

Cut a 2-pound piece of seedless watermelon into 1-inch-thick triangular wedges, leaving the green rind attached. In a large stainless-steel bowl or pot, combine 8 cups warm water, 1/4 cup kosher salt, 1/4 cup sugar, 1/2 teaspoon cayenne pepper, and 6 smashed garlic cloves. Stir until the salt and sugar dissolve. Submerge the watermelon wedges in the mixture. Cover and refrigerate overnight. Using a slotted spoon, remove from the brine. Pat the wedges dry with paper towels to remove excess moisture. Serves 6. Serve with the pork belly and gravy.

Garlic-Studded Pork Roast in Milk

SERVES 4 TO 6

This recipe has more of an Italian influence than French or Southern. When in my early twenties, I took the night train from Paris by myself and met my mother and two friends in Rome. It was one of the more adult events of my life at that point. It always seemed a bonus when getting on a "fast train" to actually arrive at the correct destination. Board the wrong one and you are a long way from where you need to be. I was a little terrified, but I got there. So, now when faced with a challenge, I consider myself most fortunate if I speak the language and have the currency.

We enjoyed this simple country dish while traveling from Florence to Venice. Traditionally, pork shoulder is braised and slow cooked. Since the shoulder muscle gets exercise, it's tough and needs long, slow cooking. By adapting this recipe to using a loin, the cooking time is drastically reduced.

1 (4-pound) center-cut boneless pork loin

2 cloves garlic, very thinly sliced and seasoned with salt and pepper

Coarse salt and freshly ground black pepper

2 tablespoons pure olive oil

1 tablespoon unsalted butter

1 onion, preferably Vidalia, chopped

1 tablespoon all-purpose flour

2 cups whole milk, or 1 cup whole milk and 1 cup heavy cream, warmed

Bouquet garni (1 sprig flat-leaf parsley, 2 sprigs thyme, and 4 fresh sage leaves, tied together in cheesecloth)

Fresh sage leaves, for garnish

Cut several slits in the pork and insert the garlic slivers in the slits. Set aside to come to room temperature. Season the roast on all sides with salt and pepper.

Heat the oil and butter over high heat in a large, heavy pot until shimmering. Add the meat and brown on all sides, about 8 minutes. Remove to a plate. Decrease the heat to medium. Add the onion and cook, stirring occasionally, until golden brown, about 5 minutes. Add the flour and cook, stirring occasionally, for 2 minutes. Add the warmed milk and bring to a boil, whisking until smooth. Add the bouquet garni, the pork, and any juices that have collected on the plate. Decrease the heat to simmer.

Simmer, uncovered, turning the meat occasionally and scraping the bottom of the pot. (As the milk cooks, it starts to curdle and form small curds.) Stir often to keep the curds from sticking and cook until the pork is tender and an instant-read thermometer inserted into the center of the meat registers 140°F to 145°F, about 1 hour. The pork will be slightly pink in the center (this is desirable).

Transfer the pork to a cutting board, preferably with a moat. Tent with aluminum foil to keep warm. Let it rest for about 10 minutes. Meanwhile, taste the curds and adjust for seasoning with salt and pepper. Transfer to a warmed serving platter. Slice the pork loin about 1/4 inch thick and place on the curds. Garnish with sage leaves and serve.

Brilliant Short Recipe
Pork Roast Stuffed with Sausage

This presentation looks pretty impressive, but it's very simple to do.

Using a knife, cut a slit in one end of the roast. Then, take a knife-sharpening steel and create a hole through the center length of the pork loin. Repeat with the other end. Widen the tunnel using your fingers and by rotating the steel in the loin at both ends. Insert 2 or 3 fully cooked sausages (about 8 ounces total—I like Aidell's Italian-style with mozzarella, but any cooked sausage will do). Proceed with the Basic recipe. The presentation and added flavor at the center is Brilliant.

Spicy Carolina Pork Shoulder

SERVES 6 TO 8

Despite the name, pork butt does not come from the rear end of the hog—it is cut from the shoulder. The terminology for pork shoulder can vary widely depending on what part of the country you live in. Generally, the upper part of the shoulder is called the Boston blade roast or Boston butt and contains the shoulder blade bone. The lower "arm" portion of the shoulder is most commonly called the arm picnic.

I once prepared this recipe far north of the Mason-Dixon Line and was surprised not to be able to readily find a pork shoulder this large. (We've got pig all over down here.) Displaced Southerners may want to order ahead from a butcher.

1 (8- to 10-pound) bone-in pork shoulder or
   Boston blade roast
1 onion, preferably Vidalia, thinly sliced
2 (28-ounce) cans whole tomatoes with juice
1½ cups apple cider vinegar
½ cup Worcestershire sauce
½ cup bourbon
¼ cup firmly packed dark brown sugar
2 tablespoons red pepper flakes, or to taste
Coarse salt and freshly ground black pepper

Place the pork, fat side up, in a roasting pan and using a sharp knife, score the surface of the meat and fat with small slits. Allow the meat to sit at room temperature for 30 minutes before cooking.

Preheat the oven to 325°F.

Combine the onion, tomatoes, vinegar, Worcestershire, bourbon, brown sugar, and red pepper in a large bowl. Season heartily with salt and pepper. Stir to combine and to slightly break up the tomatoes. Pour the tomato mixture over the pork. Transfer to the heated oven. Roast until an instant-read thermometer inserted into the center of the meat registers 180°F to 185°F for sliced pork, about 5 hours, or 190°F to 205°F for pulled pork, about 4 hours. Baste with the sauce throughout the cooking process.

Remove from the oven and transfer the meat to a cutting board. Cover with foil and let rest for 20 minutes. Slice or pull meat. Meanwhile, place the roasting pan over medium-high heat. Reduce the sauce to thicken, stirring occasionally. Taste and adjust for seasoning with salt and pepper. Serve on the side with the pork.

Brilliant: Technique
Tomato Bourbon Jus

White-tablecloth restaurants have to watch their laundry bill. Instead of finger-licking sauce on the side with a role of paper towels, try a Tomato Bourbon Jus.

Transfer the meat to a cutting board, preferably with a moat. Tent with foil to keep warm and let rest. To the roasting pan with sauce, add 4 cups homemade chicken stock (page 9), or reduced-fat, low-sodium chicken broth. Add 2 teaspoons bourbon, or to taste. (Remember, it's raw and won't be cooked any further. I am not trying to get it drunk; I just want to make the flavor of the original sauce pop.) Whisk until smooth, then strain through a fine-mesh sieve into a saucepan. Taste and adjust for seasoning with coarse salt and freshly ground black pepper. Adjust the consistency by reducing the liquid over simmering heat or adding more stock, as needed. (It should be thin, like a cooking liquid, almost brothlike, not like a sauce.) When you are ready to serve, place the pork shoulder in the middle of a warmed shallow bowl. Spoon the Tomato Bourbon Jus around the meat and serve immediately.

Peach Dijon–Crusted Pork Tenderloin

SERVES 4 TO 6

A grill pan is all you need to make a simple supper in 30 minutes or less with this recipe. I return to this recipe again and again. Mama even keeps the sauce already made in the refrigerator and uses it on pork chops as well as chicken. The key is not to start brushing the meat until it's almost cooked; otherwise, the sweet glaze will burn.

1/4 cup Kosher salt

3/4 cup firmly packed dark brown sugar

2 cups boiling water

3 cups ice cubes

2 (11/2- to 2-pound) pork tenderloins

1/2 cup peach preserves

1 tablespoon finely chopped fresh rosemary leaves

1/2 cup Dijon mustard

Freshly ground black pepper

Combine the salt and brown sugar in a heatproof bowl. Add the boiling water and stir to dissolve. Add the ice cubes and stir to cool. Add the tenderloins, cover the bowl with plastic wrap, and refrigerate to marinate, about 30 minutes. Remove from the brine, rinse well, and pat thoroughly dry with paper towels. (Do not brine any longer or the pork will be too salty.)

Meanwhile, stir together the peach preserves, rosemary, and mustard in a small bowl.

Prepare a medium-hot charcoal fire (see page 119). Or preheat a gas grill to high or grill pan over high heat. Season the tenderloins with pepper. Place the meat on the grill, and grill, turning once, until the internal temperature reaches 145°F, about 15 minutes. Brush with the peach-mustard mixture during the last few minutes. Remove to a cutting board and cover with aluminum foil to rest and let the juices redistribute, about 5 minutes. Slice on the diagonal and serve immediately with the remaining sauce on the side.

Brilliant: Short Recipe
Chive Cornmeal
Griddle Cake Sandwiches

This Brilliant version started as an impromptu sandwich in a TV studio several years ago when I was too busy to sit. Now, I love to serve it as a Brilliant main course.

Whisk together 1 cup white cornmeal, 1 cup all-purpose flour, 1 teaspoon baking soda, 1 teaspoon finely chopped fresh chives, 1/2 teaspoon fine sea salt, 1/2 teaspoon baking powder, and 1/4 teaspoon cayenne pepper in a bowl. Whisk together 1 cup buttermilk, 1/2 cup sour cream, and 1 large egg in a small bowl until smooth; add to the dry ingredients, stirring just until moistened. Pour about 3 tablespoons batter for each cake onto a hot, lightly greased griddle. Cook the griddle cakes until the tops are covered with bubbles and the edges look cooked, about 3 minutes; turn and cook until golden brown, about 2 minutes. Transfer to a plate lined with paper towels and pat dry with a paper towel to remove the excess oil. Sandwich slices of the pork between 2 griddle cakes with any remaining sauce. Serve immediately. Makes 12 griddle cakes for 6 sandwiches.

Grilled Spiced Butterflied Leg of Lamb

SERVES 10

When I lived in the French countryside, the "exotic" cuisine was pretty limited. Even the local pizza parlor "Frenchified" the thin, crisp pies by topping the pizzas with an egg. There was a *restaurant chinois* about 30 minutes away, but even in metropolitan Paris, Mexican food might as well have been from Mars. However, due to the colonial relationships with Morocco and Senegal, it was not unusual to find vendors selling North African food and spices even in the small towns across France.

Sometimes our employers, Anne and Mark, would go away for a few days, and we young Americans would be left to our own devices. We yearned for spice and, yes, honestly, sometimes craved *anything* but buttery rich French food. Often that's when we'd prepare nachos or burgers. We'd buy beer and leave the wine in the cellar. At the time, this swarthy Mediterranean combination of spices was practically a walk on the wild side.

1 (4- to 5-pound) butterflied leg of lamb, trimmed of excess fat and sinew (from one 6 1/2-pound bone-in leg of lamb)

1 teaspoon coarse salt, plus more to season

1/2 teaspoon freshly ground black pepper, plus more to season

1 tablespoon cumin seeds

1 teaspoon ground cinnamon

1/2 teaspoon ground allspice

1/2 teaspoon ground turmeric

1/2 cup whole or low-fat plain Greek-style yogurt

2 tablespoons extra-virgin olive oil

1 onion, preferably Vidalia, quartered

8 cloves garlic

Place the lamb on a cutting board. Cover with plastic wrap. Using a meat pounder or small skillet, pound the meat to an even thickness. Using a paring knife, stab the lamb all over on both sides. Season both sides with salt and pepper. Place the lamb in a large bowl or baking dish. Set aside.

In a small skillet over medium-low heat, combine the cumin seeds, cinnamon, 1 teaspoon salt, 1/2 teaspoon pepper, allspice, and turmeric. Cook, stirring constantly, until toasted and fragrant, 2 to 3 minutes. Remove from the heat and set aside.

In a food processor fitted with a metal blade, combine the yogurt, oil, onion, garlic, and reserved toasted spices. Purée until smooth. Pour the purée over the lamb and turn to coat.

Cover and refrigerate, turning occasionally, preferably for 8 hours or up to overnight. If you are refrigerating overnight, let the lamb stand at room temperature for 1 hour before grilling. (Or, for a real shortcut, simply marinate the lamb in the yogurt at room temperature for 1 hour before cooking.)

Prepare a medium-hot charcoal fire (see page 119). Or, for a gas grill, turn on all burners to high, close the lid, and heat until very hot, 10 to 15 minutes.

Remove the lamb from the dish and brush off any excess marinade. Grill the lamb, flipping every 5 minutes for even cooking, until an instant-read thermometer inserted into the center registers 130°F to 135°F for medium-rare, about 10 minutes per side. Transfer to a cutting board. Tent with aluminum foil and let rest for at least 5 minutes before slicing. Slice the lamb across the grain. Serve immediately.

Brilliant: Short Recipe

Pecan Mint Pistou

Mint and lamb are traditional, but this Pecan Mint Pistou is by no means ordinary. A dab of this on the grilled lamb is positively Brilliant.

In a food processor fitted with a metal blade, combine 2 cups fresh mint leaves, 2 cups fresh flat-leaf parsley leaves, 4 cloves garlic, 1/2 cup pecans, and 3/4 cup pecorino-romano cheese; season with salt and pepper. Blend until smooth, scraping down the sides of the bowl as necessary. With the machine running, slowly pour in 1/2 cup pure olive oil until it is thoroughly incorporated and the mixture is smooth. Makes 1 1/2 cups. The Pecan Mint Pistou can be stored in the refrigerator in an airtight container for up to 2 days or frozen for up to 1 month. Serve alongside the lamb.

8

Rice, Grits, and Potatoes

The primary grains of the South have always been rice and corn. Rice farming started on the coastal Sea Islands of South Carolina and Georgia in the late 1600s. For the next one hundred years, the economy of South Carolina was overwhelmingly based on the cultivation of rice, making it one of the richest of the North American colonies. As a result, the capital and its principal port, Charleston, became one of the wealthiest and most fashionable cities in early America. Later, because of the extraordinary success in South Carolina, the rice plantation system was extended farther south into coastal Georgia, where it also prospered.

Food folklore has it that the first rice was delivered to Charleston by a ship weathering a storm. That may have been a spot of luck, but it ended there. Initially, the South Carolina planters were ignorant as to how to grow and cultivate rice. They soon began importing slaves from the traditional rice-growing regions of West Africa and were willing to pay higher prices for slaves from the "Rice Coast." A bit of Georgia history trivia is that the trustees of the Georgia colony initially desired that Georgia be slavery free, but the prospect of growing rice with slave labor for immense profit quickly changed that lofty goal.

Undoubtedly, European recipes and techniques have heavily influenced the food of our nation and the South, but the impact of the foodways of these African slaves cannot be emphasized enough. The Gullah, African Americans who live in the Low Country region of South Carolina and Georgia, are descendants of these early slaves. The Gullah people are also known as Geechee, a term some historians consider to be related to the Ogeechee River near Savannah, Georgia. Both terms refer to several things: the people, their language, and the culture. The culture originally reached north to the Cape Fear, North Carolina, and south to the vicinity of Jacksonville, Florida, the location of some of the richest plantations in the South. To this day, the descendants of these slaves still live in small farming and fishing communities on the chain of barrier islands known as the Sea Islands. Because of their geographical isolation and strong community life, the Gullah have been able to preserve more of their African cultural heritage and foodways than any other group of Black Americans.

With the end of slavery and a series of devastating hurricanes in the late 1800s, rice production ended in the Low Country. By the early 1900s, rice farming disappeared altogether. Meanwhile, corn was becoming increasingly important as the primary Southern grain. It wasn't as labor-intensive and was not dependent on slavery. Corn was eaten fresh in the summer and dried and ground into grits for boiling and into cornmeal for baking in the winter.

Corn in the form of grits has become iconic in Southern cooking. There's a silly little phrase marketed on tea towels, shirts, aprons, and coasters. It says "GRITS: Girls Raised in the South." There are stories about pulling the leg of an unsuspecting visitor, most often a Yankee, about where grits originate. It's the Grits Tree, of course, where millions of the tiny, little pieces are harvested by hand. It's not just folklore. Quaker Oats sells 85 million pounds of grits a year, more than half in the South.

The tragic fact is that most of those grits are instant. Instant grits are offensive. Quick or instant grits taste more like wallpaper paste than sweet, earthy-tasting ground corn. I've never had wallpaper paste, but I do know instant grits don't taste like corn. They may be popular, but consider this: They are also a popular, but ineffective remedy for controlling fire ants. Supposedly, the menacing devil ants consume the offensive bit of instant grit and it swells in their abdomens, bursts, and kills the scourge. Too bad they are not good for something. It's one of those garden tales that only sounds good.

Here's the scoop on ground corn. First, imagine a rounded kernel of corn. The outside is called the hull or bran. (That's the part that gets stuck in your teeth when you eat popcorn.) The starchy inside is called the endosperm and that makes everything from cornmeal to candy—as well as shoe polish and explosives, but that's another story. Finally, inside the kernel at the very center where the kernel attaches to the cob is the germ. The germ is used to make corn oil. So, the germ contains all the oil, which can go rancid.

There are two kinds of grits: corn grits and hominy grits. Corn grits are made from whole-grain kernels of dried corn that are ground into a meal. They can be medium or coarse grind, as opposed to cornmeal, which can be fine or medium grind. For the best-quality cornmeal and grits, the corn is allowed to fully ripen, then dry on the stalks in the field before harvesting. The ears are then removed and placed (while still in their husks) in a cool, dry place, known as a crib, for their final drying. When they are ready to be ground, the ears are shucked and the kernels are removed from the cob. The corn kernels are run through the millstone, where they are ground to a desired texture and then sifted through wire-mesh screens. It's best to refrigerate perishable whole-grain grits after opening to extend their shelf life.

Hominy grits are made from whole kernels of corn that have had the outside shell and germ removed. Hominy is corn that is soaked in lye or potash, a potassium compound, which causes it to swell and the outer shell or hull to loosen. The kernels are then hulled, the germ is removed, and the remaining corn kernel is dried. These branless, germless dried kernels are then ground into hominy grits. Hominy grits with the germ removed have a longer shelflife than ground corn grits. Instant and quick grits are made from hominy corn that has had the hulls and germ removed. They are cooked, spread into a thin paste (I am not being dramatic; it's true), dried, then pulverized again to become like ground corn.

Instant potatoes are about as appealing as instant grits. We did use them in culinary school—to practice piping. Even copious amounts of butter render them barely edible. Scotch-Irish folk primarily settled the South, so there's not a complete lack of love for potatoes. Potatoes have never been as important an agribusiness crop, but people have historically grown them for their own consumption. Dede always had a few rows in his vegetable garden. He'd harvest them and store them in large burlap sacks in the basement. Monsieur Milbert, the gardener and caretaker at Château du Fëy, did the same. It always made me smile, seeing the similarities: two old country men, happy as can be puttering about their gardens, tending to their plants, and putting food on the table.

Grits, rice, and potatoes are simple starches that have comforted many and have long fed the poor of the world. Cheesy, creamy bowls of comfort or crispy brown buttered spuds can be a satisfying side or a simple supper. In this chapter we'll see that even a Basic recipe for humble porridge can be elevated into something Brilliant through a bit of chef-inspired creativity and classic French technique.

Low Country Risotto

SERVES 4

Traditionally, short-grain Arborio or medium-grain Carnaroli rice is slowly cooked by adding warm broth a little at a time to make a risotto, a creamy rice dish. Carolina Gold, from the Low Country, is an aromatic long-grain rice and is the granddaddy of South Carolina rice, supposedly the very rice that docked in Charleston all those centuries ago. Long-grain rice isn't traditional for risotto, but will still produce a creamy rice if basic risotto technique is followed.

When my first book, *Bon Appétit, Y'all*, came out, the folks at Paula Deen gave me a call and asked me to be a guest on her show. Paula and *Midnight in the Garden of Good and Evil* have put Savannah and the Low Country on the map. The thing about Paula? She's *exactly* what you see on TV. After being in food television for years and ages, let me just say not everyone is as genuine. And, frankly, so are her beautiful blue eyes. I am not sure, but her eyes are about as close as I would imagine to Elizabeth Taylor's and her violet gaze. At the end of the taping, sweet Paula said I was a darn good cook, and I could park my shoes next to her stove any time. I left not only happy that I had met her, but also felt like I had made a friend.

4 cups homemade chicken stock (page 9) or reduced-fat, low-sodium chicken broth

2 tablespoons unsalted butter

1 onion, preferably Vidalia, chopped

1 medium leek, finely chopped

2 celery stalks, finely chopped

1 cup long-grain rice

Coarse salt and freshly ground white pepper

3/4 cup dry white wine

2 cups lightly packed watercress, tough stems removed, or baby spinach (about 2 ounces)

2 tablespoons freshly grated Parmigiano-Reggiano cheese

1/4 cup chopped mixed fresh herbs (such as flat-leaf parsley, chives, and tarragon)

1/4 cup toasted sesame seeds

Heat the stock in a saucepan over medium heat and keep warm.

Melt the butter in a large, shallow saucepan over medium heat. Add the onion, leek, and celery and cook, stirring often, until they are soft and tender, 3 to 5 minutes. Add the rice and season with salt and white pepper. Stir to coat until it absorbs the butter and looks almost transparent, about 2 minutes. Add the wine and simmer until it is almost all evaporated.

Add the broth 1/2 cup at a time, allowing the broth to be absorbed before adding more and stirring frequently, until the rice is creamy and tender, 20 to 25 minutes.

Remove the risotto from the heat; add the watercress, Parmesan, and herbs. Taste and adjust for seasoning with salt and pepper. Serve the risotto in warmed shallow bowls, sprinkled with the sesame seeds.

Brilliant: Technique
Add an Egg Yolk for Creaminess

Risotto isn't a recipe as much as it is a technique. The broth is warmed because cold liquid stops the swelling of the starch, and the result would not be rich and creamy. An additional technique chefs use to bolster the creaminess of the risotto and to elevate our risotto to Brilliant is to add an egg yolk. At the very end of cooking, after adding the watercress and cheese, remove from the heat. Add 1 lightly beaten large egg yolk and stir until smooth. (The starch prevents the egg yolk from curdling.) Taste and adjust for seasoning with salt and pepper. Serve immediately in warmed shallow bowls, sprinkled with the sesame seeds.

Savory Rice Gratin

SERVES 4 TO 6

This savory dish is a satisfying side dish or a hearty, filling vegetarian main course paired with Mushroom Ragout (page 194). I employ a béchamel (page 11) to bind the rice. If you wanted, you could use chicken stock instead of the milk, transforming the sauce into a velouté. This dish reminds me of a dish my roommate used to prepare in college that consisted of rice, cream of mushroom soup, and boneless, skinless chicken breasts. Forget the canned soup, but if you did want to make this a one-dish meal, nestle 4 boneless skinless breasts, seasoned with salt and pepper, into the gratin before baking.

2 tablespoon canola oil

3 shallots, finely chopped

2 tablespoons all-purpose flour

2 cups low-fat or whole milk, warmed

1/4 teaspoon freshly grated nutmeg

Pinch of cayenne pepper, or to taste

2 cups cooked brown rice

1 tablespoon chopped fresh flat-leaf parsley

Coarse salt and freshly ground white pepper

1/2 cup grated Gruyère cheese (about 2 ounces)

Preheat the oven to 350°F. Brush a medium gratin dish with oil. Set aside.

Heat the oil in a large skillet over medium-low heat. Add the shallots and cook until translucent, 3 to 5 minutes. Add the flour and stir to coat and combine. Whisk in the milk and bring to a boil over high heat. Add the nutmeg and cayenne pepper. Fold in the rice and parsley. Taste and adjust for seasoning with salt and white pepper. Transfer to the prepared gratin dish. Sprinkle over the cheese.

Bake until a rich golden brown, about 30 minutes. Remove to a rack to cool slightly before serving.

Brilliant: Short Recipe
Savory Rice Timbales

Transform cheesy rice goodness into sophisticated vegetarian fare by wrapping it in tender chard.

Follow the Basic recipe up until you are ready to sprinkle the cheese. Instead, add the cheese to the rice mixture. Set aside. Brush six 1-cup ramekins with canola oil. Set aside. Line a rimmed baking sheet with paper towels. Set aside. Bring a pot of salted water to a boil over high heat. Decrease the heat to a simmer. Rinse 12 or so smallish Swiss chard leaves under cold water. Using a pair of tongs, dip the chard leaves one at a time into simmering water until pliable, 20 to 30 seconds, and refresh in a basin of cold water. Drain, then place on the prepared baking sheet to drain. Line each ramekin with 2 leaves of blanched chard, leaving enough overhang to cover the top. Add the filling and fold the leaves to seal. Repeat with remaining leaves and filling. Discard the paper towels. Cover each ramekin with foil and place on the rimmed baking sheet. Bake until set, about 20 minutes. Remove to a rack to cool slightly. Invert the ramekins onto warmed serving plates and serve immediately.

Freezing Whole Casseroles

I wholeheartedly recommend using reusable freezer-safe, oven-to-table casserole dishes for baking and storing. But, if you do like to make ahead, you might find yourself short on dishes. Try this helpful hint: Line the baking dish with heavy-duty aluminum foil. Brush the foil with oil or butter. Assemble the casserole and freeze. Once it's frozen solid, lift out the foil-covered casserole. Wrap the block tightly with more foil and return to the freezer. When it's time to thaw the casserole, unwrap it from the foil and simply pop it back into the casserole dish. Thaw completely in the refrigerator before baking.

Wild Rice Salad with Dried Fruit and Nuts

SERVES 4 TO 6

Wild rice is actually not true rice; it is an aquatic grass that produces an edible seed and grows in the shallows of lakes and rivers throughout eastern and north central United States. Wild rice has been harvested and eaten by Native Americans for centuries. It's prized for its distinctive natural flavor, texture, and unique, almost nutty flavor.

What I remember most about wild rice was toting about twenty-five pounds of it in my luggage to make Bob Lynn's Wild Rice Salad for a wedding Nathalie Dupree and I catered in Washington, DC. We—I mean—I hauled up ten beef tenderloins on top of that. It doesn't make a lick of sense now—DC had grocery stores—but I just did as I was told. I never actually met Bob, and I didn't eat wild rice for years after.

1/2 cup wild rice (makes 2 cups cooked rice)

2 cups water

1/2 teaspoon coarse salt, plus more to season

1 tablespoon unsalted butter

1 onion, preferably Vidalia, finely diced

1 carrot, finely diced

1 celery stalk, finely diced

1/2 teaspoon chopped fresh thyme

Freshly ground black pepper

1 Granny Smith apple, cored and finely diced

Juice of 1/2 lemon

1/4 cup pecans, toasted and chopped

2 cups mixed young tender winter greens (such as mizuna, kale, collards, and mustard greens)

1 cup fresh flat-leaf parsley leaves

1 cup snipped fresh chives (1/2-inch lengths)

Shallot Vinaigrette (page 14), warmed

1/4 cup dried cherries, cranberries, or diced dried plum, for garnish

In a heavy saucepan, combine the rice, water, and salt over medium-high heat. Cover and reduce heat to simmer and cook until tender, about 30 minutes. Remove from the heat and let rest, covered, for an additional 30 minutes. Drain the rice in a colander. Set aside.

Heat the butter in a heavy skillet over medium heat. Add the onion, carrot, celery, and thyme. Season with salt and pepper. Cook, stirring occasionally, until translucent, 5 to 7 minutes. Meanwhile, toss the apple in a small bowl with the lemon juice to prevent browning. Add the drained rice, apple, and pecans to the skillet and stir to combine. Taste and adjust for seasoning with salt and pepper. Remove from the heat and set aside.

Combine the greens, parsley, and chives in a large bowl. Season with salt and pepper. Drizzle over some of the vinaigrette and toss to evenly coat and slightly wilt the greens. Divide the salad among serving plates. Top with a spoonful of the warm rice mixture. Drizzle additional warmed vinaigrette over the rice. Garnish with the dried fruit. Serve immediately.

Brilliant: Short Recipe
Wild Rice Cakes

These cakes are nutty and sweet and take our make-ahead Wild Rice Salad to Brilliant.

Place the rice salad in a large bowl. Add 1/2 cup all-purpose flour, 1 large egg, and 2 tablespoons low-fat milk. Stir to combine. Heat 1 tablespoon canola oil in a large nonstick skillet over medium-high heat. Working in batches, scoop the batter by 1/4-cup measures into the skillet. Flatten the pancakes slightly, and cook until golden, 1 to 2 minutes on each side. Transfer to a plate lined with paper towels. Makes 12. Divide the salad among plates. Top each serving with 2 or 3 Wild Rice Cakes. Garnish with the dried fruit.

Nathalie's Cheese Grits Soufflé

SERVES 8

When I started my first cooking job, under Nathalie Dupree, I was a scared, hardworking, novice thirsting for knowledge. She has been my friend and guide all along the way, but she's a very complicated woman. While apprenticing in her home, she used to drive me absolutely, positively crazy, leaving her peanut butter–covered knife on the counter after making a sandwich, or mixing her lady garments into the laundry with my kitchen towels. Several months after I left her apprenticeship, she called me in DC to ask me how to work her microwave.

Pat Conroy once wrote that Nathalie was "more like a fictional character than a flesh and blood person." That still makes me *howl* with laughter. But it's not because she putters about uttering epithets like "do as I say, not as I do" or "oops, I dropped my diamond" when she drops a bowl. It's because it's impossible to imagine that anyone could truly be that generous and loving and be a real-life person. She's one of my dearest friends ever, and I love her. Try her grits, and you will love her, too.

5 cups low-fat or whole milk

1 cup (2 sticks) unsalted butter, plus more for the baking dish

1 cup stone-ground grits

1 teaspoon fine sea salt, plus more as needed

1/4 teaspoon cayenne pepper, plus more as needed

4 cups grated sharp white Cheddar cheese (1 pound)

1 tablespoon Dijon mustard

1/8 teaspoon ground mace

6 large eggs, separated

Preheat the oven to 350°F. Generously butter a 9 x 13-inch ovenproof baking dish.

Bring the milk to a boil in a large, heavy saucepan over medium-high heat. Stir in the grits and return to a boil. Season with the 1 teaspoon salt and cayenne pepper. Decrease the heat to low and simmer until creamy and thick but still loose and saucy, 45 to 60 minutes. Remove from the heat. Stir in the cheese, butter, mustard, and mace. Cool slightly. Taste and adjust for seasoning with salt and pepper.

Lightly beat the egg yolks in a small bowl. Stir a little of the grits into the yolks to heat them slightly, then add the yolks to the grits mixture and combine thoroughly. (This technique is called tempering; it makes the temperatures of two mixtures—one

containing raw egg—more similar, so the eggs don't curdle in the presence of the hot grits.)

In the bowl of a heavy-duty mixer fitted with the whisk attachment, beat the egg whites with a pinch of sea salt on medium speed until foamy. Increase the speed to high and whip until stiff peaks form, 2 to 3 minutes.

Add about one-quarter of the beaten egg whites to the grits mixture and stir until well mixed. Pour this lightened mixture over the remaining whites and fold them together as gently as possible.

Pour into the prepared baking dish. (The soufflé may be made several hours ahead to this point, covered, and set aside or refrigerated. When you are ready to finish it, return the soufflé to room temperature.)

Bake the soufflé until it is puffed and lightly browned, 40 to 45 minutes. Spoon onto warmed serving plates and serve immediately.

Brilliant: Short Recipe
Butter Shrimp Sauce

Basic shrimp and grits are a Low Country classic, but Nathalie's Cheese Grits Soufflé topped with her Butter Shrimp Sauce is undoubtedly Brilliant and certainly a heart-stopping indulgence.

Just before serving, so as not to overcook the shrimp, melt 1 cup (2 sticks) unsalted butter in a large skillet. Add 1¹/₂ pounds small shrimp (31/35 count), peeled and deveined, and cook until they start to turn pink, 3 to 4 minutes. Add 2 to 3 tablespoons chopped fresh mixed herbs such as flat-leaf parsley and basil. Taste and adjust for seasoning with fine sea salt and cayenne pepper. Serves 8. To serve, temove the soufflé from the oven and spoon onto warmed serving plates. Ladle the shrimp and their sauce over each serving. Serve immediately.

Sweet Potato Grits

The first time I had sweet potato grits, it was a revelation. Two of the ultimate Southern sides were married into one—delicious. I've mentioned cooking has taught me a lot about life, and it sure keeps trying to teach me patience.

Anyone who has burned his or her mouth tasting a spoonful of hot grits before they cool knows the importance of patience. Remove a steak from the grill and cut into it before it has rested? The juices run all over the board and the steak is dry and tough. Even more dire is to cut a cake or a loaf of bread before it cools sufficiently and it crumbles. Open the oven door too often to check on cooking, and your dish ceases to cook because all the heat has escaped. Patience is a key ingredient. These flavorful grits are a reward for being patient.

2 cups water

2 cups low-fat or whole milk

1 cup stone-ground grits

2 medium sweet potatoes, peeled and grated

Coarse salt and freshly ground white pepper

1/4 teaspoon ground ginger

Pinch of ground cinnamon

1 tablespoon unsalted butter

In a large, heavy saucepan, combine the water and milk and bring to a gentle boil over medium-high heat. Slowly add the grits, whisking constantly. Add the sweet potato. Season with salt and white pepper. Decrease the heat to low and simmer, stirring often, until the grits are creamy and thick, 45 to 60 minutes.

Taste the grits and sweet potato to make sure both are cooked and tender. Add the ground ginger, cinnamon, and butter. Taste and adjust for seasoning with salt and white pepper. Serve immediately.

Brilliant: Short Recipe
Sweet Potato Spoonbread

Add a bit of technique and our Basic country classic is transformed into a Brilliant soufflélike spoonbread. Preheat the oven to 375°F. Butter an ovenproof casserole or round 2-quart soufflé mold. To the sweet potato-grits mixture, add 2 large egg yolks, one at a time, stirring after each addition. In a separate bowl, using a handheld mixer, beat 2 large egg whites with a pinch of salt on high speed until stiff peaks form. Gently fold the egg whites into the warm sweet potato mixture. Transfer the lightened mixture to the prepared pan; smooth the surface with a spatula. Bake until the outside is puffed and risen, the inside is firm but moist, and the top is golden brown, 35 to 40 minutes. Serve immediately while still puffed. Serves 4 to 6.

Spiced Sweet Potato Mash

SERVES 4 TO 6

Sweet potatoes are good and good for you. Most Southern recipes drown them in butter and sugar, but they are *so good* with a just a whisper of butter. In this recipe the potatoes are first roasted, then scooped and mashed. You can use the microwave if you are pressed for time, but roasting brings out the complex flavors.

4 medium sweet potatoes (about 2 pounds)

2 tablespoons sorghum, cane, molasses, or maple syrup (see right)

1 tablespoon unsalted butter

Finely grated zest and juice of 1/2 orange

1/2 teaspoon ground cinnamon

1/2 teaspoon ground allspice

1/4 teaspoon freshly grated nutmeg

Pinch of cayenne pepper

Coarse salt and freshly ground black pepper

Preheat the oven to 400°F. Line a rimmed baking sheet with a silicone baking liner or parchment paper. (This will help with clean up.)

Using a fork, pierce the sweet potatoes in several places and place on the prepared baking sheet. Bake until fork-tender, about 50 minutes. Set aside to cool.

When the potatoes are cool enough to handle, peel the potatoes, discarding the skin. Place the pulp in large bowl. (If you really want them creamy, press them through a fine-mesh sieve or food mill.) Add the syrup, butter, orange zest and juice, cinnamon, allspice, nutmeg, and cayenne. Season with salt and pepper. Using a potato masher, heavy-duty whisk, or handheld mixer, beat until smooth. Taste and adjust for seasoning with salt and pepper. Transfer the sweet potatoes to a warmed serving bowl. Serve immediately.

Brilliant: Presentation

Twice-Baked Sweet Potatoes

Meme peeled hers; discarding the skin, and Mama does, too, but I like the leathery skin. It's the extra step of stuffing these that makes this recipe Brilliant.

Using an oven mitt or folded kitchen towel to hold the cooked potatoes, cut the potatoes in half. Using a spoon, scoop the flesh from each half into a bowl, leaving a 1/8-inch to 1/4-inch thickness of flesh in each shell. Arrange the shells on a baking sheet and bake until dry and slightly crisped, about 10 minutes. Meanwhile, prepare the mash as in the Basic recipe. Spoon the still-warm potato mixture into the crisped shells, mounding slightly at the center. Sprinkle 1/2 cup pecans equally over the filled sweet potatoes. Bake until slightly brown and crisp on top, about 10 minutes. Serve immediately. Serves 4 to 8.

Pour it On

The traditional Southern syrups are molasses, cane, and sorghum.

Molasses is a by-product of sugar refining, the syrup remaining after sugarcane juice has been processed or boiled to produce granulated sugar. The more times molasses is boiled, the less sweet it becomes. The last processes produce blackstrap molasses, a dark, bitter syrup with the highest nutritional value.

Cane syrup is made from the juice boiled down from sugarcane, similar to how maple sap is boiled down to make maple syrup. Cane syrup is thicker than sorghum syrup and tends to have a fuller, sweeter taste. It is delicious.

Sorghum is a canelike grass related to millet. When crushed, the juice is boiled down to produce sorghum syrup. Sorghum is vitamin rich with iron, calcium, and potassium and has a earthy, slightly vegetal flavor.

Yukon Gold Mash with Coarse-Grain Mustard

SERVES 4 TO 6

Several years ago, I traveled to Dijon to shoot the making of mustard, where it has been made for hundreds of years. The air is amazingly pungent and goggles are actually necessary in the factories. Mustard belongs to the same genus, *Brassica,* as broccoli, collards, and kale, all greens strong in flavor with a touch of heat and a hint of bitterness.

There are different types of mustard seed; yellow and brown are the most common. Milder yellow seeds are used to make American mustard. Brown seeds are hotter and used for Dijon mustard as well as spicy Asian mustard. The word *mustard* comes from an ancient Roman condiment of crushed mustard seed and "must," or unfermented grape juice. The French word *moutarde* is derived from a contraction of *moust*, or "must," and *ardent*, meaning "blazing" or "burning"—as in hot. This little kiss of heat with the creamy potatoes is just enough to make this Basic every-night supper dish more than the same old, same old.

2 pounds Yukon gold potatoes, peeled and cut into large chunks

Coarse salt

1 1/3 cups low-fat or whole milk

1/4 cup (1/2 stick) unsalted butter

1/4 cup coarse-grain Dijon mustard

Freshly ground white pepper

Place the potatoes in a large, heavy saucepan and cover with cold water. Season with salt, bring to a boil over high heat, then decrease the heat to low. Gently simmer until the potatoes are fork-tender, about 25 minutes.

Meanwhile, in a second saucepan, combine the milk, butter, and mustard over low heat. Cook until the butter is melted; cover and keep warm.

Drain the potatoes in a colander and return them to the saucepan over medium heat. Cook, stirring constantly, until a floury film forms on the bottom of the pan, 1 to 2 minutes. Remove from the heat. Pass the potatoes through a ricer or food mill, or mash with a potato masher until smooth. Add the warm milk mixture, stirring vigorously until well combined. Taste and adjust for seasoning with salt and white pepper. Serve immediately.

Brilliant: Short Recipe
Pommes Mont d'Or

Pommes Mont d'Or translates to Golden Potato Mountain. Sounds pretty Brilliant, doesn't it?

Preheat the oven to 350°F. Grease a gratin dish with 1 tablespoon unsalted butter. To the saucepan containing the slightly cooled potato mixture, add 3 lightly beaten large eggs and 1 tablespoon chopped fresh thyme. Stir to combine. Pour into the prepared gratin dish and spread gently with a spatula. Sprinkle 1/4 cup (1 ounce) grated Gruyère cheese on top and bake until a rich golden brown, about 30 minutes. Remove to a rack to cool slightly, then serve. Serves 4 to 6.

Parmesan Potatoes

SERVES 4

Mama tells the story of Aunt Lee offering to bring homemade potato chips to a school function. This was long before the age of food processors, so the potatoes had to be thinly sliced by hand. A mandoline may seem like a fancy gourmet appliance, but Meme actually had one she had purchased at the county fair when Mama was a little girl. Meme had made those chips before, but this time was one too many, so she delegated the task to Aunt Lee. Mama says that was the last time Aunt Lee offered homemade potato chips for parties.

You won't find this recipe nearly that labor-intensive. Serve this as a side dish at supper or for breakfast. It's just buttery and cheesy enough without being overly rich like many potato gratins.

2 tablespoons unsalted butter, melted, plus more if needed

1 tablespoon extra-virgin olive oil

2 pounds Yukon gold potatoes

Coarse salt and freshly ground black pepper

1/4 cup finely grated Parmigiano-Reggiano cheese (about 1 ounce)

1 teaspoon chopped fresh thyme

Preheat the oven to 450°F.

Combine 1 tablespoon of the butter and the oil in a large bowl. Thinly slice the potatoes with a chef's knife or on a mandoline and place in the bowl as you slice, without rinsing. (The potato starch will help bind them, instead of adding lots of cream or cheese.) Season with salt and pepper and toss to combine.

Heat the remaining 1 tablespoon butter in a 10-inch heavy, ovenproof skillet over medium-high heat. Place about one-third of the potatoes in one slightly overlapping layer in the skillet.

Toss the remaining potatoes with the cheese and thyme. Season with salt and pepper. Spread evenly over the first layer of potatoes in the skillet, pressing with a spatula. Cook for 3 minutes over medium heat, then transfer the skillet to the oven and roast, uncovered, until the potatoes are tender and the top is starting to brown, 20 to 25 minutes. Brush with additional butter, if desired.

Place on a rack to cool slightly. Invert onto a cutting board, cut into wedges, and serve.

Brilliant: Short Recipe
Pithiviers Savoyarde

Pithivier is a fancy word for an enclosed pie. Think "hot pocket." I once worked in the French alpine region of Savoie, where the hearty dishes are dubbed *savoyarde* style and often include potatoes, cheese, and ham.

Preheat the oven to 375°F. Line a rimmed baking sheet with a silicone baking liner or parchment paper. Whisk together 1 large egg and 1 tablespoon water in a small bowl. Set aside. Using a cookie cutter, cut out four 4-inch rounds of potatoes from the skillet. Set aside. On a lightly floured work surface, roll out 1 pound Quick Puff Pastry (page 19) or 1 (14-ounce) box store-bought puff pastry 1/8 inch thick. Using a 5-inch cookie cutter or a plate as a guide, cut out 8 pastry circles. Place on the prepared baking sheet. Refrigerate or freeze until firm, about 15 minutes. Meanwhile, using a 4-inch cookie cutter, cut out 4 circles from 4 slices of thinly sliced country ham, prosciutto, Serrano ham, or even deli ham. Remove one of the pastry circles. Brush with Dijon mustard. Top with a disk of potatoes, then a slice of ham. Scatter 1 tablespoon grated Gruyère on top. Brush the outer edges of the pastry circle with an egg wash made from 1 large egg and 2 tablespoons cold water. Top with a second pastry circle and press to seal. Brush the top with more egg wash. Scallop the sealed edges with the backside of a knife. Repeat with remaining ingredients. Bake until a rich golden brown, 20 to 25 minutes. Makes 4. Serve immediately or at room temperature.

Southern-Style Home Fries

SERVES 4 TO 6

We don't always serve grits for breakfast in the South. Sometimes there isn't time. Some recipes for home fries call for precooking the potatoes. My preference, especially since I'm not a morning person, is that simple is best. I find that covering the potatoes while they brown steams them at the same time.

1 tablespoon unsalted butter

1 tablespoon canola oil

2 pounds Yukon gold potatoes, diced

Coarse salt and freshly ground black pepper

1 onion, preferably Vidalia, chopped

1/2 teaspoon paprika

2 tablespoons chopped fresh flat-leaf parsley

Heat the butter and oil in large cast-iron skillet over medium-high heat until shimmering. Add the potatoes and shake the skillet to evenly distribute them in a single layer; make sure that one side of each piece is touching the surface of the skillet. Season with salt and pepper. Cook, without stirring, until the potatoes are golden brown on the bottom, 4 to 5 minutes, then turn potatoes with an offset spatula. Decrease the heat to medium and cover with a lid. Continue to cook, turning every 4 to 5 minutes, until potatoes are tender and browned on most sides, an additional 15 minutes. Add the paprika and parsley and stir to combine. Taste and adjust for seasoning with salt and pepper. Serve immediately.

Brilliant: Short Recipe

Scattered, Smothered, and Covered Home Fries

The first Waffle House opened in 1955, in Avondale Estates, Georgia. Today, the Waffle House chain of twenty-four-hour restaurants is a Southern institution. Everyone, from hardworking laborers to hung-over frat boys to blue-haired society ladies to soccer moms, loves the food and friendly service. As the name implies, the restaurants serve a lot of waffles. Equally popular, however, are their hash browns. There is a whole lingo for ordering that makes them "scattered" (spread on the grill, so they are really crispy), "smothered" (with onions), or "covered" (with cheese). Brilliant doesn't even begin to describe it. Although the Waffle House uses shredded potatoes for their hash browns, the results are equally Brilliant with diced potatoes.

After cooking the potatoes for about 10 minutes, add 1 onion, preferably Vidalia, chopped, and stir to combine. Continue to cook, turning every 4 to 5 minutes, until potatoes are tender and browned on most sides, about 15 more minutes. Add the paprika and parsley and stir to combine. Add 1 cup grated Cheddar cheese (about 4 ounces) and toss to coat. Taste and adjust for seasoning with coarse salt and freshly ground black pepper. Serve immediately. Serves 4.

Gnocchi à la Parisienne

SERVES 4

It seems every culture in the world has its version of dumplings. In the South, it's a biscuitlike dough rolled out and added to simmering broth. Gnocchi are Italian dumplings often made of potato and sometimes wheat flour. This French recipe uses the kitchen workhorse, *pâte a choux*, also used to make the gougères in *Bon Appétit, Y'all*, as well as éclairs and profiteroles. *Parisienne* means many things in French cooking. First and foremost, it means "in the manner of Paris," which automatically denotes sophistication.

A note of encouragement: Don't panic when you are adding the eggs and the dough starts to look awful. Just keep stirring and it will come together.

1 cup low-fat or whole milk

1/4 cup (1/2 stick) plus 1 tablespoon unsalted butter, plus more for the baking sheet and gratin dish

1/2 teaspoon fine sea salt, more for the cooking water

1 cup all-purpose flour

3 large eggs, at room temperature

1/4 cup chopped mixed fresh tender herbs (such as flat-leaf parsley, chives, and basil)

1/3 cup grated Gruyère cheese (about 1 1/3 ounces)

1/3 cup freshly grated Parmigiano-Reggiano cheese (about 1 1/3 ounces)

Freshly ground white pepper

Preheat the oven to 375°F. Lightly butter a rimmed baking sheet and a large gratin dish. Set aside.

To make the dough, in a saucepan, combine the milk, 1/4 cup of the butter, and the 1/2 teaspoon salt and bring to a gentle boil over high heat. Immediately remove the pan from the heat, add the flour all at once, and beat vigorously with a wooden spoon until the mixture is smooth and pulls away from the sides of the pan to form a ball, 30 to 60 seconds. (This mixture is called the *panade*.) Beat over low heat for an additional 30 to 60 seconds to dry the mixture.

With a wooden spoon, beat the eggs into the dough, one at a time, beating thoroughly after each addition. (The dough will come together, I promise.) Beat until the dough is shiny and slides from the spoon. Add the herbs and Gruyère.

Bring a pot of water to a boil over high heat. Add a little salt and decrease the heat to simmer for gentle poaching. I've found that using a small ice cream scoop about the size of a gumball is by far the easiest way to prepare these gnocchi. Or, for traditional (and a bit more troublesome) gnocchi, transfer the dough to a large pastry bag. As you squeeze the back of the bag with your right hand, hold a small knife in your left hand and cut off 1-inch lengths of dough, allowing the gnocchi to drop into the pot.

Keep the water at a gentle simmer, not at a rolling boil. Working in batches so as not to overcrowd the pot, add the dough to the simmering water. First, the gnocchi will sink to the bottom, then rise to the top after a few minutes. Poach them until they are cooked all the way through (cut one open to check and taste; it shouldn't be doughy), about 5 minutes. Remove them with a slotted spoon to the prepared baking sheet. Repeat with the remaining dough.

To serve, toss with the remaining 1 tablespoon butter. Taste and adjust for seasoning with salt and pepper. Arrange the gnocchi in one layer in the prepared gratin dish. Top with the Parmigiano-Reggiano. Bake until puffed and lightly browned, 20 to 25 minutes. Serve immediately.

CONTINUED

Gnocchi à la Parisienne, *continued*

Brilliant: Short Recipe
Zucchini Spaghetti

This recipe turns things inside out with the pasta and vegetables, and the results are Brilliant.

Trim off the ends from 4 zucchini squash. Using the julienne blade of a mandoline, slice the zucchini into long julienne strips. Transfer the zucchini to a colander set in the sink. Toss the strips with 1 teaspoon coarse salt. Set aside for 15 minutes at room temperature. Gently squeeze the zucchini to extract excess water. Heat 1 tablespoon pure olive oil over medium-high heat. Add 1 clove garlic, mashed to a paste, and cook until fragrant, 45 to 60 seconds. Add the zucchini and 2 tablespoons chopped fresh basil and cook just until heated through, about 1 minute. Taste and adjust for seasoning with salt and pepper. Serves 4. To serve, make a nest of zucchini on warmed serving plates. Fill with a spoonful of the gnocchi. Serve immediately.

Pasta Gratin with Sauce Mornay

SERVES 6 TO 8

Sure sounds fancy, doesn't it? It's just simple macaroni and cheese made with béchamel (pictured on page 111), but we've got a twist. As soon as cheese is added to a béchamel, it becomes Mornay sauce. (For more about the mother sauces, see page 11.) I've noticed more recipes from the northern states use this technique. Most Southern mac and cheese recipes call for a custard base of sorts with egg and milk, rather than a roux-based sauce. I do not discriminate; I like browned, bubbly cheesy goodness any way it comes.

2 cups low-fat or whole milk

Bouquet garni (5 sprigs thyme; 4 sprigs flat-leaf parsley; 2 bay leaves, preferably fresh; and 10 whole black peppercorns, tied together in cheesecloth)

¼ cup (1/2 stick) unsalted butter, plus more for the baking dish

¼ cup all-purpose flour

1¼ cups grated Gruyère cheese (about 5 ounces)

Coarse salt and freshly ground black pepper

3 tablespoons chopped fresh mixed herbs (such as flat-leaf parsley, chives, and basil)

1 pound pasta (such as penne, farfalle, or rigatoni), cooked and well drained

1/2 cup plain or whole-wheat fresh or panko (Japanese) breadcrumbs

¼ cup freshly grated Parmigiano-Reggiano cheese (1 ounce)

Heat the milk in a small pot until just simmering. Add the bouquet garni. Remove from the heat and set aside to steep for 10 minutes.

Meanwhile, preheat the broiler. Butter a large gratin dish and set aside.

Melt the butter in a saucepan over medium heat. Whisk in the flour and cook for a minute or two until foaming. Remove and discard the bouquet garni, pour in the milk, and bring to a boil, whisking constantly until the sauce thickens. Season with salt and pepper and simmer for 2 minutes. The sauce should coat the back of a spoon. Remove the sauce from the heat and stir in half the Gruyère cheese until it melts. Taste and adjust for seasoning with salt and pepper. Place the pasta in a large bowl, add the herbs, spoon the sauce over, and stir to combine.

Spoon the mixture into the prepared gratin dish. Combine the remaining Gruyère, breadcrumbs, and Parmigiano-Reggiano. Sprinkle over the top of the gratin. Transfer the gratin to the broiler and broil until browned and bubbling, 8 to 10 minutes. Remove from the oven and let cool slightly before serving.

Brilliant: Short Recipe
Chicken and Broccoli Bake

This Basic pasta gratin is easily a match for all sorts of additions, some of which will render it Brilliant. In summer, a chopped heirloom tomato and, if I'm feeling luxurious, perhaps shrimp or lump crabmeat. Yes, of course, truffle shavings and lobster will do the trick, but one of my all-time favorites is to simplify, not elevate, to make this a Brilliant recipe. Southerners love casseroles, and the top two ingredients for casseroles are undoubtedly broccoli and chicken. Why not marry them all?

Cut 1 head broccoli into 1-inch florets. During the last few minutes the pasta is cooking, add the broccoli to the pot. Drain the pasta and broccoli well and proceed as directed in the recipe. Just before spooning the mixture into the gratin dish, add the meat, in bite-size pieces, from 1 rotisserie or roast chicken (about 3 cups). Spoon into the gratin dish and bake as directed. Serves 6.

9

Vegetables

As the kitchen director for various cooking shows on PBS, network, and cable television, I was responsible for all the food on the show. That meant I was responsible for everything from the ramekins of salt and pepper by the stovetop to the beautiful cake being pulled from the oven to the six-foot-long hero sandwich. Sometimes I was following the host's body of recipes, as with Bobby Flay or Nathalie Dupree. For Martha Stewart, I made recipes from her magazine and books. I was also managing the internal development of recipes within my kitchen that fed back into the magazine, *Martha Stewart Living.*

Whenever I am asked about what would be surprising about food television to most people, I always comment on the volume of groceries and food we went through. In general, most traditional format television cooking shows feature four recipes per show. Each recipe requires that we shop as though we would make the recipe four times. The first recipe's worth of groceries is easy; it's what the chef uses on camera. A second is preparing the recipe to a midstage point. Anything that takes longer than a couple of minutes and can't be executed on camera is going to need a "swap out." That's when the host says something like, "Here, I have one we've done ahead." The food for the third recipe is for the final dish, what is known as the "hero" or "beauty." Finally, food for a fourth recipe is shopped for as a backup. You never know when the light is going to blow or the mic is going to die—or when someone in the kitchen is going to drop a bag of groceries. (I won't even mention a cameraman pilfering a plate of food; that makes me crazy. I don't touch your camera, don't mess with my food!) I digress.

To demonstrate a recipe for taping on camera, the grocery list needs to be written multiplying the recipe four times. Therefore, using the first recipe in this chapter, a fairly short and simple one for Asparagus with Blender Hollandaise as an example, it's not 1 pound of asparagus I need, it's 4 pounds; not 1 cup of butter, but 2 pounds; not 3 eggs, but 1 dozen; and not $1/2$ lemon, but 2. And that's not including the pantry items. Since most shows feature four recipes, just for simplicity (not that anyone would ever make the same recipe four times), multiply that amount times four to see how much food there is per show. That makes 16 pounds of asparagus, 8 pounds of butter, 4 dozen eggs, and 8 lemons.

Want to make it even more apparent how much food there is? More than one episode is shot in a day. I've worked on shows where we shot seven shows a day, which is absolute hell, to two shows a day, which is very civilized. Let's just say our fictitious show tapes three shows a day. Using that same asparagus recipe, four recipes per show, shopping each recipe four times and taping three shows a day equals 48 pounds of asparagus, 24 pounds of butter, 12 dozen eggs, and 24 lemons. That's for one day of taping. Most shows tape between three and five days a week. So ramp that up yet again for each day of taping. Astonishing, isn't it? (Before I go a drop of ink further, let me tell you that any show I ever worked on, once it was shot, if the food was safe to eat, it was either fed to the crew or donated to the local food bank.)

When I was in charge of the kitchen at Martha Stewart, I was the one who did most of the shopping. At first, that might not seem to make much sense. I was in charge of all that food? All the food prepared on a national television show that cost hundreds of thousands of dollars to produce, a major part of the public face for a national brand, but I bagged my own groceries?

Exactly. Good food depends on good ingredients. Even though it was for the altered reality of television, Martha knew if it was good or not, as did I. Being in charge meant that I handpicked the groceries to my exact specifications. So, I was the one at dawn at the Union Square Greenmarket on shooting days with the restaurant chefs, picking out unblemished zucchini blossoms or perfect Sugar pumpkins with stems.

Food that is fresh is alive. It's electric and inspiring. Its flavor is directly related to its freshness. My cooking belief system is to use really good ingredients and to do as little to them as possible. The farmer is the one who makes the major decisions: what kind of variety to plant, where to plant it, when to harvest it. The cook's decision, minor in the scheme of things, is what to do with the food when it is in the kitchen.

It wasn't always possible with television, but in "real life," I like to go to the market to see what is available before I plan my menu. Sure, I may have an idea that since it's fall, I am likely to find butternut squash and kale, so I can plan loosely around that; but I am also open to seeing what I can do with an early stalk of Brussels sprouts. In a weird way, it's part of living in the moment. Sometimes I laugh at myself on a sleepy Saturday morning as I wake up thinking about what I am going to cook that night. Then I can't wait to get to the farmer's market.

In this chapter, you'll find a selection of recipes for inspiration to guide you when you return home from the market with farm-fresh produce, whether you need one pound of asparagus or forty-eight.

Choosing Produce

If you don't grow your own vegetables, you can shop at farmer's markets, a chain like Whole Foods Market that has a commitment to local foods, or a "pick your own" farm. You can even have it delivered by subscribing to a CSA (Community Supported Agriculture), an increasingly popular way to purchase fresh, seasonal food from a local farm. Do be aware that some farm stands sell food that isn't really from the farmer. Some stands may seem to be offering local, fresh food, but they are not. They may have simply picked up a couple of cases of product at a wholesale market terminal. It's possible that the produce was shipped in from out of state, but it's also possible the produce is local. The way to find out is to ask. It's your food; find out where it came from.

One concern with the origin of your food and how it was grown involves pesticides. There's a list called the Dirty Dozen, made of foods believed to be most susceptible to absorbing pesticides because they have soft skin. Nefarious vegetable members of this list include celery, bell peppers, spinach, kale and collard greens, potatoes, and lettuce. Fruits include peaches, strawberries, apples, blueberries, nectarines, cherries, and grapes. A pesticide is a mixture of chemical substances used on farms to destroy or prevent pests, diseases, and weeds from affecting crops. The government tells us that consuming pesticides in small amounts doesn't harm you, but some studies show a correlation between pesticides and health problems. Health experts suggest that when it comes to the Dirty Dozen list, choose organic if it's available.

Asparagus with Blender Hollandaise

SERVES 4 TO 6

Traditionally, hollandaise is whisked together in a double boiler, which can easily result in a wicked steam burn for the cook and a curdled sauce if it is overheated, neither of which is appealing. Regardless of how it's described—curdled, broken, or separated—an overheated hollandaise looks pretty much like scrambled eggs floating in oil and tastes about as good. A blender—and a dollop of stabilizing mustard—makes this magical emulsion a breeze to prepare and everyone, friends and family both, will think you are a culinary genius.

For best results, I always use Land O Lakes butter in this recipe. Cheap butter contains more water and expensive butter contains more fat; Land O Lakes is consistent and works like a charm. Also, this recipe makes about 1 cup of sauce. If you need more, it's best to make a second batch, as opposed to doubling the recipe.

1 cup (2 sticks) Land O Lakes unsalted butter

3 large egg yolks

Juice of 1/2 lemon

1 teaspoon Dijon mustard

Coarse salt and and freshly ground white pepper

Pinch of cayenne pepper

1 pound asparagus, ends trimmed

1 teaspoon canola oil

Melt the butter in a small, heavy saucepan over medium-high heat. Cook until bubbling but not brown.

Meanwhile, combine the egg yolks, lemon juice, mustard, salt, and cayenne in a blender and blend for a few seconds at high speed until you have a smooth, frothy mixture.

Turn the blender off and replace the centerpiece of the lid with a funnel. Turn the blender on high and add the hot butter through the funnel in a thin, steady stream, but not too slowly. (You can transfer the butter to a heatproof measuring cup if it's easier for you to pour into the funnel, but do it at just the last minute so the butter is as hot as possible.)

As you add the stream of butter, the sauce will emulsify and thicken. Continue blending until almost all the butter is used, leaving just the milk solids in the bottom of the saucepan.

Meanwhile, preheat the broiler. Spread out the asparagus spears in a single layer on a rimmed baking sheet. Drizzle with the oil and shake the pan to evenly coat the spears. Season with salt and pepper.

Broil until the spears are just tender, 4 minutes for thin and up to 10 minutes for thick asparagus.

Serve immediately, or hold the sauce in a warm water bath or thermos to keep warm for up to 2 hours. Discard any remaining sauce after serving. (It will only curdle and is impossible to reheat.)

Brilliant: Presentation
Wrap Asparagus Bundles with Smoked Salmon

The ease of making a blender hollandaise allows this luxurious vegetable dish to be considered Basic. So, what will make it Brilliant? Marry it with a natural partner: smoked salmon. You will need 4 to 6 ounces, depending on how many you are serving.

Divide the warm cooked asparagus into 4 to 6 servings, wrap 1 slice of salmon around each bundle, and place on warmed plates. Spoon over the Hollandaise and serve immediately. Serves 4 to 6.

Glazed Spring Vegetables

SERVES 4 TO 6

As much as I love winter food like braised meats and long simmered stews, by the time springtime rolls around, it is a real treat to go to the farmer's market and see the baskets of spring vegetables. The trick here is to cook what's fresh and available, and not worry about the recipe. These vegetables are glazed from the natural sugars present in them, not by dousing with sugar or honey. The butter is gilding the lily, and optional, but well worth it.

8 ounces fingerling potatoes, halved lengthwise

8 ounces baby carrots, with greens trimmed to 1/2 inch

8 ounces French breakfast radishes, with greens trimmed to 1/2 inch

3 cloves garlic, thinly sliced

8 sprigs thyme

1/4 cup canola oil

11/4 cups water

2 tablespoons unsalted butter, optional

1 tablespoon chopped fresh mint

Coarse salt and freshly ground white pepper

Combine the potatoes, carrots, radishes, garlic, thyme, and oil in a large, straight-sided skillet and toss to coat with the oil. Add the water to the skillet and bring to a boil. Cover the skillet tightly and simmer vigorously over medium heat, shaking the skillet occasionally, until the vegetables are tender, about 10 minutes.

Transfer the vegetables to a warmed platter with a slotted spoon, discarding the thyme sprigs, then boil the cooking liquid for 1 minute to emulsify the oil. Remove from the heat and add the butter, swirling the skillet until the butter is incorporated. Add the mint and adjust for seasoning with salt and white pepper. Pour the sauce over the vegetables and serve.

Brilliant: Short Recipe
Shaved Raw Asparagus

When asparagus is fresh and incredible in spring, I love to shave it and serve it raw. Holding a single asparagus spear by its tough end, lay it flat on a cutting board. Using a vegetable peeler, create long shavings of asparagus by drawing the peeler from the base to the top of the stalk. Repeat with the remaining spears and don't worry if some pieces are unevenly thick (such as at the end of the stalk, which might be too thin to peel). Discard the tough stem ends. Prepare the Basic recipe. At the end of cooking the vegetables, add the shaved asparagus and toss to coat.

Meme's Yellow Squash Casserole

SERVES 6

This good, old-fashioned squash casserole has been on our family dinner table more times than I can remember. I love it and make a point to ask Mama to fix it during the holidays. It's important to cook the squash before assembling the casserole. Squash has a very high water content. If you do not cook the squash first, it will exude water as it bakes, and you will have a soggy mess.

2 tablespoons unsalted butter, plus more for the baking dish

2 tablespoons canola oil

1 onion, preferably Vidalia, chopped

3 yellow squashes, sliced 1/4 inch thick

2 zucchini, sliced 1/4 inch thick

Coarse salt and freshly ground black pepper

2 large eggs

1 cup low-fat or regular evaporated milk

1 cup shredded Cheddar cheese (4 ounces)

2 cups Club cracker crumbs or plain or whole-wheat fresh or panko (Japanese) breadcrumbs

Preheat the oven to 400°F. Brush a medium casserole dish with butter.

Heat the oil in a large skillet over medium-high heat. Add the onion and cook until translucent, 3 to 5 minutes. Add the yellow squashes and zucchini. Season with salt and pepper. Cook until just tender, 3 to 5 minutes. With a slotted spoon (leaving the cooking juices behind), transfer the vegetables to a bowl. Add the eggs, evaporated milk, and cheese; stir to combine. Transfer the vegetable mixture to the prepared baking dish. Sprinkle with cracker crumbs and dot with the butter. Bake until the vegetables are tender and the topping is lightly browned, about 30 minutes. Transfer to a wire rack to cool slightly. Serve warm.

Brilliant: Technique
Grilled Squash

Instead of sautéing the squash, shake things up by grilling the squash. This is also a great use for leftover grilled vegetables. Slice the squash lengthwise approximately 1/4 inch thick. Season generously with coarse salt and freshly ground black pepper Grill the squash, turning frequently, until the slices are well browned on both sides and soft but still slightly firm, about 6 minutes. Slice into bite-size pieces. Transfer to a bowl and proceed with Mama's recipe. Serves 4 to 6.

Grilled Okra Skewers

SERVES 4 TO 6

I like okra every which way—raw, boiled, steamed, fried—you name it, I love it. Not everyone does. Grilled or broiled okra is a revelation. This recipe is an official Okra Converter. When buying okra, choose firm, brightly colored pods that don't exceed four inches in length; larger pods are more likely to be tough and fibrous.

Many recipes suggest soaking bamboo skewers in water to use on the grill. This never seems to work well enough for me, and they always burn to a crisp. My suggestion is to buy some stainless-steel skewers and be done with it.

4 jalapeños

1 1/2 pounds okra, stems trimmed

1 tablespoon canola oil

Coarse salt and freshly ground black pepper

Prepare a charcoal fire using about 6 pounds of charcoal and burn until the coals are completely covered with a thin coating of light gray ash, 20 to 30 minutes. Spread the coals evenly over the grill bottom, position the grill rack above the coals, and heat until medium-hot (when you can hold your hand 5 inches above the grill surface for no longer than 3 or 4 seconds). Or, for a gas grill, turn all burners to high, close the lid, and heat until very hot, 10 to 15 minutes.

Meanwhile, slice the jalapeños into coins about 1/4 inch thick. Thread the okra crosswise onto 2 skewers, building a ladder of sorts so the okra won't spin on the skewer and inserting slices of jalapeño every other pod or so, depending on how much kick you want. Brush with canola oil and season with salt and pepper. Transfer to the grill and cook until bright green and tender, 2 to 3 minutes per side. Remove from the grill and serve immediately.

Brilliant: Short Recipe

Roasted Jalapeño Dipping Sauce

To heighten this Basic combination of smoky grilled okra and jalapeño, make a Brilliant dipping sauce. Omit slicing the jalapeños; before grilling the okra, place the jalapeños on the prepared grill and roast until blackened and charred. Peel, seed, and core. Place in the jar of a blender, with 1 clove garlic and 1/4 cup canola oil. Purée until smooth. Season with coarse salt and freshly ground black pepper. Makes about 1/2 cup. Proceed with grilling skewered okra as above. Remove the okra from the skewers and place on a warmed serving plate. Serve the dipping sauce on the side.

Okra Cornmeal Cakes

MAKES 12 (3-INCH) CAKES

The inspiration for these delicious okra cakes came from Gloria Smiley, a friend and professional food stylist in Atlanta. Her okra cakes have a rice base, maybe because she's got rice in her blood since she's from the Low Country. I felt compelled to use corn, maybe because I'm from farther inland. In fact, in the middle of summer, I like to add fresh corn cut off the cob, as well. The amount of water to use will depend on the size grind of the cornmeal. Serve these in bite-size bits for a cocktail nibble or larger cakes for a side dish.

2 cups fine yellow cornmeal

2 teaspoons baking powder

1 teaspoon fine sea salt

1 large egg, lightly beaten

1 1/2 cups water, plus more if needed

8 ounces okra, stems trimmed and sliced 1/4 inch thick

1 jalapeño, cored, seeded, and finely chopped

1 clove garlic, mashed into a paste

1/4 cup corn oil, for frying

Line a plate with paper towels. Set aside.

To prepare the batter, in a large bowl, whisk together the cornmeal, baking powder, and fine salt. In a second bowl or large liquid measuring cup, combine the egg and water. Add to the dry ingredients and whisk until smooth. Add the okra, jalapeño, and garlic. Stir to combine. (The batter is thick, but should be wet, not dry. Add water as needed; the amount will depend on the size grind of the cornmeal.)

To fry the griddle cakes, heat the oil in a cast-iron skillet over medium heat. Scoop 1/4 cup of batter onto the heated skillet and press into an even layer. Repeat with additional batter, without crowding. Cook the cakes until the bottoms are brown and bubbles form on the tops and edges, 2 to 3 minutes. Turn and brown the other side, an additional 2 to 3 minutes. Transfer to the paper towel–lined plate. While hot, season with salt and pepper. Repeat with remaining batter. Serve immediately.

Napoleon

A Napoleon is traditionally a stacked dessert of Puff Pastry (page 19), Pastry Cream (page 21), and fruit, but the term has come to mean pretty much anything stacked. Sometimes the concept is taken a bit too far and the stack becomes towering and difficult to eat, more akin to a Napoleon complex, but it's a very restaurant way of presenting a thin little cake or vegetable. Our Basic Okra Cornmeal Cakes are Brilliant layered with a soft, creamy cheese, such as fresh goat cheese or ricotta; thickly sliced tomato; and perhaps the Warm Summer Shrimp Salad (page 61).

Garlic Paste

I find the bitter heat of coarsely chopped garlic easily overwhelms a dish, so I prefer it very finely chopped, grated on a Microplane, or mashed into a paste with salt. First, halve a peeled garlic clove lengthwise and remove any of the green shoot, if present, as it is bitter. Coarsely chop the garlic, then sprinkle it with coarse salt. (The salt acts as an abrasive and helps chop the garlic.) Then, using the flat side of a chef's knife like an artist's palette knife, press firmly on the garlic, crushing a little at a time. Repeat until the garlic is a fine paste.

Green Beans with Buttery Peaches

SERVES 4 TO 6

A couple of years ago Mama called in the middle of the night to tell me my sister, Jona, had been burned and was left with third-degree burns over 20 percent of her body. I remember going back to bed and, of course, doing the math poorly. "Ok, she's 5 foot, 8 inches, so 20 percent is a little more than a foot." I just couldn't wrap my head around it.

The doctors wouldn't perform skin grafts until she was consuming a certain amount of calories. Every day without the skin grafts was dangerous. She was practically comatose from the heavy-duty narcotics. I tried to feed her. She fought me, of course, feisty and mad as hell. I shoved green beans in her mouth, furious at her, crying. I was so mad I could hardly breathe. We yelled and screamed at each other. Now, she absolutely hates green beans. Green beans are one of the reasons she's alive. You know what? I love them.

1½ pounds green beans, ends trimmed

1 tablespoon unsalted butter

1 tablespoon canola oil

4 peaches, pitted and sliced

Coarse salt and freshly ground black pepper

1 clove garlic, crushed to a paste

1 teaspoon fennel seeds

Make an ice-water bath by filling a large bowl with ice and water. Line a plate with paper towels.

To cook the beans, bring a large pot of salted water to a rolling boil over high heat. Add the beans and cook until crisp-tender, about 3 minutes. Drain well in a colander, then set the colander with beans in the ice-water bath (to set the color and stop the cooking), making sure the beans are submerged. Once chilled, remove the beans to the prepared plate.

In the same pot, heat the butter and oil over medium-high heat until shimmering. Add the peaches and season with salt and pepper. Cook, turning once, until browned on both sides, about 4 minutes, depending on the tenderness of the peaches. Add the garlic and fennel seeds; cook until fragrant, 45 to 60 seconds. Add the reserved green beans and toss to coat. Taste and adjust for seasoning with salt and pepper. Serve hot, warm, or at room temperature.

Brilliant: Short Recipe

Savory Almond Toffee Nougatine

Green beans with peaches may seem a bit unusual to be Basic, and indeed, I first had this interesting combination at L'Arpège, a 3-star Michelin restaurant in Paris. For the Brilliant, I wanted to play off the peach component by using its cousin, the almond.

Combine ¼ cup sugar, ¼ cup water, and ¼ teaspoon fine sea salt in a small, heavy-bottomed saucepan over high heat. Cook to the pale caramel stage (see page 23), 330°F, 5 to 7 minutes, depending on the thickness of the pan. Add 2 tablespoons unsalted butter and season with ¼ teaspoon freshly ground black pepper. Add 2 tablespoons toasted sliced almonds. Pour onto a silicone baking liner. (If it hardens before it is sufficiently thin, keep it on the silicone liner and place it in a 300°F oven to slowly soften.) Let cool completely. Break into shards, then chop to pulverize with a knife or in a food processor fitted with a metal blade. Makes about ¾ cup. To serve, sprinkle over the green beans with peaches.

Meme's Green Beans with Potatoes and Ham

SERVES 4 TO 6

Old-fashioned, comfort, country, soul food—it doesn't matter what you call this dish, it's good. Granted the beans are army green and quite soft, but that's what it is. I simply trim the stem ends of the beans, leaving the bean whole and the curly tip intact. Meme made these green beans in the summer, essentially cooking two side dishes at once. The smoky broth is rich and meaty, perfect for receiving a dip from a buttery wedge of cornbread (page 230). If you'd like to lighten it up a bit, you can use smoked turkey neck instead of the ham hocks; for ease of shredding the meat, use the end piece of a hunk of country ham.

4 cups water

2 smoked ham hocks

1 tablespoon canola oil

3 pounds green beans, stem ends trimmed

1 onion, preferably Vidalia, chopped

Coarse salt and freshly ground black pepper

2 pounds small red new potatoes, halved

In a large pot, combine the water, ham hocks, and oil and bring to a boil over high heat. Decrease the heat to low and simmer until the flavors have married, at least 30 minutes. Add the green beans and onion. Season with salt and pepper. Continue cooking until the green beans are just tender, about 25 minutes. Add the potatoes and cook until the potatoes are tender, about 20 minutes more. Remove the hocks from the pot and remove the meat from the bone. Return the meat to the pot and stir to combine. Taste and adjust for seasoning with salt and pepper. Serve immediately.

Brilliant: Short Recipe
Salted Chiles

A bit of pungent, salty heat, similar to old-school pickled peppers, is just the trick to elevate this Basic country classic to Brilliant.

Wearing rubber or latex gloves, finely chop 10 serrano chiles, seeds included. Place in a glass jar. Add $1/4$ cup distilled white vinegar and 2 teaspoons kosher salt. Cover loosely with a lid, or with cheesecloth and a rubber band. Refrigerate for 5 days, then close the lid tightly. Makes $3/4$ cup. Keep stored in the refrigerator; the chiles will last for several weeks or months. Serve as a condiment with Meme's Green Beans with Potatoes and Ham.

Jona's Tomato Pie

MAKES 1 (9-INCH) PIE

When I was a very young girl, my grandparents did not have air-conditioning. It sounds so primitive, doesn't it? Yes, they had indoor plumbing! No jokes about me being a hick. Not having AC when the heat index is 110°F is pretty serious stuff. Meme would sprinkle the sheets with baby powder. Oscillating fans, window fans, and the terrifyingly large attic fan ran at all hours of the day and night. The attic fan was situated in the center of the house in the ceiling; once the switch was flipped, the levered doors would groan open, the motor would hum, and the blades would begin to twirl-thump, thump— as the big brass blades pushed the air.

Hot, dry summers make for uncomfortable people, but it is pretty much heaven for tomatoes. As long as there is enough water to prevent them from drying up and dying, tomatoes love the heat. This pie is a great side dish or even main dish during tomato season and can be served hot, warm, or at room temperature.

All-American Pie Crust (page 18), baked blind

4 to 5 ripe tomatoes, preferably heirloom, cored and
　　thinly sliced

Coarse salt

1 tablespoon canola or pure olive oil

1 onion, preferably Vidalia, sliced

Freshly ground black pepper

1/2 cup mixed chopped fresh herbs (such as chives,
　　flat-leaf parsley, and basil)

1/2 cup freshly grated Gruyère cheese (2 ounces)

1/2 cup freshly grated Parmigiano-Reggiano cheese
　　(2 ounces)

1/4 cup mayonnaise (page 15)

Coarse salt

Preheat the oven to 350°F. Place the tomatoes in a colander in the sink in a single layer. Sprinkle with salt and allow to drain for 10 minutes.

Meanwhile, heat the oil in the skillet over medium heat. Add the onion and season with salt and pepper. Cook until translucent, 3 to 5 minutes.

Layer the tomato slices, cooked onion, and herbs in the pie shell. Season each layer with pepper. Combine the grated cheeses and mayonnaise. Spread this mixture on top.

Bake until lightly browned, about 30 minutes. Remove to a rack to cool. Serve hot, warm, or at room temperature.

Brilliant: Short Recipe
Tomato Powder

Amp up the tomato flavor of this Basic recipe with a very chef-inspired and Brilliant tomato powder. It's almost a bit of silliness, cooking something for more than 5 hours to get 2 tablespoons of results. You won't believe it when you taste it. It's the pure essence of tomato flavor.

Position a rack in the middle of the oven and preheat to 175°F. Line a rimmed baking sheet with a silicone baking liner. Cut 3 plum or heirloom tomatoes crosswise into 1/8-inch slices, discarding the core end. Arrange in a single layer on the prepared baking sheet. Dehydrate the tomato slices in the oven, turning once at the halfway point with an offset spatula, until completely dry and crisp, 5 to 5 1/2 hours. Remove to a rack to cool completely. Crumble the tomato into a spice grinder and grind to a fine powder. Transfer to a fine-mesh sieve set over a bowl. Shake the powder through the sieve, then discard any large pieces. Makes about 2 tablespoons. Garnish the edges of the plate with the tomato powder.

Broiled Tomatoes Stuffed with Cornbread

SERVES 4

What is it about tomatoes and mayonnaise? A blissful marriage made in heaven, I think. It's a very Southern combination, but we don't have a lock on it. It's like Southern hospitality. I am a firm believer that what folks call Southern hospitality is just as simple as making someone feel welcomed and comfortable. The minute someone walks in my door, I ask if he or she would like a glass of tea or water. Or bourbon. Or a bite to eat. Hospitality and good manners are the social lubrication the world needs to run more smoothly. It's just a matter of being polite.

Serve this on a bed of romaine lettuce or spinach for a special lunch or light supper for a hot summer night.

3 slices bacon, cut into lardons (see page 54)

2 large ripe tomatoes, preferably heirloom

1 cup crumbled Jalapeño Cornbread Muffins (page 230)

1/4 cup mayonnaise (page 15)

2 green onions, white and pale green parts only, sliced

Leaves from 2 sprigs thyme, chopped

Coarse salt and freshly ground black pepper

Preheat the oven to 350°F. Line a plate with paper towels.

Heat a large ovenproof skillet over medium heat. Add the bacon and cook until crisp and brown, 5 to 7 minutes. Using a slotted spoon, transfer the bacon to the plate. Discard the bacon grease or save for another use. Wipe the skillet clean with paper towels. Set aside.

Using a serrated knife, halve the tomatoes horizontally. Carefully scoop out the pulp and reserve. In a small bowl, combine the tomato pulp, cornbread, mayonnaise, bacon, green onions, and thyme. Season with salt and pepper. Spoon the mixture into the tomato shells. Place the filled tomato shells in the reserved skillet. Bake for about 20 minutes, until heated through. Serve immediately.

Brilliant: Short Recipe
Sauce Verte

So if a little mayonnaise makes something good, does a lot of mayonnaise make it great? No, it makes it Brilliant! Don't take a shortcut and skip the herb blanching step. It keeps the sauce bright green, hence the name, which translates as "green sauce."

Bring a small saucepan of salted water to a boil over high heat. Add 1 cup chopped fresh mixed herbs (such as flat-leaf parsley, basil, tarragon, chives, and watercress or spinach). Drain immediately in a fine-mesh sieve, shock under cold running water, and dry well. Place the herbs in a bowl. Add 2 tablespoons finely chopped cucumber and 1 cup mayonnaise (page 15). Stir to combine. Taste and adjust for seasoning with coarse salt and freshly ground black pepper. Makes about 1 1/4 cups. Store in an airtight container in the refrigerator for up to 2 days. To serve, spoon a dollop of the sauce in the center of a plate. Top with the broiled tomato.

Mustard Greens with Smoked Turkey Neck

SERVES 4 TO 6

When I worked in France, I lived near a hillside covered with large fields planted with rape, a green that yields seeds for pressing into canola oil. I would gather the tender greens and simmer them with end pieces of Bayonne ham. Other greens may be substituted, but mustard greens will make the most rewarding pot likker. Smoked turkey neck provides smoky flavor, but without as much fat as ham, bacon, or salt pork. Meme, who lived to be ninety-two, always used fatback, an exceptionally Southern ingredient. For those worrywarts fretting about any carcinogens in smoked meats, I suggest an equally Southern snort of bourbon to calm your nerves.

2 tablespoons canola oil

1 onion, preferably Vidalia, quartered

4 cloves garlic, smashed

1 pound mustard greens, tough stems removed
     and chopped

2 cups fruity white wine (such as Riesling or
     Gewürztraminer)

4 cups homemade chicken stock (page 9) or reduced-fat,
     low-sodium chicken broth

4 cups water

1 smoked turkey neck

Coarse salt and freshly ground black pepper

Heat the oil in a large stockpot over medium heat. Add the onion and cook until golden, 8 to 10 minutes. Add the garlic and cook until fragrant, 45 to 60 seconds.

Add the greens and cook until the greens are slightly wilted, about 5 minutes. Add the wine and bring to a boil; cook until reduced by half, about 10 minutes. Add the stock, water, and smoked turkey neck; season lightly with salt and pepper. Bring to a boil; decrease the heat to medium-low and simmer, stirring occasionally, until the greens are very, very tender, about 1 hour. Taste and adjust for seasoning with salt and pepper. Ladle into warmed serving bowls with plenty of the flavorful broth. Serve immediately.

Brilliant Presentation
Croutons

Bump up these Basic mustard greens to Brilliant by contrasting the tender texture of the cooked greens with a scattering of crisp croutons. Preheat the oven to 350°F. In a bowl, mash 1 clove garlic with 1 teaspoon coarse salt to form a smooth paste. Remove the crust from 4 ounces rustic bread (half a small loaf) and cut into 1-inch cubes. Add to the garlic and toss to combine with 1 to 2 tablespoons of melted butter or pure olive oil. Spread the cubes in a single layer on a rimmed baking sheet. Bake, turning once, until crisp and golden brown, about 20 minutes. Spoon the greens into a warmed serving bowl. Scatter the croutons on top and serve immediately.

Winter Greens and Butternut Squash Gratin

SERVES 8 TO 10

The amusing thing about Thanksgiving is that it is the one meal that is almost immovable in terms of menu. Each family member has that one dish that is his or her favorite, and for some, the entire holiday is absolutely, positively ruined if the sweet potatoes are topped with something other than toasty brown marshmallows or if the squash casserole is missing. The deal is, dishes can be added, but nothing can be removed from the menu. I learned this the hard way. I have had, without fail, some form of cooked winter greens at every Thanksgiving meal of my entire life. In late November, the fields have been kissed with a touch of frost, something that Meme said brings out their sweetness. I added this dish several years ago, and it has become a family favorite.

2 teaspoons unsalted butter, plus more for the gratin dish

2 butternut squashes, (about 3 pounds total), cut in half lengthwise and seeded

1 (10-ounce) bag chopped kale

2 tablespoons pure olive oil

6 cloves garlic, very finely chopped

Coarse salt and freshly ground black pepper

1/2 teaspoon freshly grated nutmeg

Pinch of ground allspice

Leaves from 4 sprigs thyme, chopped

1 1/2 cups heavy cream

3 tablespoons plain or whole-wheat fresh or panko (Japanese) breadcrumbs

2/3 cup freshly grated Parmigiano-Reggiano cheese (about 2 1/2 ounces)

Preheat the oven to 400°F. Butter a large gratin dish.

Peel the squash, then cut crosswise into 1/4-inch slices; set aside.

Bring a large pot of salted water to a rolling boil. Add the kale and cook until just tender, about 5 minutes. Drain well in a colander, then squeeze out any excess water.

Heat the oil in a large sauté pan over medium-high heat. Add the garlic and the well-drained greens. Cook until the greens are slightly wilted, 3 to 4 minutes. Taste and adjust for seasoning with salt and pepper.

Meanwhile, place half the sliced squash in the prepared dish and season with salt and pepper. Combine the nutmeg, allspice, and thyme in a small bowl.

Spoon the kale over the squash and sprinkle with half the seasoning mixture. Top with remaining squash and sprinkle with the remaining seasoning.

Pour the cream over the gratin and cover with a piece of aluminum foil. Bake for 25 minutes, remove the foil, and press down on the squash with a spatula to compress. Cover and continue baking until the squash is soft when pierced with the tip of a knife, about 20 minutes.

Meanwhile, combine the breadcrumbs and cheese in a small bowl. Season with salt and pepper. Decrease the oven temperature to 375°F. Remove the foil from the gratin dish and sprinkle the breadcrumb mixture over the squash. Dot with the butter and continue baking, uncovered, until golden brown, about 10 minutes. Transfer to a wire rack to cool for about 10 minutes before serving.

Brilliant: Short Recipe
Slow Cooker Turkey

I went round and round on how to elevate this interesting and delicious dish to Brilliant. What I kept returning to was how many people have commented to me that they have added this recipe to their Thanksgiving repertoire. Quite the feat, I think, since that's an almost impenetrable list of recipes to infiltrate. I decided that turkey must be the key. This is a bit more complex than some of my Brilliant suggestions, but

CONTINUED

it's also the only one that calls for a slow cooker, and it still uses just a handful of ingredients.

Season a 4- to 6-pound boneless turkey breast with coarse salt and freshly ground black pepper. Place the breast, skin side up, in a slow cooker. Pour over 1/4 cup Madeira; add 1 onion, preferably Vidalia, sliced, 1 sprig thyme; 1 garlic clove; and 1 tablespoon of honey. Seal with the lid. Cook on high heat, turning once, until tender, 3 to 4 hours.

Remove to a clean cutting board and cover with foil. Let the turkey rest before slicing. Pour the broth into a fat separator or remove the grease with a spoon. Strain the broth into a small saucepan and bring to a boil. Taste and adjust for seasoning with salt and pepper. Keep warm over low heat. Remove the skin, slice the turkey, and place on the bottom of a warmed serving plate. Top with a spoonful of Winter Green and Butternut Squash Gratin. Serves 8 to 10.

Summer Vegetable Galette

SERVES 4 TO 6

There are gadgets to cut the corn kernels off the cob, but a sharp knife will do the job just fine. Most people stand the corn vertically on the cutting board and the kernels go everywhere. Instead, set the ear of corn on its side and, using a chef's knife, slice away the kernels on four "sides," squaring off the round ear. The kernels will fall away, but not having far to go, will not scatter. Then, stand the ear on one end and cut away the remaining "corners" of the cob.

All-American Pie Crust (page 18), rolled into a 12-inch
    circle about 1/4 inch thick
2 teaspoons pure olive oil
2 small zucchini (about 8 ounces total), sliced lengthwise
    1/4 inch thick
2 small yellow squashes (about 8 ounces total), sliced
    lengthwise 1/4 inch thick
Coarse salt and freshly ground black pepper
Scraped kernels from 1 ear fresh sweet corn (about 1/2 cup)
2 tablespoons Pistou (page 206) or store-bought pesto
2 ounces fresh goat cheese, Neufchâtel, or cream cheese,
    at room temperature
1 large egg
5 grape tomatoes, sliced 1/4 inch thick, or 1 medium
    ripe tomato, preferably heirloom, cored, seeded, and
    chopped
1/4 cup freshly grated Parmigiano-Reggiano cheese (1 ounce)
5 leaves basil, cut in chiffonade (see right)

Preheat the oven to 450°F. Line a baking sheet with a silicone baking liner or parchment paper.

Place the dough on the prepared baking sheet. Roll up the edge to create a 1/2-inch rim. Set aside.

Heat the oil in a large skillet over medium-high heat. Add the zucchini, yellow squash, and corn. Season with salt and pepper. Cook until lightly browned, about 5 minutes. Remove to a bowl to cool. Add the Pistou and stir to combine. Meanwhile, combine the goat cheese and egg in a bowl with a fork until almost smooth (some lumps are okay). Season with salt and pepper.

Using an offset spatula or the back of a spoon, spread the egg-cheese mixture over the pie crust. Top with the cooled vegetables. Evenly disperse the tomato over the top and sprinkle with the Parmigiano.

Bake until the pastry is a rich golden brown, about 20 minutes. Transfer to a rack to cool slightly. Garnish with the basil. Serve hot or at room temperature.

Brilliant: Short Recipe
Tomato Confit

The fresh tomatoes make this recipe a Basic supper, but add a few pieces of flavorful Tomato Confit and it's Brilliant. The tomatoes oven dry with herbs and oils into confit. The gentle heat of the oven concentrates their sugars, rendering the simple orbs into tomato candy.

Heat the oven to 200°F. Line a rimmed baking sheet with a silicone baking liner or parchment paper. Cut 1 pint grape tomatoes in half lengthwise. In a medium bowl, combine the tomato halves; 1/2 cup extra-virgin olive oil; 2 cloves garlic, very thinly sliced; 2 thyme sprigs; and coarse salt and freshly ground black pepper. Place the mixture in a single layer on the prepared baking sheet. Transfer to the oven and cook until soft but not caramelized, about 1 1/2 hours. Remove to a rack to cool. Transfer the tomatoes in oil to a sealable container and store in the refrigerator for up to 2 weeks.

Chiffonade

This recipe uses a technique called chiffonade. To chiffonade is to slice an herb or leafy vegetable into very thin strands. To do this, stack the leaves and roll up tightly into a cylinder. Slice the cylinders crosswise into thin strips.

Mushroom Ragout

SERVES 4 TO 6

I once found a single morel in my backyard, so tiny it was about the size of a thimble. Encouraged to extend my mushroom cultivation, I purchased a shiitake log for about thirty-five dollars. Following the instructions, I soaked it and set it out in a shaded area. A few weeks later I harvested a few mushrooms. They were amazing. I waited for more, and nothing happened. I thought it was a little too much effort and money for a handful of mushrooms. Then, one day I was standing on the deck and noticed a squirrel flitting by with a shiitake mushroom in his mouth. I was being robbed! Being the country girl and chef that I am, all I could think of was how good that shiitake-fed squirrel would taste on a bed of fresh shiitake mushrooms.

2 pounds mixed mushrooms (such as chanterelle, morel, portobello, cremini, oyster, and shiitake), trimmed

1 tablespoon canola oil

1 tablespoon unsalted butter

4 cloves garlic, mashed into a paste

1/4 cup homemade chicken stock (page 9) or reduced-fat, low-sodium chicken broth

1/4 cup dry red wine

2 tablespoons heavy cream (optional)

1/4 cup chopped fresh flat-leaf parsley

Coarse salt and freshly ground black pepper

Cut medium-size mushrooms in half and large mushrooms into quarters.

Heat the oil and butter in a large skillet over medium-high heat. Add the mushrooms and sauté until brown and just tender, about 10 minutes. Add the chicken stock, wine, and cream and bring to a boil. Cook, uncovered, until the mushrooms are fully tender and the sauce coats the mushrooms, about 5 minutes. Add the parsley and toss to coat. Taste and adjust for seasoning with salt and pepper. Serve immediately.

Brilliant: Short Recipe
Topped with a Poached Egg

Transform this Basic recipe into a Brilliant appetizer with the simple addition of a poached egg.

Poach four eggs following the instructions in Poached Eggs in Red Wine Sauce (page 72). Spoon the mushrooms onto warmed serving plates. Top each plate with a poached egg. Shave over curls of Parmigiano-Reggiano. Season with finishing salt (see page 50) and freshly ground black pepper. Serve immediately. Serves 4.

Sautéed Brussels Sprouts with Apples and Bacon

SERVES 4 TO 6

When students say something like, "I don't like _____," I always ask when was the last time they tried it. My mantra is I will try anything once. I am not sure what the weirdest thing I have ever eaten was—it may be the crispy batch of deep-fried cod tongues in Nova Scotia. I was ten. Admittedly I was an odd little girl and a very adventurous eater. I have always also loved Brussels sprouts. Of course you don't like them if the only way you've ever had them was cooked to stinky mush. Give this recipe a try (pictured on page 111). The sweetness of the apple and the gently salty, smoky flavor of the bacon will win you over. Promise.

1 pound Brussels sprouts, trimmed and cut in half
    lengthwise

2 slices thick-cut bacon, cut into lardons (see page 54)

1 onion, preferably Vidalia, chopped

1 Granny Smith apple, peeled, cored, and cut into
    $1/4$-inch dice

Leaves from 2 sprigs thyme, chopped

1 tablespoon chopped fresh flat-leaf parsley

Coarse salt and freshly ground black pepper

Bring a large pot of salted water to a boil. Add the Brussels sprouts and cook until bright green and just tender, about 5 minutes; drain and set aside.

In a skillet, cook the bacon over medium heat until crisp, 5 to 7 minutes. Decrease the heat to medium, add the onion, and sauté until translucent, 3 to 5 minutes. Add the apple and thyme and cook, stirring occasionally, until the apple is golden brown, about 3 minutes. Add the Brussels sprouts and toss to combine. Cook, stirring occasionally, until tender,

about 5 minutes. Taste and adjust for seasoning with salt and pepper. Transfer to a warmed serving platter and serve immediately.

Brilliant: Technique
Peeling the Sprouts

Even die-hard haters of Brussels sprouts will like this Brilliant version. The trick is to peel the sprouts.

Cut about $1/4$ inch off the stem end of each sprout and begin peeling off the leaves. When difficult to peel further, trim off another $1/4$ inch and continue removing leaves. Repeat to peel all the leaves from the sprouts; discard the tiny cores. Follow the procedure for the Basic recipe, but no need to blanch the sprouts. Add the leaves to the onion and apple. Sauté until the leaves are bright green and slightly wilted but still crunchy, about 3 minutes. Taste and adjust for seasoning with coarse salt and freshly ground black pepper. Serve immediately.

Pinto Beans with Side Meat

SERVES 6 TO 8

Side meat. Pretty descriptive terminology—it sounds rough and hardworking. Side meat is meat taken specifically from the sides of a pig. It may be smoked and cured, in which case it becomes bacon, or salted, in which case it becomes salt pork. Dried beans are inexpensive, rough, and hardworking, too. Country cooking, the food of the working class and poor, is pretty similar the world round. That goes for the Deep South as well as the South of France.

Chowchow is a spicy, pickled mixed fruit and vegetable relish that's traditionally served on pinto beans in the South. The relish ingredients vary recipe to recipe, but they are often the produce available at the end of the harvest. You can find chowchow at most grocery stores in the South, or online and in specialty markets in other parts of the country.

1 pound dried pinto beans, washed and picked over
    for stones
12 ounces salt pork, cubed
1 onion, preferably Vidalia, chopped
10 cloves garlic
8 cups homemade chicken stock (page 9) or reduced-fat,
    low-sodium chicken broth
2 sprigs thyme
2 bay leaves, preferably fresh
Coarse salt and freshly ground black pepper
Chowchow, for serving

Place the pinto beans in a large bowl and add water to cover. Soak overnight. Or, place the beans in a large pot of water and bring to a boil over high heat. Once the beans come to a boil, remove from the heat and set aside for 1 hour. Before cooking, discard any floating beans and drain.

To prepare in a slow cooker, combine the drained soaked beans, salt pork, onion, garlic, chicken stock, thyme, and bay leaves in a slow cooker. Heartily season with freshly ground black pepper. Cook over low heat until the beans are tender, about 6 hours.

To prepare on the stovetop, heat a large Dutch oven over medium heat. Add the salt pork and cook until it starts to crisp and brown, about 5 minutes. Add the onion and cook until translucent, 3 to 5 minutes. Add the garlic and cook until fragrant, 45 to 60 seconds. Add the chicken stock, thyme, and bay leaves. Bring to a boil over high heat. Decrease the

heat to simmer and cook until the flavors are well-blended, 20 to 30 minutes.

Add the beans. Bring to a boil over medium-high heat, then decrease the heat to low. Simmer, covered, until the beans are tender, about 3 hours. Taste and adjust for seasoning with salt and pepper. Spoon into warmed serving bowls and top with chowchow. Serve immediately.

Brilliant: Short Recipe
Crusty Bread Topping

This thick, meaty *garbure* calls for crusty bread to soak up the flavorful juices. To transform this dish from hardworking, but Basic, to Brilliant, add a crusty bread topping.

Preheat the oven to 350°F. Using your fingers, tear a medium loaf (about 12 ounces) of country bread into large pieces and place in a bowl. Drizzle over 1/4 cup melted unsalted butter. Season the bread with coarse salt and freshly ground black pepper. Toss to coat. About 30 minutes before the beans are finished cooking, remove the lid and scatter the buttery bread across the top of the beans. (If you are cooking in a slow cooker, you will need to transfer the beans to an oven-proof pot.) Transfer the pot of beans to the oven and bake, uncovered, until the bread is crisp and golden brown, about 30 minutes. You won't believe how good this tastes.

10

Soups and Stews

The first thing a budding chef learns in cooking school is how to make soup. Soup is so much more than tossing a bunch of stuff in a pot, topping it with water or stock, and boiling away. Having said that, a perfect stew, when put on the right course, practically cooks itself. Soup is one of my favorite dishes to prepare. Following proper techniques and using good ingredients pretty much ensures a satisfying bowl of soup.

Just about everything in French cooking but ice cream starts with a mirepoix (even then that is questionable given the boundaries of modern French cooking). The mirepoix is a combination of vegetables that creates a solid base for the soup. With a stew, most often the meat is browned and then the vegetables are cooked in the brown bits of goodness to take on the flavor of the meat. With soups, the vegetables are the first flavor, the first step, the first brick in the foundation. With both, the vegetables must be "sweated"—cooked over low heat—to reduce the liquid and concentrate the flavors. Aromatics are then added—the bouquet garni, a bundle of herbs and spices—to enhance the flavors. The stock is the vehicle for all the flavors. It's what drives the soup, so using the best-quality stock is essential.

However, even as a culinary professional, I don't always use homemade stock. Meme always used bouillon cubes, and Mama does the same. I generally stay away from those because they are far too high in sodium. If I am using store-bought stock, I look for reduced-fat, low-sodium broth in the box, not the can. In those instances, I also add ingredients to the broth to augment and boost the flavor. When I am prepping my mirepoix, I save the peels and trimmings. If I am taking apart a chicken, I reserve the neck bone and wing tips. I may chop a fresh onion or carrot or add a bunch of herbs. I add these fresh ingredients to the store-bought broth to help boost the flavor.

In terms of thickeners, most Southern soups and stews use all-purpose flour. French soups often use rice or potato. Of course, the most classic way to thicken a Southern soup is with a roux. The most celebrated use of a roux is in gumbo. When I was growing up in Louisiana, Mama made gumbo throughout the fall and winter, using shrimp, duck, quail, and chicken. I remember as a child our neighbor made a pot of gumbo. Peering into the pot I was shocked by a squirrel's head, with his ratlike curved teeth smiling back at me. Mama still laughs and says my eyes were big as saucers. It may sound rustic and primitive, but even proper techniques must be followed to make squirrel gumbo. (Personally, I think not using the head may be one of them.)

Southern soups like gumbo or Brunswick stew are traditionally hearty and filling, often serving as the entire meal, paired with cornmeal griddlecakes or a buttered biscuit. Many French soups are served as the first course of a meal. The French have a litany of words to describe soup and stews, including *soupe, potage, garbure, consommé, purée, velouté,* and *crème.*

The French definition of *soupe* is much like our own, a predominantly liquid dish made by cooking meat, seafood, or vegetables in water or stock. A *potage* is a thick soup. *Crème* is close to *potage*, but not quite. Generally a *crème* is a purée of meat or vegetables that has been thinned, or loosened, with stock or broth. When a *crème* is enriched with the velvety soft caress of eggs and cream, it is deemed a *velouté*. At the most simple, we have *garbure*, a hearty stew that often includes cabbage, beans, and salted or preserved duck, goose, turkey, or pork. In the opposite direction is *consommé*, a classically clear composition.

My hope is that by the end of this chapter, you will be as clear as consommé about how to prepare a satisfying bowl of *soupe.*

Tomato Consommé

I love, love, love making consommé. It's the technical prowess, somewhere between cooking and a science experiment that makes me "jump up and down" happy. I learned to use canned tomato juice from my chef, a Chinese gentleman named Sam, when I worked at Asia Nora, owned by Nora Pouillon. I don't remember his last name; I only ever called him chef. He left shortly after I started, but he taught me a great deal in a short period of time. I drank in his wisdom like a sponge. Chefs can appear sometimes like caped crusaders, superheroes in uniform. The whites confer automatic authority. Only some deserve to own superhero status, and, believe me, it has nothing to do with being on television.

1 onion, preferably Vidalia, coarsely chopped

1 carrot, coarsely chopped

1 celery stalk, coarsely chopped

2 cloves garlic

4 sprigs flat-leaf parsley

1 1/2 cups egg whites (from 1 dozen large eggs)

Coarse salt and freshly ground white pepper

4 cups tomato juice

4 cups V-8 juice

Combine the onion, carrot, celery, garlic, and parsley in a food processor fitted with a metal blade. Pulse until finely ground. Transfer to a large bowl. Add the egg whites and stir to combine. Season with salt and freshly ground white pepper. Set aside.

Combine the tomato juice and V-8 juice in a tall, straight-sided pot. Add the vegetable mixture and whisk to combine. (Yes, whisk it all together and make a real mess.) Bring the mixture to a low boil over medium heat. Adjust the heat to maintain a simmer and cook, uncovered, for 20 minutes. The protein will coagulate and a solid "raft" of the vegetables will form.

Using your ladle, make a small opening in the top of the raft. Ladle the consommé out of the stockpot one ladle at a time and pour through a sieve lined with a double thickness of cheesecloth (or with paper towels or a coffee filter) into a second saucepan. The consommé should be crystal clear. Taste and adjust for seasoning with salt, but not pepper. (Pepper will not dissolve and will mar the perfect clarity of the soup.) Heat until quite hot over medium-high heat. Ladle into warmed bowls. Serve immediately.

Brilliant: Short Recipe
Parmesan Tuile

This prissy, sexy little Brilliant twist takes the classic tomato soup and cheese sandwich flavor combination to a whole new level.

In a bowl, toss together 1 1/2 cups freshly grated (not powdered or ground) Parmigiano-Reggiano cheese (about 6 ounces) and 2 teaspoons all-purpose flour. Heat a large nonstick skillet over medium-low heat. Sprinkle about 1 1/2 tablespoons of the cheese mixture into the skillet to form a 4-inch round. Cook until the cheese starts to melt and become firm, 1 1/2 to 2 minutes. Using a small offset spatula, turn; continue cooking until firm and slightly golden, 15 to 30 seconds more. Immediately drape the softened cheese round over a lightly greased wine bottle or rolling pin, and let cool slightly to set the shape. Repeat with the remaining cheese mixture. (If the skillet gets too hot, remove it from the heat for several minutes before continuing.) Makes about 1 dozen. To serve, ladle the consommé into warmed bowls. Garnish with a Parmesan tuile. Serve immediately.

Roasted Tomato Soup

SERVES 4

Roasting the tomatoes with a little brown sugar intensifies the flavors. The acidity of the tomatoes combines with the sweetness of the sugar and takes this dish to a whole new level. But what really makes this recipe sing is a little chemistry. Tomatoes contain alcohol-soluble flavors that can only be delivered to your taste receptors in the presence of alcohol. The red wine makes this basic recipe shine.

2 (28-ounce) cans whole tomatoes, drained, with juices reserved

2 tablespoons firmly packed light brown sugar

1 tablespoon unsalted butter

1 onion, preferably Vidalia, very finely chopped

1 tablespoon tomato paste

Pinch of ground allspice

2 tablespoons all-purpose flour

2 cups homemade chicken stock (page 9) or reduced-fat, low-sodium chicken broth

1/4 cup dry red wine

1/2 cup heavy cream or crème fraîche (optional)

Coarse salt and freshly ground black pepper

Position a rack in the upper third of the oven and preheat to 450°F. Line a rimmed baking sheet with a silicone baking liner.

Working over a fine-mesh sieve set over a bowl and using your fingers, open the whole tomatoes and squeeze as many seeds out as possible (without making yourself completely crazy), catching the juices in the bowl. Discard the seeds and reserve the juices.

Spread the tomatoes in a single layer on the prepared baking sheet. Sprinkle evenly with the brown sugar. Bake until all liquid has evaporated and the tomatoes begin to color, about 30 minutes. Cool slightly; remove the tomatoes and transfer to a small bowl.

Melt the butter in a large, heavy saucepan over medium heat. Add the onion, tomato paste, and allspice. Cook, stirring frequently, until the onions are softened, 3 to 4 minutes. Add the flour and cook, stirring constantly, until thoroughly combined. Whisking constantly, gradually add the chicken stock. Add the reserved tomato juices, wine, and roasted tomatoes;

cover and bring to a boil. Decrease the heat to simmer, and cook, stirring occasionally, for about 10 minutes.

Using an immersion blender, purée the soup. Leave it coarse and chunky if you prefer a more rustic soup, or purée until smooth for a more elegant soup. Add the cream and heat through, about 3 minutes. (If I am making the creamy flan below, I omit the cream.) Remove from the heat. Taste, adjust for seasoning with salt and pepper, and serve immediately.

Brilliant: Short Recipe
Gruyère Flans

As a child, I loved when Mama served tomato soup and grilled cheese sandwiches. Consider these cheesy, creamy flans a Brilliant grown-up version of that favorite pairing.

Preheat the oven to 350°F. Brush six 1-cup ramekins with 2 tablespoons room-temperature butter. In a blender, combine 1 cup grated Gruyère cheese, 5 large eggs, 3/4 cup whole milk, 2 ounces room-temperature cream cheese, a pinch each of freshly grated nutmeg, freshly ground white pepper, and salt. Blend until smooth. Divide the custard among the prepared ramekins, filling each one three-quarters full. Cover each ramekin with aluminum foil and place in a roasting pan. Pour enough hot water into the pan to reach halfway up the sides of the ramekins. Bake until just set but still wiggly and slightly soft in the center, 25 to 30 minutes. Using a metal spatula or tongs, transfer the ramekins to a rack. Run the blade of a thin metal spatula around the edge of each flan to loosen. When ready to serve, unmold each flan into the center of a warmed shallow soup bowl. Ladle the soup around the flan, season with salt and pepper, and serve immediately. Serves 6.

Melita's Sweet Potato Soup

SERVES 6 TO 8

There are some cooks who are borderline professionals, beyond amateur, but don't actually count on cooking to pay the bills. My friend Melita Easters is one such cook. She serves this soup in silver Jefferson cups or porcelain demitasse cups as a passed hors d'oeuvre, something I like to do with my Wild Mushroom Soup (see opposite), as well.

Melita entertains more than any one I know and is practically a professional hostess. She is an indefatigable fund-raiser and works very hard to advance her causes. I used to cater her parties, but she'd continuously pull me out of the catering kitchen to talk to her and her guests. I'd join the party under protest in my chef's whites for a bit, then scurry back to the kitchen. In true Melita fashion, the woman who works to get what she wants, she eventually fired me from catering to have me just where she wanted me.

3 tablespoons unsalted butter

1 onion, preferably Vidalia, coarsely chopped

1 teaspoon curry powder, preferably Madras

6 medium sweet potatoes, peeled and cubed

9 cups homemade chicken stock (page 9) or reduced-fat, low-sodium chicken broth

1/4 cup maple syrup

2 to 3 sprigs thyme

1/8 teaspoon freshly grated nutmeg

Pinch of cayenne pepper

Coarse salt and freshly ground white pepper

Melt the butter in a large, heavy soup pot over medium heat. Add the onion and curry powder and cook, stirring occasionally, until translucent, 3 to 5 minutes. Add the sweet potatoes, stock, syrup, thyme, nutmeg, and cayenne. Bring to a boil, then decrease the heat to simmer. Cook until the potatoes are soft, about 25 minutes. Remove the thyme sprigs from the soup.

To finish the soup in the stockpot, use an immersion blender and purée the soup. Or, ladle the soup into a blender and purée until smooth, a little at a time.

Strain the soup through a fine-mesh sieve into a second large pot, discarding any solids. Rewarm the soup over medium-low heat. Taste and adjust for seasoning with salt and white pepper. Ladle into warmed serving bowls and serve immediately.

Brilliant: Short Recipe
Rum Cream

The boozy bite of sugary rum is the adult addition to transform this Basic recipe to Brilliant. The tiny hint of the acidic lemon helps bring out the sweet flavor of the rum.

In the chilled bowl of a heavy-duty mixer fitted with the whisk attachment, whip 1 cup heavy cream until soft peaks form. Add 1/4 teaspoon finely grated lemon zest, 1/2 teaspoon freshly squeezed lemon juice, and 3 tablespoons good-quality dark rum. Continue whipping until the cream is stiff. Refrigerate until you are ready to serve. Makes about 2 cups.

To serve, heat the soup and ladle into warmed bowls. Top with a dollop of the Rum Cream.

Wild Mushroom Soup

SERVES 6

Porcini, or *cèpes* as they are known in French, are incredibly rich, meaty, and fragrant mushrooms. I like to combine an inexpensive mushroom, such as white button, with dried porcini, as the fairly benign white mushrooms will take on the earthy flavor of the porcini. Given the fact that fresh porcini are about thirty dollars a pound when you can find them, this is a very economical alternative.

During the holidays, I like to serve this soup as a passed hors d'oeuvre in demitasse cups or shot glasses.

1/2 ounce dried porcini mushrooms

1 cup boiling water

2 tablespoons unsalted butter

1 onion, preferably Vidalia, chopped

2 pounds mixed fresh mushrooms (such as white button, cremini, shiitake, morel, and chanterelle), sliced

3 cups homemade vegetable stock (page 11) or low-sodium vegetable broth

Bouquet garni (5 sprigs thyme; 4 sprigs flat-leaf parsley; 2 bay leaves, preferably fresh; and 10 whole black peppercorns, tied together in cheesecloth)

1/2 cup heavy cream (optional)

Coarse salt and freshly ground black pepper

Add the dried porcini mushrooms to the boiling hot water to plump, about 15 minutes. Remove the mushrooms and squeeze out the excess liquid. Place the mushrooms in a bowl. Strain the soaking liquid through a fine sieve or coffee filter into another bowl. Set aside.

Melt the butter in a large pot over medium heat and add the onion. Cook until the onion is translucent, 3 to 5 minutes. Add the fresh mushrooms and cook, stirring occasionally, until the mushrooms are tender, 5 to 7 minutes.

Add the stock, reserved mushroom liquid, and bouquet garni. Bring to a boil, then decrease the heat to simmer. Cook until the mushrooms are very soft, about 30 minutes.

Remove the bouquet garni. Purée the soup with an immersion blender. Leave it coarse for a more rustic soup, or purée it until smooth for a more elegant soup. Add the cream and stir to combine. Taste and adjust for seasoning with salt and pepper. Ladle into warmed bowls and serve immediately.

Brilliant: Short Recipe
Herbed Whipped Crème Fraîche

Finishing a soup with heavy cream is Basic, but topping it with Herbed Whipped Crème Fraîche is Brilliant. I don't have to feel guilty regarding sometimes hard-to-find ingredients like crème fraîche, since I've included a recipe (page 16).

In the chilled bowl of a heavy-duty mixer fitted with the whisk attachment, whip 1 cup crème fraîche until soft peaks form. Add 1/2 teaspoon finely chopped fresh thyme. Season with coarse salt and freshly ground white pepper. Continue beating until stiff peaks form. Makes about 1 cup.

To serve, ladle the Wild Mushroom Soup into warmed bowls. Add a dollop of the Herbed Whipped Crème Fraîche and serve immediately. Ummm. Doesn't that taste Brilliant?

Provençal Vegetable Soup *Soupe au Pistou*

SERVES 6

Traditional or not, it doesn't make sense to me to make soup with dried beans at the height of summer with the widespread availability of fresh, seasonal produce. So, I've substituted butter beans. Other suggestions would include fresh black-eyed peas, lady peas, crowder peas, cranberry beans, or flageolet beans. If you are without fresh beans, or want to go the traditional route, you can substitute cooked dried beans, or if you are in a real pinch for time, frozen. I find canned beans far too soft for long cooking.

Pistou is essentially a nutless pesto traditionally made in a mortar and pestle. As long as I am casting off the shackles of traditionalism, I suggest making the pistou in a food processor, a common appliance many cooks have, instead of a mortar and pestle, which many home cooks do not.

1 tablespoon pure olive oil

2 onions, preferably Vidalia, chopped

1 carrot, chopped

1 celery stalk, chopped

2 large cloves garlic, finely chopped

6 cups water, plus more if needed

1 ham hock or ham bone (optional)

Coarse salt and freshly ground black pepper

4 ounces green beans, ends trimmed and cut into
    1/2-inch pieces

1 yellow squash, chopped

1 zucchini, chopped

1 bay leaf, preferably fresh

2 tablespoons chopped fresh flat-leaf parsley

2 tablespoons chopped fresh basil

1/2 teaspoon red pepper flakes

1/2 cup elbow macaroni or orzo

Pistou (recipe follows)

In a large, heavy Dutch oven, heat the oil over medium heat. Add the onions, carrot, and celery and cook until the onions are golden, 10 to 12 minutes. Add the garlic and cook until fragrant, 45 to 60 seconds. Add 4 cups of the water and the ham hock. Season the mixture with salt and pepper Bring to a boil over high heat, and then decrease the heat to low. Simmer until the mixture is flavorful and well combined, about 30 minutes.

Add the green beans, yellow squash, zucchini, bay leaf, parsley, basil, and red pepper. Add more of the remaining 2 cups water as needed to cover the vegetables by about 1 inch. Continue to simmer slowly over very low heat until the vegetables are just tender, 20 minutes more. Add the pasta and more water, if needed. Simmer until the pasta is tender, 10 to 15 minutes.

Before serving, taste and adjust the soup for seasoning with salt and pepper. To serve, ladle the soup into warmed bowls. Finish with a dollop of pistou.

Pistou

MAKES ABOUT 1 1/2 CUPS

4 cups firmly packed fresh basil leaves (about 3 bunches), washed and dried

4 to 6 cloves garlic, finely chopped

3/4 cup freshly grated Parmigiano-Reggiano cheese (about 3 ounces)

Coarse salt and freshly ground black pepper

1/3 cup extra-virgin olive oil

Combine the basil, garlic, and cheese in a food processor fitted with the metal blade. Season with salt and pepper. Blend until smooth, scraping down the sides of the bowl as necessary. With the machine running, slowly pour in the olive oil until it is thoroughly incorporated and the mixture is smooth. Use immediately, store in the refrigerator in an airtight container for up to 2 days, or freeze for up to 1 month.

Brilliant: Short Recipe
Tomato-Scrubbed Toast

Summer capped with more summer is the gist of this Brilliant addition. It's summer, squared.

Position an oven rack 4 inches below the broiler and preheat the broiler. To make the toasts, arrange 6 slices hearty peasant bread on a baking sheet. Brush the tops with 1 tablespoon pure olive oil and season with coarse salt and freshly ground black pepper. Broil until golden brown, 2 to 3 minutes. Turn the slices over and toast the other side. Remove from the oven while warm, and lightly rub the oiled side of each toast with the cut surface of a garlic clove. Then, using a halved garden-fresh tomato, scrub the bread to absorb the juices. Makes 6 toasts.

To serve, ladle the soup into warmed bowls. Top with a toast. Doesn't that make you hungry for summer just thinking about it?

Split Pea Soup

SERVES 6 TO 8

My grandfather had false teeth. As a child I used to get him to take them out, and he'd touch his chin to his nose. My sister and I would squeal with laughter and giggles. For some reason, when he didn't feel well or had a cold, he'd leave his teeth out. (Not exactly sure how those are related, but thankfully, I have all my teeth and don't care to find out.) And, when he didn't have his teeth in, he couldn't eat much more than mash, mush, or split pea soup.

Mama taught me to save the hambone in the freezer for adding flavor to soups such as this; you can use a ham hock, too. Or, you can leave the ham out for a more subtle flavor.

2 tablespoons canola oil

2 onions, preferably Vidalia, chopped

1 large carrot, chopped

2 cloves garlic, very finely chopped

8 cups homemade chicken stock (page 9) or reduced-fat, low-sodium chicken broth

1¼ cups green split peas, rinsed

Coarse salt and freshly ground black pepper

Bouquet garni (3 sprigs flat-leaf parsley; 2 sprigs thyme; 1 bay leaf, preferably fresh; and 1 tablespoon whole black peppercorns, tied together in cheesecloth)

1 ham hock or hambone (optional)

Heat the oil in a large, heavy pot over medium-high heat. Add the onions and carrot and sauté until vegetables begin to soften, 4 to 6 minutes. Add the garlic and cook until fragrant, 45 to 60 seconds. Add the chicken stock and split peas; season with salt and pepper. Add the bouquet garni and hambone. Bring to a boil, then decrease the heat to simmer. Cook, stirring occasionally, until the peas are tender, about 1 hour. Taste and adjust for seasoning with salt and pepper. Ladle into warmed bowls and serve immediately.

Brilliant: Short Recipe
Deviled Ham Garlic Toasts

Meme often made split pea soup and deviled ham with leftover ham in the days after a big holiday. Dede loved deviled ham. In honor of him, Deviled Ham Garlic Toasts are the simple accent to take Basic Split Pea Soup to Brilliant.

In a food processor fitted with a metal blade, pulse 4 ounces coarsely chopped ham; 2 green onions, chopped; 2 tablespoons sour cream, and 1 tablespoon Dijon mustard. Season with coarse salt and freshly ground black pepper. Add a few dashes of hot sauce. Makes about ¹/2 cup. Spread on 6 to 8 garlic toasts (page 80). Ladle the soup into warmed bowls. Float the Deviled Ham Garlic Toasts on top. Brilliant.

High Cotton Brunswick Stew

SERVES 6 TO 8

The term high cotton *refers to having money, good times, and living large. Traditionally Brunswick stew is made from the tougher cuts, as well as leftover bits and pieces of the hog, maybe a scrawny old rooster, and perhaps a squirrel or rabbit or two, depending on the recipe. Brunswick stew goes hand in hand with barbecue, and for me to consider a BBQ joint worth a return visit, the stew has got to be good. I like it so full of goodness that the spoon will stand up in it. When I was a little girl, Meme made it in a large cast-iron pot over a wood fire. I think this version (pictured on page 198) would have made her chuckle.*

2 tablespoons canola oil

1 onion, preferably Vidalia, chopped

1 poblano or green bell pepper, cored, seeded, and chopped

Coarse salt and freshly ground black pepper

2 cloves garlic, very finely chopped

1 teaspoon smoked paprika, or to taste

1/2 cup dry white wine

8 fingerling potatoes

6 cups homemade chicken stock (page 9) or low-fat, reduced-sodium beef broth

1 (28-ounce) can whole tomatoes with juice

2 cups shelled fresh butter beans (about 1 1/2 pounds unshelled) or frozen butter beans

Scraped kernels from 4 ears fresh sweet corn (about 2 cups)

Bouquet garni (8 sprigs flat-leaf parsley; 6 sprigs thyme; 2 bay leaves, preferably fresh; and 10 whole black peppercorns, tied together in cheesecloth)

1 pound boneless, skinless chicken breasts or thighs, cut into 1-inch pieces

1 pound pork tenderloin, cut into medallions

Heat the oil in a large, heavy pot over medium-high heat until shimmering. Add the onion and poblano and season with salt and pepper. Cook until the vegetables are softened, 3 to 5 minutes. Add the garlic and smoked paprika. Cook until fragrant, 45 to 60 seconds. Add the wine and cook until almost dry, 3 to 5 minutes.

Add the potatoes, stock, tomatoes with juice, butter beans, corn, and bouquet garni. Bring to a boil. Decrease the heat to simmer. Cook, uncovered, until the butter beans and potatoes are just tender, about 30 minutes. Season the chicken and pork on both sides. Add the seasoned meat and continue to cook until the juices of the chicken run clear when pierced with a fork, 5 to 7 minutes. Taste and adjust for seasoning with salt and pepper. Ladle into warmed serving bowls and serve immediately.

Brilliant: Short Recipe
Served with Smoked Meat

Considering the fact that I've already taken country stew, called it High Cotton, and fancied it up, Brilliant better be pretty darn good. Well, it is. To elevate our citified High Cotton Brunswick Stew, give stovetop smoking a twirl.

Prepare the High Cotton Brunswick Stew to the point of adding the chicken and pork and keep warm. Soak 1/2 cup wood chips in 1 cup water for 5 minutes. Sprinkle them on the bottom of a stovetop smoker. Place the smoker's drip pan on top of the wood chips, and put the whole, uncut tenderloin and whole chicken pieces on the drip pan rack. Season on both sides with salt and pepper. Heat the smoker over medium-high heat until the wood begins to smoke, then close the smoker lid. Decrease the heat to medium. Smoke until an instant-read thermometer inserted into the center of the pork registers 140°F to 145°F and in the center of the chicken registers 160°F, about 20 minutes. Transfer the meat to a warmed plate and cover with aluminum foil to rest and allow the juices to redistribute. Slice the meat on the diagonal and place in the center of warmed bowls. Ladle the stew around the meat and serve immediately.

Louisiana Duck Gumbo

When I was growing up in Louisiana, my father hunted duck, and the freezer was usually filled with duck, as well as dove, quail, deer, boar, wild turkey, rabbit, and squirrel. (Don't laugh, even though Dede called squirrels "tree rats," they really are excellent panfried with gravy.) Gumbo is named for a West African word for okra, *gombo*. This flavorful stew can feature any number of main ingredients, most commonly shrimp, crab, chicken, duck, and sausage. Many of the ingredients are harvested from the Gulf, local lakes and rivers, or produced on the farm. All gumbos start with an initial browning of fat and flour, to create a roux, then are seasoned with the "holy trinity" of bell pepper, onion, and celery. Here, I commit a bit of sacrilege. I find the taste of green bell peppers too strong and substitute poblano pepper. You can choose your own sins.

1/2 cup canola oil

1/2 cup all-purpose flour

2 onions, preferably Vidalia, chopped

2 celery stalks, chopped

2 poblano or green bell peppers, cored, seeded, and chopped

4 cloves garlic, finely chopped

1 1/2 teaspoons Creole seasoning blend

2 teaspoons hot sauce, or to taste

1 1/2 teaspoons Worcestershire sauce

1 pound andouille sausage, sliced

4 cups homemade chicken stock (page 9) or reduced-fat, low-sodium chicken broth

1 (4- to 5-pound) duck, cut into 8 pieces (excess skin removed if making cracklings), neck and giblets reserved

Coarse salt and freshly ground black pepper

Hot cooked rice, for serving

1 tablespoon filé powder, for serving

1/4 cup green onions, chopped, for serving

Heat the oil in a large, heavy Dutch oven over medium-low heat. Add the flour and cook, stirring occasionally, until the roux is deep chocolate in color, 30 to 45 minutes. (Alternatively, preheat the oven to 350°F. Place the oil and flour in a 5- to 6-quart cast-iron Dutch oven and whisk together to combine. Place on the middle rack of the oven. Bake uncovered, whisking 2 or 3 times, until deep chocolate, about 1 1/2 hours.)

Combine the vegetables in a large bowl. Add half of the mixed vegetables to the roux. Cook until tender, 3 to 5 minutes. Add the Creole seasoning, hot sauce, Worcestershire, and andouille. Stir to combine. Add the stock and whisk until smooth. Add the duck and reserved neck. Season with salt and pepper. Bring to a boil, decrease the heat to a simmer, and cook covered, stirring occasionally, for 1 hour.

Add the remaining vegetables and simmer until the meat is falling off the bone, about 1 hour. (Adding half of the trinity later in cooking helps keep some of the vegetables more toothsome.) Taste and adjust for seasoning with salt and pepper.

To serve, spoon rice into warmed bowls. Ladle the gumbo over the rice and sprinkle with filé powder and green onions. Serve immediately.

Brilliant: Short Recipe
Duck Skin Cracklings and Offal Mince

There are two ways to approach this Brilliant (shown at bottom right of photo) addition to our Basic Louisiana Duck Gumbo. Wild duck is not very fatty and is quite tough, which is why it requires the long cooking time. If you are using domestic duck, using a chef's knife, remove the excess skin from the cavity and slice

CONTINUED

into strips. If you are using lean wild duck, augment the gumbo with one 7- to 8-ounce duck breast fillet. Remove the skin from the fillet and cut into $1/2$ inch strips. (Reserve the duck for another use, or halve it and add to the simmering gumbo.)

Heat a large skillet over medium heat. Add the duck skin and cook until golden and crisp, 8 to 10 minutes. Using a slotted spoon, transfer the cracklings to a plate lined with paper towels. Season with finishing salt (see page 50) and freshly ground black pepper. To the rendered fat, add 1 bay leaf, preferably fresh (be careful it will spit and spatter). Then, add the gizzard and heart. Season with coarse salt and freshly ground black pepper Cook until browned on all sides, 3 to 5 minutes. Add the liver and cook until firm, about 5 more minutes. Remove to a cutting board and let cool slightly. Chop into $1/4$-inch dice. Add to the cracklings. Makes about 1 cup.

To serve, spoon the rice into warmed bowls. Ladle the gumbo over the rice and top with the crispy mince. Serve immediately.

Charleston She-Crab Soup

SERVES 4

"She crabs" are simply female blue crabs. Once when shooting a story for television, I learned from a crusty old fisherwoman on the Chesapeake Bay how to tell the difference between a boy and a girl crab. Turn the crab over on its back. There's a flap on the underbelly. Boy crabs have flaps that look like the Washington monument, long and pointed. Girl crabs have rounded flaps with softer lines, and it looks like the dome of the capitol.

If you are truly starting from scratch, by boiling and picking crabs, make sure to save the crab roe, or eggs, found in female, or sook, crabs in the late spring and early summer. Once boiled, it's bright coral red and is a tasty treasure beyond measure in this soup. Frozen crab roe is available online and in specialty seafood stores.

1/4 cup (1/2 stick) unsalted butter

1 celery stalk, chopped

1 large carrot, chopped

1 onion, preferably Vidalia, chopped

1/4 cup all-purpose flour

1 1/2 cups low-fat or whole milk

1/2 cup heavy cream

1 cup homemade fish or seafood stock (page 13) or bottled clam juice

5 ounces jumbo lump crabmeat, picked over for shells and cartilage

2 tablespoons dry sherry, plus more for garnish

1/2 teaspoon Worcestershire sauce

Hot sauce, to taste

Coarse salt and freshly ground white pepper

2 ounces boiled crab roe

Heat the butter in a saucepan over medium heat. Add the celery, carrot, and onion and cook until softened, about 5 minutes. Sprinkle the flour over the vegetables and cook, stirring, until golden, about 3 minutes. Whisk in the milk and cream and bring to a boil. Decrease the heat to medium-low and add the stock, crabmeat, and sherry; simmer for 20 minutes. Add the Worcestershire sauce and hot sauce. Taste and adjust for seasoning with salt and pepper. If using, crumble the roe in the bottom of warmed bowls, then ladle in the hot soup. Garnish with a spoonful of sherry. Serve immediately.

Brilliant: Technique
Sherry Gelée

A nip of sherry is Basic and traditional for she-crab soup. Making a chef-inspired gelée is Brilliant. Molecular gastronomy is nothing new. Folks have been using gelatin to change textures for centuries. (Granted, chefs used to start by boiling calves' hooves.) Now, the most widely available unflavored gelatin, Knox, is packaged in premeasured individual 1/4-ounce envelopes that equal 1 scant tablespoon and will set 2 cups liquid. Gelatin is also sometimes available in sheets at gourmet markets and cookware stores and 5 sheets are equal to 1 envelope of gelatin, enough to set 2 cups liquid.

Pour 1/4 cup sherry into a small bowl. Sprinkle over 1 envelope gelatin. Set aside to "bloom" and absorb the liquid, 3 to 5 minutes. Meanwhile, heat the remaining 1 3/4 cups of sherry in a saucepan over medium heat. Season with 1/4 teaspoon coarse salt. Once the gelatin has bloomed, add it to the warm sherry and stir to dissolve. Pour into an 8-inch square pan; chill until firm, about 3 hours. Cut into 1-inch squares to serve. Use the 2 tablespoons sherry as directed when cooking the soup, but instead of garnishing the soup with the liquid sherry, spoon the sherry squares directly into the bowls of soup just before serving.

Meme's Chicken and Rice

SERVES 4 TO 6

Meme made this stew most often when we were sick, and this soothing and satisfying rice porridge will certainly cure what ails you. It's quite similar to Asian congee or *jook*. She literally just combined rice, onion, chicken, and water in a pot and cooked it. I sear the thighs for additional flavor, but keep her Basic premise.

1 teaspoon canola oil

1 (4-pound) chicken, cut into 8 pieces, or 6 bone-in, skin-on breasts or thighs

Coarse salt and freshly ground black pepper

1 onion, preferably Vidalia, chopped

1 clove garlic, mashed into a paste

1 cup long-grain white rice

4 cups homemade chicken stock (page 9) or reduced-fat, low-sodium chicken broth

Heat the oil in a large, heavy saucepan over medium heat. Pat the chicken dry with paper towels and season on both sides with salt and pepper. Add the chicken, skin side down, without crowding the pan. Cook until a rich golden brown on both sides, 3 to 5 minutes per side. Remove the chicken to a plate.

Add the onion and cook until translucent, 3 to 5 minutes. Add the garlic and cook until fragrant, 45 to 60 seconds. Add the rice and stir to combine. Season with salt and pepper. When the chicken is cool enough to touch, remove the browned skin. (The skin becomes flabby as it simmers.) Return the chicken to the pot. Add the stock. Bring to a boil over high heat. Decrease the heat to simmer and cook until the chicken is falling off the bone and the rice is completely soft, soupy, and thick, 45 to 60 minutes. Taste and adjust for seasoning with salt and pepper. Ladle into warmed serving bowls and serve immediately.

Brilliant: Short Recipe
Potage à la Reine

Given how homey the Basic version is, it's quite amusing that the French version of the same soup is *Potage à la Reine*, which translates to "Soup of the Queen." Only a queen with servants would dirty this many dishes. It's full frontal and Brilliantly French.

Bring 4 cups homemade chicken stock or reduced-fat, low-sodium chicken broth (page 9) to a boil in a stockpot over medium-high heat. Add (without first browning) a whole chicken cut into 8 pieces or 4 bone-in, skin-on chicken breasts. Decrease the heat to a simmer and cook until the juices run clear, 45 to 60 minutes. Using a slotted spoon, remove the cooked chicken to a plate to cool. Meanwhile in a second saucepan, combine 4 cups homemade chicken stock; 1 cup long-grain rice; 1 onion, preferably Vidalia, chopped; and 1 clove garlic, very finely chopped. Bring to a boil and decrease the heat to simmer. Cook until the mixture is completely soft, 45 to 60 minutes. Meanwhile, remove the chicken meat from the bones, discarding the bones and skin. Purée the meat in a food processor fitted with a metal blade until completely smooth. Place in a third saucepan with 2 cups of the chicken cooking liquid. Stir to combine. (Reserve the remaining stock for another use.) When the rice is cooked, working in batches, purée the rice in a food processor fitted with a metal blade until smooth. Add the puréed rice to the chicken-stock mixture. Bring to simmer over medium-high heat. (You can serve this now, or continue with the Escoffier-inspired pot-messing madness.) Strain the mixture through a fine-mesh sieve into a fourth pot. Bring to a simmer over medium-high heat. Meanwhile, combine 1 cup heavy cream and 2 large egg yolks in a liquid measuring cup. Whisk some of the heated puréed soup into the measuring cup, then pour that back into the soup. Stir to combine. Taste and adjust for seasoning with salt and freshly ground white pepper. Serve immediately.

Spring Lamb Stew with Vegetables *Navarin d'Agneau Printanier*

SERVES 4

Lamb has been associated with spring holidays for centuries. Symbolizing the season of rebirth, it has become a holiday feast ritual for many cuisines, French included. The lamb on the table is not a new-born lamb, but one born in the late autumn and ready to be harvested (i.e., eaten) in the spring. The Southern counterpart would be ham. After the pigs are slaughtered, traditionally after the first frost, the hams are prepared and allowed to cure through the winter. They are ready to eat, just as with the lamb, for the spring celebration. Now, that's planning ahead.

2 pounds boneless lamb shoulder, cut into 2-inch cubes

Coarse salt and freshly ground black pepper

2 tablespoons unsalted butter

1 tablespoon canola oil

1 onion, preferably Vidalia, chopped

3 cloves garlic, finely chopped

2 tablespoons all-purpose flour

1 cup dry white wine

4 ripe tomatoes, preferably heirloom, cored, seeded
    and chopped

2 cups homemade chicken stock (page 9) or reduced-fat,
    low-sodium chicken broth

2 tablespoons tomato paste

Bouquet garni (5 sprigs thyme; 4 sprigs flat-leaf parsley;
    2 bay leaves, preferably fresh; and 10 whole black
    peppercorns, tied together in cheesecloth)

8 small red new potatoes

8 baby carrots, peeled

8 small white turnips, halved

16 shallots or cipollini onions, peeled and left whole

Crusty baguette, for serving

Preheat the oven to 350°F.

Pat the lamb dry with paper towels. Season with salt and pepper.

Heat the butter and oil in a large Dutch oven over medium-high heat. Sear the lamb in two or three batches, without crowding, until nicely browned on all sides, about 5 minutes per batch. Transfer to a plate.

Decrease the heat to low, add the onion, and cook, stirring occasionally, until golden brown, 5 to 7 minutes.

Add the garlic and cook until fragrant, 45 to 60 seconds. Stirring constantly, add the flour and cook until light blond in color, 2 to 3 minutes. Add the wine and stir briskly to remove any brown bits and flour from the bottom of the pan. Add the tomatoes, chicken stock, and tomato paste.

Return the lamb with any accumulated juices to the Dutch oven and add the bouquet garni; season with salt and pepper. Bring to a boil and cover with a tight-fitting lid. Transfer to the oven and cook until the lamb is just beginning to become tender, about 45 minutes.

Remove from the oven and add the potatoes, carrots, turnips, and shallots. Cover, return to the oven, and cook until the meat and vegetables are tender, 30 to 45 minutes. Remove and discard the bouquet garni. Taste and adjust for seasoning with salt and pepper. Serve straight from the casserole with a baguette.

Brilliant: Short Recipe
Buttery English Peas

Bring a large pot of salted water to a boil over high heat. Add 2 cups shelled English peas (about 2 pounds unshelled). Cook until just tender, about 2 minutes. Drain in a colander and transfer to a medium bowl. Add 1 tablespoon unsalted butter and 1 tablespoon chopped fresh mint. Season with coarse salt and freshly ground black pepper. Makes 2 cups. Ladle the lamb stew into warmed bowls and top with a big spoonful of peas for a Brilliant garnish.

11

Daily Bread

Nothing smells as wonderful as a loaf of bread baking. The warm scent instantly triggers hunger no matter the time of night or day, no matter whether you are full or famished, and no matter the place. The smell of bread baking will make you hungry; it will make you want.

For the cook baking the bread, the hunger, the want starts before that, it starts with the immense pleasure of baking. There's something incredibly satisfying about the tactile experiences of scooping a measuring cup into a canister of flour and sweeping off the excess with a flourish, or grasping the handle of a glass measuring cup and carefully watching the side until the liquid has reached just the right level. Dipping a finger into warm water to make sure the water is just warmer than body temperature, not so hot that it will kill the yeast. The fact that these immense pleasures are so incredibly simple, generated from an almost ridiculously uncomplicated combination of water and flour, makes it all the more special. Baking bread provides food and nourishment for the body, but also the spirit.

Bread both nourishes and transports us to moments in the past. One whiff of buttery cinnamon, and I am a child again with my sister at the kitchen table watching Mama make French toast. A single bite of *pain au chocolat*—a handful of heaven—yeasty, buttery air wrapped around melting chocolate reminds me of a sleepy morning in Paris sipping café crème at a corner café. One mouthful of chewy baguette swiped with butter and slathered with jam, and I am in France, sipping hot coffee in the cool kitchen overlooking the foggy Yonne River Valley. Toasted bagels topped with cream cheese and smoked fish take me to a crowded Jewish deli on the Upper West Side. Ah, and of course, there's nothing, absolutely nothing like the smell of biscuits. The smell of a biscuit is a time-travel machine for me, taking me back to when I was three years old, making biscuits with Meme, standing on the stool by her side, dusted in flour as only a little girl cooking with her grandmother can be, just starting my love affair with the kitchen. Bread both feeds me and carries me to places I have once been.

Bread is poetry and artistry, capable of evoking wonderful memories, but there's science in bread, too. Most western bread is made of wheat flour. Gluten is the generic name for certain types of proteins, including gliadins and glutelins, found in common cereal grains, mainly wheat, barley, rye, and spelt. These proteins are not soluble in water and give wheat dough its elastic texture. They are activated by the addition of water and movement. Gluten provides the framework for dough to rise, by stretching and trapping the gas bubbles given off by the leavener as the dough expands.

Flours react differently in their ability to absorb moisture, depending on the type of grain, humidity, temperature, and even where the grain was grown. The amount of flour needed in a recipe may vary by as much as a cup or two! It is best to start with a smaller amount and slowly add more while kneading to achieve a smooth, satiny dough.

Wheat flour is the most common grain used in Southern and French baking, and several types are used for bread making. First of all, a gentle reminder that there are different varieties of wheat, like there are different varieties of apples. Just as there are Granny Smith, Mutsu, and Red Delicious apples in the bin, there are Turkey Red, Avalon, and Harvard bags of wheat. You may never see the name of the wheat variety listed on a bag of flour, but it's important for a baker to know that wheat cultivars are defined in terms of protein content, such as hard wheat (high-protein content) versus soft wheat (high-starch content), and growing season, such as winter wheat versus spring wheat.

Hard wheat is higher in gluten-producing proteins than soft wheat. It is best used for yeast-leavened baked goods. Soft wheat has plump wheat berries with less protein and therefore fewer gluten-forming capabilities. Soft wheat is best used for baked goods that don't need a highly developed web of gluten, such as cakes, biscuits, and pastry.

Southern flours have traditionally been milled from soft winter wheat. Soft wheat is the reason why the South is well known for cakes, biscuits, and pie crusts over yeast breads, which require the gluten strength of high-protein flour. Soft red winter wheat was once grown in Georgia, Tennessee, North Carolina, and South Carolina. In the days before national food distribution companies, it was the only wheat widely available in the South. We Southern bakers still take that business quite seriously. While living in France and shooting photographs for Anne Willan's how-to tome *Cook it Right*, I had Mama ship me White Lily flour to create the biscuit photographs. We chuckled and wondered whether it would be held up by French custom agents.

In 2008, the parent company of White Lily, The J.M. Smucker Company, moved the mill that had been based in Knoxville, Tennessee, for more 125 years to the Midwest. Despite the official party line of "rigorous testing," some folks insist the flour is not the same. The violation was succinctly dubbed the Second War of Northern Aggression.

The most common wheat flour is all-purpose flour, which is exactly what it sounds like: suitable for everything from yeast breads to cookies to cakes. Bread flour has a higher gluten content and is best for bread. The gluten framework that forms from bread flour is strong and does a great job of trapping the carbon dioxide produced by the yeast. Dough made with bread flour should be kneaded longer than dough made from all-purpose flour to fully develop the gluten. Whole-wheat flour, which contains the entire wheat kernel, adds a nutty taste to dough. All-purpose flour is often added to whole-wheat flour to lighten the dough. Whole-wheat flour is best stored in the refrigerator to prevent rancidity.

Three other flours that bear mentioning are pastry flour, cake flour, and self-rising flour. Pastry and cake flours are high-starch, low-gluten soft-wheat flours with a very fine texture. Cakes made with pastry or cake flour are more tender than cakes made with all-purpose flour. Typically, pastry flour is unbleached and cake flour is bleached, or chlorinated. Bleached cake flour is bright white. Self-rising flour is flour that has had a leavener—baking powder—and salt added to it. A leavener is simply what makes bread rise, usually yeast, baking soda, or baking powder.

Cornmeal, which is simply flour ground from dried corn, comes in three basic grinds, fine, medium, and coarse. Fine or medium cornmeal is generally used in baked goods and pancakes, and coarser grinds are usually labeled grits (see page 157 for more about grits). Because corn contains no gluten, baked goods made with cornmeal only, such as the muffins on page 230, are ideal for anyone who suffers from gluten intolerance.

Representing the perfect union of art and science, poetry and progress, here is a collection of recipes that I hope you will consider the best thing since sliced bread.

~ Sweet Peach Pancakes

MAKES 16

With its fertile soils and hot climate, the South yields a nearly year-round cornucopia of gorgeous produce. We've always had an emphasis on local. In recent years, there has been an increased interest in fresh and locally grown produce all over the United States. Farmers' markets are multiplying all over the country, and stores are listening to customers' requests for seasonal and local foods. Nothing makes me madder than seeing California peaches in the grocery store in Atlanta, Georgia. Nothing against California, but we're the Peach State, for goodness' sake.

The food of the South is no longer just about fried chicken and overcooked greens. Or doesn't have to be. Don't get me wrong—I love fried chicken—but we are more than that. We were country when country wasn't cool.

1½ cups all-purpose flour

2 tablespoons sugar

1 teaspoon baking soda

2 teaspoons cream of tartar

Pinch of fine sea salt

1 cup low-fat or whole milk

1 large egg

1 tablespoon unsalted butter, melted

2 tablespoons canola oil, plus more if needed

2 to 3 peaches, pitted and thinly sliced

Sorghum, cane, or maple syrup (see page 166), for
accompaniment

Combine the flour, sugar, baking soda, cream of tartar, and salt in a bowl. Combine the milk, egg, and butter in a large liquid measuring cup. Add the wet ingredients to the dry ingredients and whisk just until combined.

Preheat the oven to 300°F.

Heat a large, heavy-bottomed skillet over medium heat and lightly coat with canola oil. Add 2 peach slices, then ladle ¼ cup of batter over the peaches for each pancake, cooking only a few at a time. Cook until the bubbles on top burst and the bottoms are golden brown, about 1 minute. Flip the pancakes and cook until golden, about 1 minute. Transfer to a baking sheet and place in the oven to keep warm. Repeat with remaining batter, adding more oil to the pan as necessary. Transfer to a warmed serving platter. Serve hot or warm with sorghum, cane, or maple syrup.

Brilliant: Short Recipe
Honey Nut Butter

Peaches and almonds have a natural affinity because they are related. Pairing the flavors is Brilliant (shown at left in photo opposite).

Preheat the oven to 350°F. Place 1 cup slivered almonds on a rimmed baking sheet. Roast, shaking the pan occasionally, until the almonds are golden, about 5 minutes. Transfer to a food processor fitted with a metal blade. Purée until very finely ground. Add 1 tablespoon honey. Makes 1 cup. To serve, scoop a dollop of the honey butter on top of the peaches. Top with syrup of your choice and serve immediately.

∾ Sweet Potato Biscuits

MAKES ABOUT 16

My dear friend and colleague Rebecca Lang is also one of Nathalie's former apprentices. She has written several cookbooks, including *Quick Fix Southern: Homemade Hospitality in 30 Minutes or Less*. Our styles of Southern cooking are somewhat different, but we share the same belief in doing the work, learning, and paying our dues. We've lamented how so many culinary students don't want to learn, they just want to be on TV, a condition Rebecca dryly described as "stir until famous."

Rebecca is generally not about shortcuts, but did share with me this handy tip for making sweet potato biscuits. If you don't have time to roast the potatoes, use sweet potato baby food instead.

2 medium sweet potatoes, plus more for rolling out

2 cups all-purpose flour

1 tablespoon sugar

2 teaspoons baking powder

1/2 teaspoon fine sea salt

5 tablespoons (1/3 cup) unsalted butter, chilled and cut into small pieces

1/3 cup low-fat or whole milk

Preheat the oven to 400°F.

Bake or microwave the sweet potatoes until soft and tender, about 45 minutes in the oven or about 10 minutes in the microwave. Set aside to cool.

When the sweet potatoes are cool enough to touch, peel and mash until smooth in a food processor fitted with a metal blade or with an old-fashioned potato masher. Measure out 1 cup and reserve the rest for another use.

Line a rimmed baking sheet with a silicone baking liner or parchment paper. Set aside.

In the same bowl of the food processor, combine the flour, sugar, baking powder, and salt. Pulse in the butter until the mixture resembles coarse meal. Combine the sweet potato and milk in a small bowl and whisk until smooth. Add the potato mixture to the flour mixture, pulsing just until moist.

Turn the dough out onto a lightly floured surface; knead lightly four or five times. Using a lightly floured rolling pin, roll out the dough 3/4 inch thick. Cut out 10 biscuits with a 2-inch biscuit cutter, pressing the cutter straight down without twisting so the biscuits will rise evenly when baked. Place the biscuits on the prepared baking sheet. Gather together the scraps (by placing the pieces on top of one another in layers instead of bunching it up). Roll out 3/4 inch thick. Cut with the biscuit cutter into 5 or 6 more biscuits. Place the biscuits on the prepared baking sheet. Discard any remaining scraps.

Bake until lightly browned, about 15 minutes. Transfer the biscuits to a wire rack to cool. Serve warm or at room temperature.

Brilliant: Short Recipe
Apple Smash

The flavors of sweet potatoes and apples marry well; they're both harvested in the fall, highlighting the philosophy, "what grows together, goes together." A Brilliant quick smash of apple on a tender sweet potato biscuit may best be described as destiny.

Combine 2 McIntosh apples, peeled, cored, and chopped in a medium heavy-duty saucepan with 1/4 cup apple juice, 1 tablespoon unsalted butter, 1 teaspoon honey, and a pinch of salt. Cook over medium-high heat until very soft, about 15 minutes. Use a potato masher to mash until smooth. Makes about 1 cup. Serve warm or at room temperature. To serve, split the sweet potato biscuits with a fork or serrated knife. Spread a spoonful of Apple Smash on one half, sandwich together, and serve immediately.

Cornmeal Buttermilk Pancakes

MAKES 10

I wake up hungry. Buttered pancakes dripping with syrup? Sausage and soft-scrambled eggs? Cheese grits? Yes, please. We lived in Louisiana when I was a little girl, and we would pause at a truck stop in Mississippi on visits to see my grandparents back in Georgia. We ordered steaming bowls of scrambled eggs, grits, and sausage rudely smushed together in a glorious mess, a short stack of pancakes on the side.

To this day, every time those flavors marry in my mouth, I vividly remember the tile floors, fluorescent tubes, and vinyl booths of that roadside spectacle. Ham biscuits make me think of eating breakfast in college on the run, and cheese toast brings memories of leftover biscuits leaving dark brown crumbs on the foil-lined bottom of my grandmother's toaster oven.

3/4 cup unbleached all-purpose flour

3/4 cup fine yellow cornmeal

2 tablespoons sugar

1/2 teaspoon baking powder

1/2 teaspoon baking soda

1/2 teaspoon fine sea salt

11/4 cups buttermilk

2 large eggs

3 tablespoons unsalted butter, melted

2 tablespoons canola oil, plus more if needed

Sorghum, cane, or maple syrup (see page 166), for accompaniment

In a large bowl, sift together the flour, cornmeal, sugar, baking powder, baking soda, and salt. Whisk together the buttermilk, eggs, and melted butter in a bowl or liquid measuring cup. Add the buttermilk mixture to the dry ingredients and whisk just until combined.

Preheat the oven to 300°F.

Heat a large, heavy-bottomed skillet over medium heat and lightly coat with canola oil. Ladle 1/4 cup batter into the pan for each pancake, cooking only a few at a time. Cook until the bubbles on the top burst and the bottoms are golden brown, about 11/2 minutes.

Flip the pancakes and cook until golden, about 1 minute. Transfer to a baking sheet and place in the oven to keep warm. Repeat with the remaining batter, adding more oil to the pan as necessary. Transfer to warmed serving plates. Serve hot or warm with sorghum, cane, or maple syrup.

Brilliant: Short Recipe
Toad in the Hole Pancakes

The British version of toad in the hole is a thin Yorkshire pudding batter with sausages, but the American version, at least the one I fondly remember as a child, was toast with a circle removed from the center and an egg fried inside it. It was a special weekend treat.

To create your own Brilliant kid-friendly treat, first prepare the pancakes, undercooking them on the second side. Then, with a small biscuit cutter, remove the center from each pancake. Butter the slightly undercooked side of each pancake and place in a skillet, butter side down. Crack an egg into each pancake hole. Cook until the egg is set and the pancake is a rich golden brown on the bottom, about 2 minutes. Transfer to a warmed serving plate. Serve hot or warm with sorghum, cane, or maple syrup.

Mama's Dutch Baby Pancake

SERVES 2 TO 4

This baby is a happy, buttery offspring of the union of an ebullient popover and a levelheaded pancake. A fairly recent addition to Mama's repertoire of recipes, this pancake has become one of my favorites. It's easy, simple, and quick. It's something freshly prepared to enjoy when you don't want to hover over a skillet making individual pancakes or didn't think far enough ahead to make a breakfast casserole.

1/4 cup (1/2 stick) unsalted butter

1/2 cup all-purpose flour

1/2 cup low-fat or whole milk

2 large eggs, lightly beaten

1/4 teaspoon fine sea salt

Confectioners' sugar, for dusting

Sorghum, cane syrup, maple syrup, or jelly (see page 166), for accompaniment

Preheat the oven to 400°F. Place the butter in a 10-inch cast-iron skillet or ovenproof baking dish and heat in the oven for 10 to 15 minutes.

Whisk together the flour, milk, eggs, and salt. When the butter has melted, pour the flour mixture into the hot skillet. Return to the oven and bake until puffed and brown, 15 to 20 minutes. Remove from the oven and sprinkle with confectioners' sugar. Cut into wedges and serve with syrup or jelly.

Brilliant: Short Recipe
Spiced Honey

Sometimes what I call "just a little something-something" is enough to take Basic to Brilliant. First of all, always heat syrup for pancakes and the like. Never pour cold syrup. And, while you are heating, add some spices, and you won't believe how good your kitchen smells!

Warm 1 cup honey in a small saucepan over medium heat. Add 6 whole cardamom pods and 1 stick cinnamon. Let gently bubble at a very low simmer for about 5 minutes. Remove from the heat to steep, 3 to 5 minutes. Remove the spices. Makes 1 cup. Drizzle over the pancake. Pour yourself a second cup of coffee and enjoy.

Classic Crêpes

MAKES ABOUT 15

Seen for years in France, crêpe booths and stands seem to be popping up at our local farmers' markets. The cooks in the booths prepare the thin pancake on a large round griddle and apply the batter with a squeegee-type tool. Mama cooked crêpes for dinner parties when I was a little girl, and I have always loved them.

Crêpes may seem fancy, but they are simply a very thin pancake and may be filled with something as common as jam or a store-bought spread, such as Nutella, or as fancy as Mushroom Ragout (page 194). Another savory alternative would be Southern Ratatouille (page 27), or even Chicken Breasts with Tarragon Velouté (page 107), by simply dicing the chicken into bite-size cubes. Keep in mind that a crêpe is really just a thin piece of bread and the possibilities are endless.

1 cup all-purpose flour

1/4 teaspoon fine sea salt

3 large eggs

1 cup low-fat or whole milk, plus more if needed

2 tablespoons unsalted butter, melted

1 tablespoon sugar (optional)

2 to 3 tablespoons clarified butter (page 100)

In a bowl, whisk together the flour, salt, eggs, milk, and butter. Add enough milk to get the consistency of heavy cream. If you are making sweet crêpes, add the sugar and stir to combine. Set aside for at least 30 minutes, or up to 1 day in the refrigerator.

Heat an 8-inch nonstick skillet or crêpe pan over medium-high heat. Using a pastry brush, brush with clarified butter, then tilt to pour away excess. Stir the batter and carefully ladle about 2 tablespoons of the batter into the skillet. Rotate the skillet so the batter spreads out and thinly coats the bottom and edges. Return the skillet to the heat and cook the crêpe until the edges turn golden brown and lacy and start to pull away from the skillet, about 2 minutes. Using a knife or an offset spatula, carefully turn the crêpe over; cook the second side until just golden, 30 to 40 seconds. Slide the crêpe onto a plate. Repeat with the remaining batter, stirring it before making another crêpe. Adjust the temperature as needed. Stack cooked crêpes between sheets of waxed paper. Use immediately, or store in the freezer tightly wrapped in plastic for up to 1 month.

Brilliant Presentation

Layered Crêpe Cake

A crêpe cake is a thing of Brilliant beauty.

To assemble, place a crêpe on a serving plate and spread with 2 tablespoons jam, jelly, or Pastry Cream (page 21). Top with another crêpe and repeat until all the crêpes have been used. Do not spread filling on the top layer. Dust with confectioners' sugar. Serve immediately.

Nathalie's Sally Lunn Bread

MAKES 1 (10-INCH) CAKE

There's mixed food lore about this rich, briochelike bread: that it was brought with Protestant refugees from France, who called it sun and moon or *soleil et lune*; that it originated in Bath, England, and was baked by a woman named Sally Lunn; or finally, that it was a bread presented by Carême, and called *solilemme*. As a former history major, I find food history fascinating, but what I really care about is whether it tastes good. And, it does.

2 packets (4 1/2 teaspoons) active dry yeast

1/2 cup sugar

1 cup low-fat or whole milk, warmed

4 large eggs, lightly beaten

1 tablespoon fine sea salt

4 cups bread flour

3/4 cup (1 1/2 sticks) unsalted butter, melted, plus more room-temperature butter for the pan

In a small bowl, combine the yeast, sugar, and warm milk. Stir to combine and set aside to proof and dissolve, about 5 minutes.

Meanwhile, in the bowl of a heavy-duty mixer fitted with the dough hook attachment, combine the eggs and salt. Add the yeast mixture. With the mixer on low, add the flour to the egg mixture, alternating with the melted butter, beginning and ending with the flour. Increase the speed and beat well to combine. The batter should be thick. Cover with a clean kitchen towel and let rise in a warm place until doubled, about 1 hour.

Brush a 10-inch Bundt or tube pan with room-temperature butter.

Using your hand, punch down the dough. Turn the dough into the prepared pan. Cover again with a clean kitchen towel and return to the warm place to double again, about 1 hour.

Preheat the oven to 350°F. Bake until golden and a toothpick inserted near the center comes out clean, about 40 minutes. Transfer to a rack to cool for 10 minutes to set. Invert onto a cooling rack. To serve, slice with a serrated knife. Serve warm or at room temperature.

Brilliant: Short Recipe
Pecan–Brown Sugar Topping

Sally Lunn is rich, moist, and cakelike but not too sweet, making it a very adaptable dough for cinnamon rolls and coffee cake. For a very Brilliant version, make a Pecan–Brown Sugar Topping (pictured opposite). Combine 1/2 cup firmly packed dark brown sugar, 1/2 cup (1 stick) melted unsalted butter, and 3/4 cup chopped pecans. Spoon into the bottom of the greased Bundt pan. Proceed with the Basic recipe for Sally Lunn bread. Bake, transfer to a rack to cool slightly, then invert onto a serving plate.

Is It Done?

The poetic way to tell when a bread is done baking is to tap the bottom; it should sound hollow. A more pragmatic way is to insert an instant-read thermometer. Most breads are finished baking at about 190°F. Breads enriched with butter, eggs, or milk are finished when the internal temperature is closer to 200°F. For both, turn the loaves onto racks immediately after baking to prevent sogginess.

Savory Monkey Bread

MAKES 1 (10-INCH) LOAF

Once I was a guest on Paula Deen's show, and the premise was to play up the difference between us. They had me chop, fast and faster. I spoke French, and Paula teased me, smiling her big, pretty smile. We made Paula's Monkey Bread with canned biscuits, Italian seasoning, and shredded cheese. Let me be perfectly clear, I am not being snotty about Paula. Some of our food is quite different, but we are working for the same goal, to get people to the table.

She asked me to open the can of biscuits. I banged it on the side of the counter. It exploded, and I screamed. I rolled the biscuit dough into balls, and Paula dipped them in melted butter, then cheese. She ummed and yummed, making a tasty fuss, and started to lick her fingers. Next thing I knew she reached her buttery fingers in the direction of my lips for me to taste. I couldn't help it. I just couldn't do it. I arched away my mouth from her, raised my face to the heavens, and said, "I don't know you!" I mean, seriously, the list of people whose fingers I would lick is pretty short. She just laughed and smiled.

1/4 cup oil from Garlic Confit (page 14) or extra-virgin olive oil

2 tablespoons unsalted butter, melted

3/4 cup freshly grated pecorino romano cheese (3 ounces)

2 tablespoons chopped fresh flat-leaf parsley

Coarse salt and freshly ground black pepper

1 pound store-bought whole-wheat pizza dough or yeast rolls, defrosted

1 cup Garlic Confit cloves (page 14) optional

Brush a 10-inch tube pan with some of the garlic oil.

Combine the remaining oil with the butter in a small bowl. Set aside. Combine the cheese and parsley in a small bowl and season with a pinch of salt and pepper. Set aside.

Rub your hands with some of the buttery oil, then pull off equal pieces of dough about the size of apricots and shape into balls. Dip the balls in the oil mixture, then roll in the cheese. Place in the prepared tube pan, alternating with the garlic cloves. Cover with a clean kitchen towel and let rise in a warm place until doubled, about 1 hour.

Preheat the oven to 400°F. Bake until a rich golden brown, 25 to 30 minutes. Remove to a rack to cool slightly. To serve, use a butter knife or long spatula to loosen the bread from the sides of the pan. Invert onto a serving plate. Pull apart or slice with a serrated knife.

Brilliant: Short Recipe
Sauce Tomate for Dipping

Savory garlic-kissed rolls may be good, but they are Basic restaurant fare. Prepare Sauce Tomate, one of the Five Mother Sauces (page 11), for dipping and they're Brilliant.

Heat 2 tablespoons pure olive oil in a saucepan. Add 1 onion, preferably Vidalia, finely chopped, and cook until translucent, 3 to 5 minutes. Add 1 carrot, grated, and 2 cloves garlic, finely chopped. Cook until fragrant, 45 to 60 seconds. Add 1 (28-ounce) can crushed tomatoes, 1 teaspoon chopped fresh oregano, 1 teaspoon chopped fresh basil, and 1 tablespoon chopped fresh flat-leaf parsley. Season with coarse salt and freshly ground black pepper. Bring to a boil, then decrease the heat to simmer. Cook until thick, about 10 minutes. Makes 3 cups. Transfer to a warmed bowl and serve as a dipping sauce for the bread.

Mama's Sausage Swirls

MAKES ABOUT 40

Traditionally these quick and easy swirls, also known as pinwheels, are made with canned crescent roll dough, a cheater's croissant dough. Croissant dough is essentially yeasted puff pastry dough. The sausage rolls are almost the Southern equivalent to pigs in blankets, but not quite. These swirls are great to have on hand in the freezer for weekend company, tailgating, and Sunday brunch.

1 teaspoon canola oil (optional)

1 pound pork, turkey, or chicken breakfast sausage, in bulk
or removed from the casing

4 ounces Neufchâtel or cream cheese, at room temperature

4 ounces fresh goat cheese, at room temperature

1 pound Quick Puff Pastry (page 19) or 1 (14-ounce) box
store-bought puff pastry

1 large egg

1 tablespoon water

1/2 teaspoon fine sea salt

Coarse salt and freshly ground black pepper

Preheat the oven to 400°F. Line a rimmed baking sheet with a silicone baking liner or parchment paper.

If you are using turkey or chicken sausage, heat the oil in a large skillet over medium-high heat; otherwise, heat a dry skillet. Add the sausage and cook, using a wooden spatula to break up the sausage and stirring occasionally, until no longer pink, about 5 minutes. Drain off all excess fat and let cool.

Meanwhile, combine the Neufchâtel and goat cheese in the bowl of a heavy-duty mixer fitted with the paddle attachment. Add the drained, cooled sausage and whip to combine. Set aside.

In a small bowl, whisk together the egg, water, and salt. On a lightly floured surface, roll out the dough into a 14 x 10-inch rectangle. Divide in half lengthwise, then, working with one half at a time, roll out again into a very thin 12 x 8-inch rectangle. Place the long edge closest to you and brush the edges with the egg wash. Spread the cream cheese mixture over the dough rectangles. Roll up into a 12-inch log and press to seal

the edge. Place seam side down on the prepared baking sheet. Refrigerate until firm, about 30 minutes.

Trim the ends to make 10-inch logs, then slice into 1/2-inch pieces. Place cut side down on the prepared baking sheet. (At this point you can freeze them on the baking sheet until firm, then transfer them to a sealable freezer container.) Bake until golden brown and puffed, 20 to 25 minutes. Transfer to a rack to cool. Serve warm or at room temperature.

Brilliant: Technique
Danish-Style Pinwheels

Buttery dough rolled around a creamy sausage filling is a Basic; a couple of twists learned in the pastry kitchen is Brilliant.

Preheat the oven to 400°F. Line a rimmed baking sheet with a silicone baking liner or parchment paper. Roll out half the dough into a 12-inch square. Cut into twelve 3-inch squares. Brush each with the egg wash glaze. Mound 1 level tablespoon of the sausage–cream cheese mixture in the center of each square. Cut diagonally from each corner to within 3/4 inch of the center. Fold the four alternating points to the center, pressing down lightly to hold them in place. Repeat with remaining ingredients. Brush the pastries with the egg wash. Place in the refrigerator and chill until firm, about 30 minutes. Bake until golden brown, 15 to 20 minutes. Remove to a rack to cool slightly. Serve warm or at room temperature. (Heads up: You will have about 1/2 cup of the sausage–cream cheese mixture left over. Spread it on a biscuit or bagel.) Makes 24.

Jalapeño Cornbread Muffins

MAKES 12

This is my Basic buttermilk cornbread recipe as seen in my first book, *Bon Appétit, Y'all,* with jalapeño pepper added. I wanted to tell you so you didn't think I was trying to pull a fast one on you. I generally prefer to make cornbread with all cornmeal and no wheat flour. However, at the Greenbrier Resort in West Virginia, they serve Kathy Justice's Blue Ribbon Cornbread, which is combination of the two. Not just for the excellent cornbread, the Greenbrier holds a special place in my heart.

The Greenbrier hosts the Symposium for Professional Food Writers every year. It is where I shared a suite with Julia Child, making sure she didn't lose her cane as I carried her books for her. I also attended while working for Anne Willan; it is the place where the idea for *Bon Appetit, Y'all* originated. The Symposium for Professional Food Writers has continually, bar none, been the most influential guiding experience in my career.

2 tablespoons unsalted butter or bacon grease, melted,
  plus more for the muffin cups
2 cups fine white or yellow cornmeal (not cornmeal mix
  or self-rising cornmeal)
1 teaspoon fine sea salt
1 teaspoon baking soda
2 cups buttermilk
1 large egg, lightly beaten
1 jalapeño, cored, seeded, and chopped

Preheat the oven the oven to 425°F. Brush 12 standard muffin cups with butter.

In a bowl, combine the cornmeal, salt, and baking soda. Set aside. In a large measuring cup, combine the butter, buttermilk, egg, and jalapeño. Add the wet ingredients to the dry and stir to combine.

Spoon the batter into the prepared muffin cups, filling each cup no more than two-thirds full. Bake until golden brown, 25 to 30 minutes. Remove to a rack to cool slightly. Invert into a cloth-lined basket. Serve immediately.

Variation Instead of baking as muffins, this batter may be prepared in a skillet. Preheat the oven to 450°F. Place the 2 tablespoons butter in a 10½-inch cast-iron skillet or ovenproof baking dish and heat in the oven for 10 to 15 minutes. Prepare the batter as directed; remove the heated skillet from the oven and pour the melted butter into the batter. Stir to combine, then pour the batter back into the hot skillet. Bake until golden brown, 20 to 25 minutes. Remove to a rack to cool slightly. Cut into wedges and serve immediately.

Brilliant: Short Recipe
Cheddar Butter

Slather some Cheddar Butter on those warm muffins and taste just how Brilliant cornbread can be.

In a small bowl, (or in a food processor fitted with a metal blade), combine ½ cup (1 stick) unsalted butter, at room temperature; 1 cup grated Cheddar cheese (4 ounces); 1 garlic clove, finely chopped; and a dash of hot sauce. Season with coarse salt and freshly ground black pepper. Stir until smooth and well combined. Makes 1 cup. Serve at room temperature with the muffins.

Walnut Soda Bread *Pain aux Noix Rapide*

MAKES 1 LOAF

Pain aux noix, a yeast bread, is often served at the end of a meal in France with the cheese course and a selection of dried fruit, such as apricots and figs. The biscuit-making Southerner in me wanted to create bread that would be quicker, using baking soda as a leavener. Walnuts are used in France, but pecans would be very good, too. Or, if you are lucky enough to have a source for black walnuts, give those a try. Layer the flavor of the nuts by using nut oil, too. Nut oils are available online and in gourmet specialty markets. This makes an excellent make-ahead breakfast bread, too.

1 cup unbleached all-purpose flour

3/4 cup whole-wheat flour

1 teaspoon baking powder

1/2 teaspoon baking soda

3/4 teaspoon salt

4 large eggs

1/2 cup buttermilk

3 tablespoons canola or pure olive oil, plus more for
    the loaf pan

3 tablespoons walnut or pecan oil

1 cup chopped walnuts or pecans (3 ounces)

1/2 cup currants

Preheat the oven to 375°F. Brush a 8¹/2 x 4¹/2-inch loaf pan with oil.

In a large bowl, whisk together the flours, baking powder, baking soda, and salt.

Beat the eggs in a large bowl. Whisk in the buttermilk and oils. Quickly whisk in the flour, and fold in the walnuts. Transfer to the prepared pan.

Bake until nicely browned and a tester inserted near the center of the loaf comes out clean, 50 to 60 minutes. Remove from the oven; allow to cool for 10 minutes in the pan. Invert onto a rack and let cool completely.

Brilliant: Presentation
Fig and Cheese Tartines

A tartine is the French version of an open-faced sandwich. It makes my mouth water just thinking about slathering a spoonful of room-temperature Saint André, Camembert, or Brie on this bread and topping the cheese with sliced fresh figs, perhaps judiciously drizzled with a glistening spoonful of amber honey. Pop it under the broiler until warm and melted? Brilliant.

12

Desserts

Fluffy cake with thick, candied caramel icing; tottering, shaggy coconut cakes; blistered pockets of fried pies; and tins of aggressively crunchy nut brittle—it's not a Southern bakeshop, it's a Southern celebration and that's just the beginning. Meme and Dede started baking fruitcakes to enjoy and give as gifts months before Christmas, carefully tucking each one, swaddled in stained, bourbon-drenched cheesecloth, tightly in a tin. In the week before a holiday, we make cakes and pies and hold them in sealable containers, mounded high in the laundry room to keep them out of harm's way—and seclude them from premature nibbles, I am sure. Mama pulls out her candy thermometer for Christmas almost as soon as the Thanksgiving dishes are done.

The phenomenon is not limited to fall and winter; spring brings legions of tea cakes, coated in a snowy blanket of confectioners' sugar, separated and stacked on creased sheets of waxed paper. Summer is filled with buttery fruit cobblers and freshly churned ice cream on the screen porch. Weddings and baby showers mean freshly polished silver platters of meringues and mints; funerals bring foil-wrapped plates of fudge and even more layer cakes. On holidays, holy days, and gatherings of all shapes and sizes, Southerners lay out the desserts.

When Southerners are happy, we eat, and when we're sad, we eat. And it seems my people are pretty partial to sugar. Today sugar is abundant and moderately priced, but that was not always the case. There was a time when sugar was so precious and rare it was presented to royalty in jewel-covered boxes. Sugar was one of the first commodities, besides precious metals, to be transported from the colonies to Europe. Slavery was at the core of the sugar trade and ensured maximum production and maximum profits for the plantation owners.

Sugarcane has been grown in the South since colonial times. Granted, the majority of U.S. sugar is now made from beets, but more than half of the country's supply of cane sugar is currently produced in Florida; cane for sugar is also grown in Louisiana and Texas. Sugarcane grown for syrup is produced over a wider area of the country, in small pockets extending from eastern Texas to South Carolina. It's in our backyard, too. Port access to the major sugar-producing tropical islands to our south is through the Gulf of Mexico and the Atlantic coast. One way or the other, we're nearly surrounded by sugar. In today's vernacular, the Southern sweet tooth laughingly could be considered a by-product of a locavore diet.

If the South is home to sideboards filled with homemade cakes and pies, France is home to jewel box *pâtisseries* filled with exquisitely executed pastries and confections lined up like sugary soldiers, nestled in their pristine paper cups. The choices are overwhelming: perfectly sculpted pastel macaroons, exquisite crisp swirls of pale ivory meringues, petite tartlets exploding with carefully placed fruit, chocolate-glazed éclairs, layered Napoleons, sturdy cream puffs filled with *crème Chantilly*, delicate almond *calissons*, and boozy, intoxicated *babas au rhum* are just a sampling of the artist's palette.

Southern desserts have reflected a decidedly European character throughout the centuries. Even with the heavy influence of former African slaves in the savory kitchen, the sweet kitchen remained primarily Western European. Many early colonial recipes originated in cookbooks brought over from Europe, including sugar candy, candied fruits and flowers, sugar-coated nuts, marzipan, brittles, and toffee. Others include sweet cakes, cookies, and meringues. Grunts, buckles, slumps, and bread and fruit puddings would be fairly familiar to my ancestors. Layer cakes, archetypical Southern desserts, haven't been a part of American history for nearly as long. Predictable cake baking was not possible until the advent of more reliable stoves and of baking powder, commercially available in the 1850s. Many of the early Southern desserts are similar to the Sweet Biscuits with Stewed Blackberries (opposite) or Nut Brittle (page 262). It wasn't until later that sweets like Dede's Burnt Caramel Cake (page 253) and Pineapple Upside-Down Cake (page 257) became part of the Southern celebration.

Here is a collection of recipes for your own celebrations. Beignets to brittle, I think you'll enjoy every sugary bite.

Sweet Biscuits with Stewed Blackberries

SERVES 6

Blackberries are one of the more complicated summer fruits, thick in the mouth like wine, musky, and sharp with sweet and sour edges. Wild blackberries grow prolifically throughout the South, and my sister and I picked them with Dede in the woods near a pond. We would each grab one of his mighty gnarled, thick hands, and we'd all skip sort of sideways down the hill, slapping our thighs. He called it the "buzzard lope" for reasons never understood. Once we were near the bushes, he tromped through the grass first in his well-worn brown leather boots to make sure the area was free of snakes. My sister and I ate at least one berry for every berry that went into the bucket. We'd return an hour or so later with stained smiles, blackened teeth, and sweaty red faces.

Expensive store-bought blackberries can't hold a candle in my mind to the juicy jewels we harvested as kids with Dede. Those berries tasted sweeter from the love that went into picking them and the memories made from them.

Sweet Biscuits

2 cups White Lily or other Southern all-purpose flour or
  cake flour (not self-rising), plus more for rolling out

3 tablespoons sugar

1 tablespoon baking powder

1 teaspoon fine sea salt

1/4 cup (1/2 stick) cold unsalted butter, chilled and cut into
  small pieces

1 cup low-fat or whole milk, plus more for brushing

Stewed Blackberries

12 ounces fresh blackberries or thawed frozen
  blackberries

3/4 cup cold water

1/3 cup sugar

Pinch of fine sea salt

2 tablespoons all-purpose flour

1/2 teaspoon pure vanilla extract

1/2 tablespoon unsalted butter, chilled

Unsweetened whipped cream, for garnish

Preheat the oven to 500°F. Line a baking sheet with a silicone baking liner or parchment paper.

To make the biscuits, combine the flour, 1 tablespoon of the sugar, baking powder, and salt in a bowl. Using a pastry cutter or two knives, cut the butter into the flour mixture until it resembles coarse meal. Pour in the milk and mix gently until just combined.

Turn the dough out onto a lightly floured surface. Knead lightly, using the heel of your hand to compress and push the dough away from you, then fold it back over itself. Give the dough a small turn and repeat eight or so times. (It's not yeast bread; you want to barely activate the gluten, not overwork it.) Using a lightly floured rolling pin, roll the dough out into a 12-inch square about 1/4 inch thick.

Using a pastry cutter, cut the dough into strips about 2 inches wide and 4 inches long. Liberally brush the dough with milk and sprinkle over the remaining 2 tablespoons of sugar. Using an offset spatula, transfer the dough strips to the prepared baking sheet.

Bake until a deep golden brown, about 10 minutes. Remove to a rack to cool.

CONTINUED

To make the blackberries, combine the blackberries with 1/2 cup of the water, the sugar, and the salt in a saucepan. Bring to a boil over high heat and cook, stirring with a whisk or crushing with a potato masher, until the berries are pulpy, 3 to 5 minutes. In a liquid measuring cup, combine the remaining 1/4 cup water and the flour. Stir well with a fork or small whisk until well combined and no lumps remain. Whisking constantly, slowly add the flour mixture to the berries and bring to a boil. Cook until slightly thickened, another 3 to 5 minutes. Add the vanilla and remove from the heat. Add the butter and stir to combine.

To serve, divide the sweet biscuits among serving bowls and ladle over the blackberry mixture. Garnish with the whipped cream. Serve immediately.

Brilliant: Short Recipe
Blackberry Fool

A fool, at least the one found in the pastry kitchen, is a fruit and whipped cream dessert and is very simple on its own. Using it as a garnish for the Sweet Biscuits with Stewed Blackberries is a Brilliant way to layer the flavor of the fruit.

Combine 1/2 cup blackberries and 1 tablespoon sugar in a food processor fitted with a metal blade and process until puréed. Strain through a fine-mesh sieve. Discard the contents of the sieve. In a bowl set over a bowl of ice, combine 1/2 cup heavy cream and 1/4 teaspoon pure vanilla extract; whisk until stiff peaks form. Using a large rubber spatula, gently fold the berry purée into the cream. Makes about 1 cup. Spoon on top of the biscuits and stewed berries in place of the plain whipped cream. Serve immediately.

Château du Fëy Cherry Clafoutis

SERVES 6

Clafoutis is a batter pudding originally from the Limousin region of France. This country dessert is traditionally made with cherries that have not been pitted, but that's asking for a trip to the dentist. There were grand cherry trees in the garden at La Varenne, and we made this dessert often in the summer. One of the chores I had as an apprentice was to pick cherries and make jam. The traditional confiture pot is a large, solid-copper basin with sloped sides that create a large surface area for moisture evaporation. My cohort in much of the jam making was food writer Amanda Hesser. We would prepare dinner for twenty and somehow put up ten liters of jam at the same time. Sometimes, overwhelmed with the crop, we'd cheat a bit and macerate the cherries in vodka and sugar to make kirsch.

Unsalted butter for the baking dish

1/3 cup granulated sugar, plus more for the baking dish

1 pound sweet cherries, pitted

1/4 cup all-purpose flour

Pinch of fine sea salt

4 large eggs

1/2 cup low-fat or whole milk

1/2 cup heavy cream

1/4 cup kirsch, brandy, or Cognac

Confectioners' sugar, for garnish

Preheat the oven to 350°F. Butter a 1 1/2-quart shallow baking dish and sprinkle it with granulated sugar. Place the cherries in the dish; set aside.

Sift the flour, granulated sugar, and salt into a bowl and make a well in the center. Add the eggs to the well and stir with a whisk until mixed. Stir in the milk and cream and continue stirring to draw in the flour until the batter is smooth. Pour the batter over the cherries.

Bake until just set, about 35 minutes. Sprinkle the kirsch over the hot pudding. Allow to cool to room temperature. Cut into wedges and place on serving plates. Dust with confectioners' sugar and serve immediately.

Brilliant: Short Recipe
Cherry Coulis

One of the techniques that I like to employ in the kitchen is layering flavor. Not simply using the same ingredient again and again, but doing it with thought and purpose.

To take our Basic recipe to chef-inspired Brilliant, prepare Cherry Coulis. Put 8 ounces sweet cherries, pitted, in a blender and blend until smooth. Depending on the sweetness, add 1 tablespoon confectioners' sugar, or to taste. Add a dash of freshly squeezed lemon juice and a tiny pinch of fine sea salt. Strain the purée through a fine-mesh sieve. Makes 1 cup. Spoon the coulis around the edge of each serving plate. Top with a slice of the claufoutis. Serve immediately.

Meringue Pillows with Strawberries and Cream

SERVES 6

When I was eighteen, I went to visit my friend Alton Irby in London. I got a job waiting tables at an Italian trattoria. I was awful; there's a reason I work in the kitchen instead of the dining room. Alton and I spent every last pence we earned eating at fancy restaurants. One day I headed off to see Kew Gardens. On the way I stopped at a market and bought strawberries and clotted cream to enjoy in the park. When I walked up to the gate and counted my heavy English coins, I discovered I didn't have enough money to visit the gardens and also return home. So, I sat on the park bench looking through the garden gate, eating my strawberries and cream. Not very posh, silly little girl. I still think of that experience anytime I taste strawberries and cream. And, years later, I still need to make it to Kew Gardens.

Unsalted butter and all-purpose flour for the pans, if using parchment paper

4 large egg whites

1/2 teaspoon fine sea salt

1 cup granulated sugar plus 1 tablespoon, or to taste

1 teaspoon pure vanilla extract

1 to 2 pints strawberries, hulled and quartered lengthwise

2 tablespoons Grand Marnier, or to taste

Fresh mint leaves, for garnish

Confectioners' sugar, for garnish

Whipped cream, for garnish

Preheat the oven to 400°F. Line 2 rimmed baking sheets with silicone baking liners or parchment paper; set aside. (If you are using parchment paper, it is necessary to butter and flour the parchment. Then, before shaping the pillows, dab a little bit of meringue at the corners to hold the paper in place.)

In the bowl of a heavy-duty mixer fitted with the whisk attachment, beat the egg whites on high speed with a pinch of salt until frothy. Gradually add the 1 cup granulated sugar and vanilla, beating at high speed until the whites hold stiff, glossy peaks.

Using a rubber spatula, spoon three 1-cup blobs of meringue onto each prepared baking sheet, leaving 2 to 3 inches of space between the blobs. Using a small, wet offset spatula, shape the blobs into rectangles, creating 3 smooth pillows. Repeat with the remaining ingredients on the second baking sheet to make 6 pillows.

Decrease the oven temperature to 200°F. Place the baking sheets in the oven; bake until the meringues are crisp on the outside but have a marshmallow consistency inside, about 11/2 to 2 hours. Check the consistency by poking into the bottom of one meringue pillow. If the meringues start to brown, decrease the oven temperature to 175°F. Remove from the oven and let cool completely on a wire rack.

Meanwhile, combine the strawberries, Grand Marnier, and the remaining 1 tablespoon granulated sugar in a bowl. Refrigerate until ready to serve.

When you are ready to serve, using your hands or the back of a knife, gently crack the meringue pillows and place on small plates. Top with the macerated berries. Garnish with mint, a dusting of confectioners' sugar, and a dollop of whipped cream. Serve immediately.

CONTINUED

Brilliant: Presentation
Dacquoise

A *dacquoise* is a meringue "cake," often, but not always, containing nuts, and layered with fruit, cream, or frosting. It's a Brilliant presentation.

Preheat the oven to 200°F. Draw two 8-inch circles on parchment paper. Turn the paper upside down. Butter and flour the parchment paper. Instead of making home style pillows, pipe the meringue into rounds. Prepare the meringue and spoon into a piping bag fitted with a large round tip. Dab a little bit at the corners of the paper to hold the paper in place. Pipe the meringue in coils, starting at the center of a circle and working to the outside edge. Repeat on the second circle. Smooth the tops with a small, wet offset spatula. Transfer the parchment liner and meringue coils to the oven and bake until dry, about 2 hours. (As long as it is not too humid, the meringue rounds can be made several days in advance and stored in an airtight container at room temperature.)

When you are ready to serve, place a meringue round on a chilled serving plate. Spoon over the strawberries and whipped cream and top with the second round to create a cake. Dust with confectioners' sugar. Take a picture! Serve immediately.

Meringue

Meringue is a combination of egg whites and sugar whipped to form a thick, stiff foam. Different textures are achieved by varying the methods of mixing the sugar and egg whites, and varying the baking times and temperatures. Meringue can be made soft to top a pie, or dried in the oven to make a *dacquoise* or meringue cookie.

A French meringue is the simplest meringue; it is made by beating sugar into egg whites until stiff and fluffy.

A Swiss meringue is made by heating egg whites and sugar in a double boiler until the mixture reaches 110°F to 120°F. Then the mixture is beaten until stiff. This technique ensures that the sugar is completely dissolved and stabilizes the meringue.

An Italian meringue is the most stable meringue. It is made by heating a sugar syrup to the soft-ball stage, 232°F to 240°F (see page 23), then beating the hot syrup into the egg whites. Adding butter to the finished meringue makes it buttercream frosting.

Buttermilk Panna Cotta with Mint-Blueberry Compote

This recipe was inspired by my experience cooking in North Georgia at Persimmon Creek Vineyards. I made it with sheep's milk, but first, I had to milk the sheep. It's not so easy. The ewe is positioned on the milking stand and her head is secured between two wooden bars. There's a whole rhythmic movement that starts with grabbing the udder, pushing up, and then fanning your fingers and pulling down. (I will say this: the barn was clean—no take-your-breath-away animal odors.) Owner Mary Ann says her hands are too small to milk two teats at once. I have serious, thick, working chef-girl hands and still couldn't manage to get two going at once. But I did have some success, and it was very satisfying: a whole scant 3/4 cup of satisfaction!

Persimmon Creek is crystal clear, sparkling, and beautiful. I tromped down the creek bank and was overcome with the scent of crushed wild mint. Large, dark evergreen sprigs with dark, almost purple stems were growing along the bank. I encouraged the guests to eat mint bite by bite with the berries. It's more than just an obligatory garnish; it lends bright flavor. Take a nibble next time you see mint on your dessert plate.

1 teaspoon canola oil

2 cups heavy cream

1/2 cup sugar

1 cup firmly packed fresh lemon verbena, lemon balm,
    or mint leaves

2 (1/4-ounce) packets powdered gelatin (about 2 tablespoons)

6 tablespoons cold water

2 cups buttermilk

Pinch of fine sea salt

Mint-Blueberry Compote (recipe follows)

Mint sprigs, for garnish

Lightly oil eight 1-cup custard cups.

Heat the heavy cream and sugar in a small, heavy saucepan over medium heat until the sugar dissolves. Remove from the heat and stir in the lemon verbena. Cover and let steep for 10 minutes.

Sprinkle the gelatin over the cold water in a bowl; let stand for 5 to 10 minutes to "bloom" and absorb the water. Meanwhile, return the cream to the heat and bring back to a simmer. Strain, discarding the leaves. Pour the strained cream mixture over the gelatin and stir until the gelatin is completely dissolved. Add the buttermilk and salt. Stir to combine.

Divide the mixture among the prepared cups. Chill until firm, at least 2 hours, but 4 hours is even better.

To serve, run a sharp knife around the edge of each panna cotta and unmold onto chilled serving plates. Spoon over the compote. Garnish with mint. Serve immediately.

Mint-Blueberry Compote

MAKES ABOUT 1 1/2 CUPS

1/2 cup water

1/2 cup sugar

Finely grated zest of 1 lemon

2 cups blueberries (10 ounces)

1 1/2 tablespoons freshly squeezed lemon juice

Pinch of fine sea salt

1/4 cup finely chopped fresh mint

Combine the water, sugar, and lemon zest in a 1-quart heavy saucepan and bring to a boil. Boil uncovered for 5 minutes. Stir in the blueberries and simmer, stirring occasionally, until the blueberries begin to burst, 3 to 5 minutes. Remove from the heat and stir in the lemon juice, salt, and mint. Serve warm or at room temperature.

CONTINUED

Brilliant: Short Recipe
Classic Shortbread

Serve classic shortbread with the panna cotta and blueberry compote. The combination of herbs and the juxtaposition of textures, temperature, and flavors are perfectly Brilliant.

Preheat the oven to 300°F. Cream 1/2 cup (1 stick) unsalted butter, at room temperature, in the bowl of a heavy-duty mixer fitted with the paddle attachment. Add 1 cup all-purpose flour; 1/3 cup confectioners' sugar, sifted; and a pinch of fine sea salt. Mix until just combined. Pat into an 8-inch round cake pan; crimp the edges with the tines of a floured fork. Bake until firm and slightly browned, 30 to 35 minutes. Remove to a rack to cool slightly. Immediately score into 8 wedges. Let cool completely. Invert onto a clean work surface. Slice with a serrated knife. Makes 8. Serve alongside the panna cotta and blueberry compote.

French Beignets

MAKES ABOUT 32

Beignets evoke New Orleans and make my heart beat faster. I don't care how touristy it is, there's nothing like sipping a deliciously bitter cup of coffee with chicory in the French Market and licking confectioners' sugar off your fingertips—or your love's. Memories like that can last a lifetime. When my sister and I were little, Mama made beignets from the Café du Monde mix, leavened dough rolled out and cut into strips. In France, they use a version of *pâte à choux* to make beignets. Both are sugary and sublime.

1 cup water

1/2 cup (1 stick) unsalted butter

1 teaspoon plus 1 cup granulated sugar

1/4 teaspoon fine sea salt

Finely grated zest of 2 oranges

1 cup, plus 2 tablespoons all-purpose flour

4 large eggs

1 teaspoon pure vanilla extract

Vegetable shortening, for frying

Confectioners' sugar, for serving

Line a baking sheet with paper towels. Set aside. In a small saucepan, combine the water, butter, 1 teaspoon granulated sugar, salt, and half the zest and bring the mixture to a rapid boil. Remove the pan from the heat and add the flour all at once, stirring vigorously. Cook the paste over low heat, beating briskly, until the ingredients are thoroughly combined and the dough leaves the sides of the pan and forms a ball. Remove the pan from the heat. Add the eggs one at a time, beating well after each addition. By hand or with an electric mixer set at medium speed, beat the paste until it is smooth and glossy. Stir in the vanilla.

Fill a heavy-bottomed saucepan, deep fryer, or Dutch oven no more than one-third full with shortening. Heat to 370°F. Using an ice cream scoop, carefully drop the dough by teaspoonfuls into the shortening. Fry the beignets in batches, turning them once or twice, until golden brown, 3 to 5 minutes. Using a slotted spoon, remove to the prepared baking sheet to drain.

Combine the remaining orange zest and 1 cup granulated sugar in a bowl. While the puffs are still warm, roll them in the sugar and orange zest mixture until evenly coated. Just before serving, sprinkle the beignets with the confectioners' sugar. Serve immediately.

Brilliant: Short Recipe
Pets de Nonne

Pets de Nonne are a delicate dessert with an indelicate identity. Certainly coined by a mischievous schoolboy, the term translates to "nun's farts." One Brilliant bite and you won't care what they're called.

Using a paring knife, make a small hole in the bottom of each beignet. Prepare a batch of Pastry Cream (page 21) and place it in a piping bag fitted with a small round tip. Pipe the cream into the beignets. Serve immediately.

Brown Butter–Pecan Tea Cakes

MAKES 32

According to French food lore, these traditional buttery bites that are also known as financiers (pictured on page 232) originated at a bakery located in a financial district and were shaped like bars to mimic gold bullion. Other versions of the tale insinuate that they are called financiers because they are so rich. I am not certain what the real story is, but they are, in a word, addictive.

Chefs love toys—knives, pots, and pans. If the expression "she who has the most toys wins" is true, pastry chefs can go ahead and claim the victory. Silicone molds, mats, and baking liners revolutionized the pastry kitchen, and now many of those toys are available online and in cookware and gourmet shops. Mini muffin pans are great, but to give your tea cakes a restaurant touch, seek out a GastroFlex or Flexipan baking mold at your local cookware store.

1 cup (2 sticks) unsalted butter, plus more for the molds

3/4 cup ground pecans or almonds

3/4 cup all-purpose flour, sifted

2 1/2 cups confectioners' sugar, sifted

1/2 teaspoon fine sea salt

8 large egg whites, at room temperature, whisked just until frothy

1/2 teaspoon pure vanilla extract

Preheat the oven to 425°F. Using a pastry brush, butter mini muffin cups or silicone molds with butter. Set aside.

In a small heavy saucepan, melt the butter over medium heat until it stops sputtering and starts to brown, 5 to 7 minutes. (For more about clarifying and brown butter, see page 88.) Remove from the heat and let cool to lukewarm.

Thoroughly mix the pecans, flour, confectioners' sugar, and salt in a heavy saucepan. Add the egg whites and whisk until well combined. Set the saucepan over low heat and whisk constantly until the mixture is just warm to the touch. Remove from the heat and whisk in the butter, leaving behind the dark brown milk solids. Fill the prepared molds about two-thirds full.

Bake until golden brown, 18 to 20 minutes. Transfer to a rack to cool slightly and before inverting onto the rack. Repeat with the remaining batter.

Brilliant: Short Recipe
Chocolate Ganache

Many things in the world would be better, even Brilliant, if served with chocolate. Serve the tea cakes with a warm bowl of Chocolate Ganache for dipping and prepare to receive the accolades.

Combine 1 1/4 cups heavy cream and 2 tablespoons unsalted butter in a saucepan over low heat just until simmering. Remove the pan from the heat. Add 12 ounces best-quality semisweet chocolate, finely chopped, and stir until the chocolate is melted. Makes about 2 cups. Serve the tea cakes on a platter with the warm ganache on the side for dipping.

Drying Bakeware

Once bakeware, such as mini muffin tins and cake pans, are washed and dried, put them a low oven for about 30 minutes to make sure they are perfectly dry.

Wedding Cookies

MAKES ABOUT 4 DOZEN

Mama's always called these cookies tea cakes, but they are also known as Mexican wedding cookies, butternuts, butterballs, and snowballs (pictured on page 232). I don't care what you call them, they are good. Mama likes to make them so you can just pop them in your mouth, "not that big, but not so scrawny that they look undernourished." As if.

1 cup (2 sticks) unsalted butter, at room temperature

1/4 cup granulated sugar

1 teaspoon pure vanilla extract

2 cups cake flour (not self-rising)

1 cup chopped pecans

1/2 teaspoon fine sea salt

1/2 cup confectioners' sugar, for rolling

Preheat the oven to 300°F. Line a rimmed baking sheet with a silicone baking liner or parchment paper.

In the bowl of a heavy-duty mixer fitted with the paddle attachment, beat the butter, granulated sugar, and vanilla on medium speed until light and fluffy. Add the flour, pecans, and salt, beating on low speed after each addition until well blended. Using a small ice cream scoop, shape the dough into 1-inch balls. Place 1 1/2 inches apart on the prepared baking sheets.

Bake until the bottoms of the cookies are lightly browned, about 30 minutes. Transfer to a wire rack to cool slightly. While still warm, roll the cookies in the confectioners' sugar until evenly coated. Transfer to a wire rack set on top of a rimmed baking sheet to cool completely. Store in a tightly covered container at room temperature for up to 1 week.

Brilliant: Presentation
Shape into Tartlet Shells

The cookie melts in your mouth in a flood of sugared butter. A Brilliant addition to your dessert repertoire is to use the dough for a tartlet base.

Place about 1/4 cup dough in a 4-inch tartlet shell. Smooth the bottom and sides. Bake for 15 minutes until golden brown. Fill with Pastry Cream (page 21) or whipped cream and top with fruit. Serve immediately. Makes 12.

Mama's Pecan Tassies

MAKES 2 DOZEN

I've used the same pecan company, Pearson, for more than a decade. For many years, Mary Pearson and I never met, but we talked often on the phone. Funny thing is, she actually lives right down the street from my cousin. When we finally did meet, sweet Mary grabbed my cheeks and said, "You are real!"

These petite pies are a holiday staple and keep well in an airtight container for a week or so (pictured on page 232). To bring out their flavor after they've been in storage for a few days, simply pop them in a 350°F oven for a few minutes, and they will taste freshly baked.

Crust

1/2 cup (1 stick) unsalted butter, at room temperature

1 (3-ounce) package cream cheese, at room temperature

1 cup all-purpose flour

1/4 teaspoon fine sea salt

Filling

1 large egg

3/4 cup firmly packed dark brown sugar

1 tablespoon unsalted butter, melted

1/2 teaspoon pure vanilla extract

1/8 teaspoon fine sea salt

1/2 cup chopped pecans

2 dozen perfect pecan halves, for decoration

Preheat the oven to 350°F. Set out a nonstick mini muffin tin or grease a standard mini muffin tin.

To make the crust, in a heavy-duty mixer fitted with the paddle attachment, cream together the butter and cream cheese on medium speed until smooth. Add the flour and salt and continue to beat on low speed until a dough forms. Divide the dough equally into 24 balls, each about the size of a gumball. Press the balls of dough into the muffin cups, using your thumb to press the dough against the sides to form a shell. Set aside.

To make the filling, combine the egg, brown sugar, butter, vanilla, and salt in a bowl. Sprinkle 1/2 to 1 teaspoon nuts into each shell. Top with a teaspoon of the egg mixture. Place a pecan half in the center.

Bake for 15 minutes. Then decrease the temperature to 325°F and bake until set, 10 to 15 minutes more. Remove to a rack to cool.

Brilliant: Technique
Bourbon-Soaked Pecans

I generally like my bourbon in a glass with ice, but it does belong in the kitchen, as well. Smoky, sweet bourbon enhances the flavor of the rich, fatty pecans, taking a simple home-style holiday favorite to Brilliant.

Placet the pecans in a bowl, cover with 3/4 cup bourbon, and let soak for at least 30 minutes. Drain the bourbon-soaked pecans through a fine-mesh sieve, reserving the bourbon for another use. (See first sentence.) Preheat the oven to 350°F. Spread out the nuts in a single layer on a rimmed baking sheet and toast, shaking once or twice, until toasted and fragrant, about 5 minutes. Watch closely to avoid burning the nuts. Proceed with the recipe. Sip and savor.

Skillet Blondie

MAKES 1 (10-INCH) PAN

The flavor of this cookie resembles the taste of a Snickers bar—even without the caramel, and especially so when you follow my chef-inspired Brilliant suggestion to refrigerate the dough. If you do want to use caramels, I suggest using the old-fashioned Brach's caramels. Unwrapping the caramels is a perfect job for the kids while you are measuring out the ingredients. When I was a little girl, my grandfather always had a pocketful of caramels or peppermint candy. We played a game where he put one in his closed palm. Holding out both hands he said, "Jack in the bush." My sister and I squealed and giggled, "Cut 'em down!" He then asked, "How many licks?" I replied, "One," tapping the hand I thought contained my sweet prize. Of course, my sweet, doting grandfather always gave his grandchildren the prize whether we guessed correctly, or not.

My first forays into baking, like many aspiring young chefs, involved chocolate chip cookies. This blondie is essential a big chocolate chip cookie. If you don't have a cast-iron skillet, run out and get one. No, seriously, you can use an 8-inch square pan, but you still do need to own a cast-iron skillet.

1 1/2 cups all-purpose flour

1/2 teaspoon baking soda

1/2 teaspoon fine sea salt

1/4 teaspoon baking powder

1/2 cup (1 stick) unsalted butter

1 cup firmly packed dark brown sugar

1 teaspoon pure vanilla extract

1 large egg, lightly beaten

1 cup semisweet chocolate chips

1/2 cup unsalted peanuts, chopped

15 caramel candies, halved (optional)

Preheat the oven to 350°F.

Whisk together the flour, baking soda, salt, and baking powder in a bowl.

Heat the butter in a 10-inch cast-iron skillet over low heat. Add the brown sugar, stirring until dissolved.

Add the butter mixture to the flour mixture. Add the vanilla and egg. Fold in the chocolate chips, peanuts, and caramels. Transfer the batter to the buttery skillet, smoothing the surface with a spatula.

Bake until a cake tester inserted into the center comes out clean, 20 to 25 minutes. Place on a wire rack to cool. Slice while still slightly warm.

Brilliant: Technique
Chill, Baby

This may seem ridiculous for a dump-and-stir chocolate chip bar cookie, but covering and chilling the dough in the refrigerator for a minimum of 24 hours, and preferably 36 hours, allows the dough and other ingredients to fully soak up the liquid of the eggs. A long hydration time is important for two reasons. Eggs, unlike water, are gelatinous and slow moving, and the butter coats the flour, deterring the absorption. Giving the cookie dough a resting time in the refrigerator solves those problems. The result is a cookie richer with the flavors of toffee and caramel.

Claire's Dark Chocolate Cake

MAKES 3 (8-INCH) ROUND LAYERS

My dear friend Claire is a very talented cook and pastry chef. Our friendship took root in the hours commuting to Connecticut where she was my supervisor when we worked for Martha Stewart. She is strong minded, direct, to the point, and was a fierce boss at times, but quickly became one of the people in my life I love most. Looking for shells on the beach with Claire and her precious daughter, Ruby, is one of my favorite activities. Whenever I visit her in South Florida, I plead with her to make me this cake.

Claire and I have an "escape route." We've always said that if life becomes too absurd, we'll just move to France, open a BBQ joint, and call it Ruby-Doo BBQ. I'll tend the pit, and she'll make this dark chocolate cake to serve with milk and fried pies. Personally, I think the idea of a French BBQ joint is wonderfully absurd enough to work, and that, in a nutshell, is our business plan.

This amount of batter will also make a 13 x 18-inch sheet cake.

1 tablespoon unsalted butter, at room temperature, for the pans

1 1/2 cups unsweetened cocoa powder, plus more for the pans

3 cups all-purpose flour

3 cups sugar

1 tablespoon baking soda

1 1/2 teaspoons baking powder

1 1/2 teaspoons fine sea salt

1/2 teaspoon ground ginger

3 large eggs

1 1/2 cups warm water

1 1/2 cups buttermilk

3/4 cup canola oil

1 1/2 teaspoons pure vanilla extract

Chocolate Ganache Frosting (recipe follows)

Preheat the oven to 350°F. Butter a 13 x 18-inch sheet cake pan or three 8-inch round or square cake pans. Line the bottoms with parchment paper, butter the parchment, and dust with cocoa.

Combine the cocoa powder, flour, sugar, baking soda, baking powder, salt, and ginger in the bowl of a heavy-duty mixer fitted with the paddle attachment. Give it a turn or two with the paddle to mix and combine. Then, with the mixer on low speed, add the eggs, water, buttermilk, oil, and vanilla. Beat on low speed until smooth, stopping and scraping down the sides of the bowl once or twice. Divide the batter among the prepared pan(s).

Bake, rotating the pans once, until a tester inserted into the center comes out clean, 25 minutes for the baking sheet, 35 to 45 minutes for 8-inch layers. Remove to racks to cool, about 20 minutes. For cake rounds, once partially cooled, invert and lift off the pans, turn right side up on the rack, and let cool completely.

To make a layer cake, when you are ready to frost, place the first layer on a cake stand. Using a long serrated knife, trim the top off the cake layer to make a flat surface. Set the layer aside. Repeat with the second layer. Using a small offset spatula, evenly cover the top of the first layer with 1 cup of the frosting. Spread the frosting so that it extends beyond the edges of the layer. Place the second cake layer, cut side down, on top of the frosting; press to make it level. Cover with 1 cup of the frosting. Top with the third cake layer. With the small offset spatula, spread the entire cake with about 1 1/2 cups of the frosting, creating a "crumb coat," a thin layer that seals in the crumbs. Refrigerate until firm, about 15 minutes. Then, using a clean offset spatula, generously coat the chilled cake with the remaining frosting. Store in an airtight container in the refrigerator up to 3 days.

Chocolate Ganache Frosting

MAKES 6 CUPS

12 ounces best-quality semisweet chocolate, finely chopped

12 ounces best-quality bittersweet chocolate, finely chopped

3 cups heavy cream

1 teaspoon pure vanilla extract

1/4 teaspoon fine sea salt

Combine the chocolates in a large bowl. Heat the cream in a heavy saucepan over medium-high heat until simmering and small bubbles appear at the edge of the saucepan. Add the vanilla and salt. Stir to combine. Pour over the chocolate and let sit for 3 minutes. Using a spatula, stir until completely smooth. Transfer to the refrigerator and chill, stirring every 20 minutes, until cool enough to spread, about 2 hours.

Brilliant Technique
Freezing Cake Layers

Freezing cake layers is a simple but Brilliant technique for sealing in moisture and tightening the cake's crumb. Bakers swear by it. This creates an easier surface to frost and prevents a lot of crumbs from forming. Crumbs in icing will quickly ruin the overall look of a cake. Once the cake rounds have cooled completely on the wire rack, wrap them tightly in plastic film. Freeze until completely firm, several hours or up to overnight.

Bittersweet Chocolate Bread Pudding

SERVES 8 TO 10

You know how the world is divided into two camps? People who like chocolate and people who don't? I am firmly in the likes chocolate camp. I am not so much a dessert person as a chocolate person. Menu planning is more involved than just assembling a collection of dishes that taste good. They have to taste good together. This rich, decadent, over-the-top dessert is best after a full-flavored dinner. It would be a perfect ending to a meal with the Garlic-Stuffed Prime Rib Roast (page 140) or the Pork Belly with French Market Red-Eye Gravy (page 147), two main courses that need something substantial to end the meal.

2 tablespoons unsalted butter, cut into small pieces, plus more for the pan

3 baguettes, sliced 1/2 inch thick and halved crosswise

1 1/2 cups whole milk

1 1/2 cups heavy cream

1/2 cup sugar

1/2 teaspoon fine sea salt

10 ounces best-quality bittersweet chocolate, finely chopped

1 teaspoon pure vanilla extract

1/4 teaspoon ground cinnamon

6 large eggs

Whipped cream, vanilla ice cream, or crème fraîche (page 16), for serving

Preheat the oven to 325°F. Generously butter a large baking dish.

Place the bread in the prepared baking dish. Set aside.

Combine the milk, cream, sugar, and salt in a saucepan over medium-low heat. Cook, stirring occasionally, until the sugar is dissolved; do not allow it to boil. Remove from the heat and add the chocolate, vanilla, and cinnamon; whisk until smooth.

Whisk the eggs in a large bowl. Slowly whisk in the chocolate mixture until combined. Pour the mixture over the bread and let soak at room temperature for 1 hour, pressing down on the bread occasionally. Distribute the butter evenly over the soaked bread.

Place the baking dish in a roasting pan. Pour in enough hot water to reach halfway up the sides of the dish. Bake until the center is just set, about 50 minutes. Transfer to a wire rack to cool slightly. Serve warm with a dollop of whipped cream.

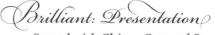

Brilliant: Presentation
Served with Chèvre Caramel Sauce

The intense bittersweet chocolate in the pudding is matched in intensity with rich Caramel Sauce made with fresh goat cheese (page 22).

Make the sauce, using goat cheese instead of cream. Spoon the warm bread pudding onto warmed serving plates. Top with vanilla ice cream and drizzle some sauce over the top. It's over-the-top Brilliant.

Cream of the Crop

Cream is the layer of butterfat that rises to the top of milk before homogenization. There has to be a certain amount of fat present for cream to whip. Some substitutions can be made in cooking, even baking, but without some kind of stabilizer, a dairy product with less than 30 percent butterfat will not whip.

Half-and-half: 10.5 to 18 percent fat

Light, coffee, or table cream: 18 to 30 percent fat

Medium cream: 25 percent fat

Whipping or light whipping cream: 30 to 36 percent fat

Heavy whipping cream: 36 percent fat or more

Extra-heavy, double, or manufacturer's cream: 38 to 40 percent fat or more. Available in specialty stores and gourmet markets.

Anne's Cornmeal Cake

MAKES 1 (8-INCH) CAKE

The original version of this recipe was in Anne Willan's *Cooking with Wine*. It's made in a food processor, which makes for a very simple "dump and stir" cake. Another benefit is that it is amazingly moist and will last for several days tightly wrapped in plastic wrap.

There's something autumnal about this cake—perhaps it is the rich golden brown color. I like to serve a wedge of this cake with a slice of pear and drizzle the yogurt with honey.

1¹/2 cups all-purpose flour

1 cup sugar

3/4 cup medium-grind yellow cornmeal

3/4 cup pecan halves

Finely grated zest of 2 lemons

4 teaspoons baking powder

1/2 teaspoon fine sea salt

1/2 cup (1 stick) butter, chilled and cut into pieces, plus
    more for the cake pan

2 large eggs, lightly beaten

1 cup dry white wine

1 cup low-fat or whole-milk plain Greek-style yogurt,
    for serving

Preheat the oven to 350°F. Generously butter an 8-inch round cake pan. Set aside.

In a food processor fitted with a metal blade, combine the flour, sugar, cornmeal, pecans, zest of 1 lemon, baking powder, and salt. Pulse to combine. Add the butter and pulse until the mixture forms crumbs that start to clump together, about 30 seconds. Add the eggs and wine and pulse just until smooth. Pour the batter into the prepared cake pan.

Bake until the cake starts to shrink from the sides of the pan and springs back when lightly pressed in the center with a fingertip, about 45 minutes.

Transfer to a wire rack to cool slightly for about 10 minutes, then turn out onto a wire rack to cool completely. Meanwhile, combine the yogurt and the remaining lemon zest and set aside. Serve the cake warm or at room temperature, garnished with the yogurt.

Brilliant Technique
Candied Zest

A garnish of candied lemon zest elevates this cake to Brilliant and echoes the zest in the batter and in the lemony yogurt dollop.

Line a rimmed baking sheet with a silicone baking liner or waxed paper. Set aside. Use a sharp vegetable peeler to remove the zest from 2 lemons, reserving the fruit for another use. Using a small paring knife, scrape off the bitter white pith and discard. Cut the peel into 1/4 x 3-inch strips. Meanwhile, bring a small pot of water to a boil over high heat. Add the zest and cook for 2 minutes. Drain. In the same saucepan, combine 1/4 cup sugar and 2 tablespoons water and bring to a boil over medium heat, stirring constantly until the sugar dissolves. Add the blanched zest, cover, decrease the heat, and simmer for 3 minutes. Remove from the heat; cool completely. Strain through a fine-mesh sieve; discard the syrup. Separate the pieces of zest and allow to dry on the prepared baking sheet. Sprinkle over 1/4 cup sugar and, using your fingers, toss well to coat. Use as a garnish for the lemon yogurt. Keeps for up to 2 days in an airtight container.

Dede's Burnt Caramel Cake

MAKES 3 (9-INCH) ROUND LAYERS

Dede's diminutive nickname was not indicative of his size; he was an absolute mountain of a man. Tall and with broad shoulders and massive trunks for arms, he was very handsome in his youth. I know he swept my grandmother off her feet with his dark hair and sapphire blue eyes. She was a college-educated Southern lady and he was a country boy with a limited education. His larger-than-life physical presence commanded respect. In truth, he was a gentle giant who experienced only one fight in his entire life. He cried at the sound of an organ playing or the moving piano chords of a well-played hymn. He loved this caramel cake and sat in the kitchen with Meme as she baked it, then whipped the icing for her by hand.

Dede was the father of three girls, and my mother was his baby girl. He had his own unique sort of language, a potpourri of nicknames and personal colloquialisms. His wife, Meme, was referred to as "Beloved." Mama's special nickname was "Frazz Horn." She was spoiled absolutely rotten by him, as were we. This manly man lavished attention on his brood of women and always said he never wanted sons, scoffing, "Boys are nothing but trouble."

1 cup (2 sticks) unsalted butter, at room temperature, plus more for the pans

3 cups all-purpose flour, plus more for the pans

1 teaspoon baking powder

2 cups sugar

4 large eggs, at room temperature, well beaten

1 cup whole milk

1 teaspoon pure vanilla extract

Burnt Caramel Icing (recipe follows)

Preheat the oven to 350°F. Butter and flour three 9-inch round cake pans and line the bottoms with waxed or parchment paper. Butter and flour the paper. Sift together the flour and the baking powder.

In the bowl of a heavy-duty mixer fitted with the paddle attachment, cream the butter and sugar on medium speed until light and fluffy, about 3 minutes. Add the flour mixture to the butter-sugar mixture, alternating between the dry and wet ingredients in three portions, starting and ending with the dry ingredients. Pour into the prepared pans.

Bake until a cake tester inserted into the center of each cake comes out clean and the cakes start pulling away from the sides of the pans, about 25 minutes. Remove to a rack to cool slightly. Invert onto the rack to cool completely.

To assemble the cake, place one cake layer on a cardboard cake round. Spread with the still-warm frosting. Repeat with remaining layers, placing the final layer bottom side up. Working quickly, use a small offset spatula to spread the icing gently around the cake. Let stand for 2 hours to allow the icing to set before serving. Store in an airtight container for up to 1 week.

Burnt Caramel Icing

MAKES ABOUT 2 CUPS

2 1/2 cups sugar

1/2 cup (1 stick) unsalted butter

1 cup heavy cream, plus more if needed to loosen

2 teaspoons pure vanilla extract

1/4 teaspoon fine sea salt

In a heavy cast-iron skillet, heat 1/2 cup of the sugar over medium-high heat. Stir until dissolved, then do not stir again; simply shake the pan occasionally until the mixture reaches the caramel stage 320°F to 335°F on a candy thermometer.

Meanwhile, in a heavy saucepan, combine the remaining 2 cups sugar, the butter, and the cream Bring to a boil, stirring occasionally.

CONTINUED

When the sugar reaches the caramel stage, immediately pour it into the cream mixture and stir to combine. Cook over medium heat, stirring once or twice, until the mixture reaches the soft-ball stage, 232°F to 240°F. Remove from the heat; add the vanilla and salt and stir to combine. Place on a rack and set aside until just cool enough to touch, 10 to 15 minutes.

Transfer the mixture to the bowl of a heavy-duty mixer fitted with the whisk attachment. Beat on high speed until creamy, 5 to 7 minutes.

I'll be honest, this icing is a bear. That's why caramel cakes are so special. A couple of helpful hints: when you are ready to frost the cake, place the bowl of icing in a bowl of warm water to keep it loose and fluid. Also, if it starts to set too firmly, you may need to add warm heavy cream to loosen it. That, holding your tongue right, and practice are the keys to a successful caramel frosting.

Brilliant: Short Recipe
Apple Hazelnut Compote

Claire helped me come up with this sophisticated addition to the quintessential Southern dessert. I wanted to accompany the very sweet cake with a savory apple mixture. She took it one step further by inserting the apple mixture between the layers. A Brilliant idea that only a French-trained pastry chef would do. You have permission to serve it on the side.

Heat 2 tablespoons unsalted butter in a large skillet. Add 2 small Granny Smith apples, cored and diced. Sprinkle over 1 tablespoon sugar. Cook until just tender, about 5 minutes. Add 1 cup hazelnuts, toasted and skins removed (page 58), then chopped, and 1 teaspoon finely chopped fresh rosemary. Season with 1 teaspoon fleur de sel or coarse salt. Stir to combine. When assembling the cake, spread 1 cup Apple Hazelnut Compote between the layers. Once the cake is fully decorated, garnish the top with 8 whole hazelnuts and tiny rosemary sprigs.

❧ Coca-Cola Cake

MAKES 1 (9 X 13-INCH) CAKE

We didn't grow up drinking soft drinks, but Mama made this cake for family gatherings and special occasions. Southern sweet tea famously has its place, but occasionally only the "pause that refreshes" will do. To my mind, there is nothing better than an ice-cold Coke Classic served in the iconic little six-ounce bottle. That quick *pssst* when the bottle top is pried from the lid, the crackling of the bubbles, and best yet? The icy slush that forms in the neck of the bottle when it's superchilled? Heaven. Some crazy Southerner thought it would be good in a cake, too.

Cake

½ cup (1 stick) unsalted butter, plus more for the pan

2 cups granulated sugar

2 cups all-purpose flour

3 tablespoons unsweetened cocoa powder

1 cup Coca-Cola

1 teaspoon baking soda

½ cup buttermilk

2 large eggs

1 teaspoon pure vanilla extract

Frosting

1 (16-ounce) box confectioners' sugar

½ cup (1 stick) unsalted butter

3 tablespoons unsweetened cocoa powder

¼ cup Coca-Cola

1 teaspoon pure vanilla extract

1 cup chopped pecans

Preheat the oven to 350°F. Butter a 9 x 13-inch glass baking dish.

To make the cake, in a bowl, sift together the granulated sugar and flour.

In a saucepan, combine the butter, cocoa, and Coca-Cola. Bring to a boil over medium-high heat. Pour over the dry ingredients; stir to combine. Combine the baking soda and buttermilk in a liquid measuring cup. Add the buttermilk mixture, eggs, and vanilla to the flour mixture and stir to combine. Pour into the prepared pan.

Bake until a cake tester inserted into the center comes out clean, about 35 minutes.

Meanwhile, prepare the icing. (It needs to go onto a still-warm cake.) Sift the confectioners' sugar into a large bowl. Combine the butter, cocoa, and Coca-Cola in a heavy saucepan. Bring to a boil, then pour over the sifted sugar. Stir to combine, then stir in the vanilla and pecans. Spread over the warm cake. Set aside to cool completely. When cool, cut into squares and serve.

Brilliant: Short Recipe
Coca-Cola Cupcakes
with Toasted Meringue

Some recipes for this cake contain miniature marshmallows. I abhor store-bought marshmallows and think they are far too sweet for this cake. However, I couldn't resist the Brilliant idea of a toasted topping of Seven-Minute Frosting.

Line 20 standard muffin cups with paper liners. Prepare the Coca-Cola cake and frosting. Divide the batter evenly among the lined cups, filling each cup three-quarters full. Bake, rotating the tins halfway through, until a cake tester inserted into the center of a cupcake comes out clean, about 25 minutes. Remove the muffin tins to a rack to cool slightly, then remove the individial cupcakes to the rack to cool completely. Meanwhile, prepare the Seven-Minute Frosting. Combine 1½ cups sugar with ⅔ cup water and 2 tablespoons light corn syrup in a small saucepan; clip a candy thermometer to side of the pan. Bring to a boil over medium heat, stirring occasionally until

CONTINUED

Coca-Cola Cake, *continued*

the sugar dissolves. Continue boiling, without stirring, until the syrup reaches 230°F. In the bowl of a heavy-duty mixer fitted with the whisk attachment, whip 6 large egg whites on medium-high speed until soft peaks form. With the mixer running, add 2 tablespoons sugar, beating to combine. As soon as the syrup reaches 230°F, remove from the heat. With the mixer on medium-low speed, pour the syrup down the side of the bowl in a slow, steady stream. Increase the speed to medium-high; whisk until the mixture is completely cool (test by touching the bottom of the bowl) and stiff peaks form, about 7 minutes.

Spoon the frosting into a pastry bag fitted with a large open-star tip. Pipe the frosting onto each cupcake, swirling the tip slightly and releasing as you pull up to form a peak. Hold a small kitchen blowtorch about 4 inches from the surface of the frosting and wave it back and forth until the frosting is lightly browned, like a toasted marshmallow. Serve immediately. Makes about 20 cupcakes.

Pineapple Upside-Down Cake

MAKES 1 (10¹/2-INCH) CAKE

My dear friend, the lovely and talented Angie Mosier, is an amazing baker, writer, and teacher. As a food and prop stylist, her phenomenal simple, clean, and refined sense of style shines through. But for all her fancy pedigree, Angie is the absolute "salt of the earth," with an intelligent and inspiring relationship with food. She gets it.

Angie has a very egalitarian view of the upside-down cake, and has expressed appreciation for the canned yellow fruit and garishly red maraschino cherries. Admittedly, my recipe is prissy, maybe even somewhat elitist, using fresh pineapple and dried cherries and topped with boozy whipped cream. You know, I don't think Angie would disapprove. She would simply reach into her cupboard for the absolutely perfect plate.

1 pineapple (about 3¹/2 pounds), peeled and left uncored

1 cup cake flour (not self-rising)

3/4 teaspoon baking powder

1/4 teaspoon baking soda

1¹/4 cups granulated sugar

3/4 cup (1¹/2 sticks) unsalted butter, at room temperature

1/2 cup firmly packed light brown sugar

1 vanilla bean, split and scraped, or 1 tablespoon pure
    vanilla extract

2 large eggs

1/2 cup sour cream

Whipped cream, for serving

Preheat the oven to 350°F. Line a baking sheet with a silicone baking liner or parchment paper.

Using a wide mandoline or a chef's knife, slice the pineapple as thinly as possible. Set aside.

Sift together the flour, baking powder, and baking soda.

Heat ¹/2 cup of the granulated sugar in a 10-inch cast-iron skillet. Cook until deep amber, about 5 minutes. Remove the pan from the heat. Add ¹/4 cup of the butter, stirring vigorously with a wooden spoon. Spread the caramel evenly over the bottom of the skillet, and sprinkle with the brown sugar.

Center 1 pineapple slice in the skillet. Place pineapple slices around it in a tightly overlapping circle. Layer a second circle, completely covering the bottom and at least halfway up the sides. Place a final slice in the center of the skillet.

In a heavy-duty mixer fitted with the paddle attachment, cream the remaining ¹/2 cup butter, remaining 3/4 cup granulated sugar, and the vanilla. Add the eggs one at a time, mixing well after each addition, and the sour cream. Slowly add the sifted flour, scraping down the sides of the bowl with a rubber spatula as needed. Pour the batter into the pineapple-lined skillet.

Place the skillet on the prepared baking sheet and transfer the baking sheet to the oven. Bake until golden brown and a cake tester inserted into the center comes out clean, about 45 minutes.

Remove from the oven and pour the excess liquid from the skillet into a measuring cup. Carefully invert the cake onto large plate and drizzle the reserved liquid over the top. Set aside to cool slightly. Using a serrated knife, cut into wedges and place on serving plates. Top with the whipped cream and serve.

Brilliant: Short Recipe
Dark Rum Crème Anglaise

Adding some rum to crème anglaise adapts it Brilliantly to the Pineapple Upside-Down Cake.

Prepare the Basic Crème Anglaise (page 20). Add 2 tablespoons dark rum. Stir to combine. Makes about 2 cups. Spoon ¹/4 cup of the Dark Rum Crème Anglaise onto chilled serving plates. Top with a wedge of the cake. Serve immediately.

Old-Fashioned Lemon Meringue Pie

MAKES 1 (8-INCH) PIE

One of my worst mistakes in the kitchen involved lemon filling. My boss requested several quarts of lemon curd. At the time I had never had lemon curd; all I knew was lemon meringue pie. So, I looked up the recipe for lemon filling, whipped up a batch, and packed it up for her weekend party. Monday rolled around, and my head almost rolled, too. Lemon curd is a lemon-flavored custard thickened only with eggs and butter. Lemon pie filling has cornstarch and, it seems, was completely unacceptable. Believe me, I got on top of that one so as not to make that mistake again. No mistake about it, you'll love this Old-Fashioned Lemon Meringue Pie.

This intensely lemon-flavored filling is balanced by a heaping mountain of sweet meringue.

6 large egg yolks

Finely grated zest of 1 lemon

Juice of 4 to 6 lemons (1/2 cup)

1 1/2 cups sugar

4 teaspoons cornstarch

3 large egg whites

French Pie Crust (page 16), blind baked and cooled

Whisk together the egg yolks, lemon zest, lemon juice, 1 cup of the sugar, and cornstarch in a saucepan. Place over medium heat and bring to a boil. Cook, whisking constantly, until thick, about 5 minutes.

Pour the mixture into a baked and cooled pie shell. Refrigerate until firm and set, at least 45 minutes and up to 2 hours; any longer and the crust will become too soggy.

To brown the pie in the oven, preheat the oven to 350°F. Put the whites in the bowl of a heavy-duty mixer fitted with the whisk attachment. Beat on high speed until frothy. With the mixer on high speed, add the remaining 1/2 cup sugar in a slow, steady stream and beat until stiff peaks form, 3 to 5 minutes.

Remove the pie from the refrigerator and top with meringue, covering the entire surface. Transfer to the oven and bake until browned, 3 to 5 minutes. Alternatively, hold a small kitchen blowtorch about 4 inches from the surface of the pie and wave it back and forth until the meringue is lightly browned. Serve immediately.

Brilliant: Short Recipe
Lemon Ice

Old-Fashioned Lemon Meringue Pie is a diner-worthy Basic; serve it with a scoop of lemon ice on the side, and you have white-tablecloth-restaurant Brilliant.

In a saucepan, combine 1 cup sugar, 1/2 cup light corn syrup, and 2 1/2 cups water; bring to a boil over medium-high heat. Cook until the sugar completely dissolves, about 2 minutes. Remove from the heat; add 1 cup freshly squeezed lemon juice. Pour the mixture into a bowl; chill over an ice bath or overnight in the refrigerator. Freeze the mixture in an ice cream maker according to the manufacturer's directions. Makes 1 quart. Store in an airtight container in the freezer for up to 1 month.

Country Apple Tart

SERVES 8

Simple free-form tarts can be as beautiful as the finest carefully prepared pastry. I love using pâte sucrée, *essentially a sugar cookie dough, in this recipe. It will crack and break while you are working with it, but it's really like modeling clay in that you can just pinch it back together.*

La Varenne Sweet Pie Pastry (page 17)

1 1/2 pounds Granny Smith apples (about 5)

1/3 cup sugar, plus more for sprinkling

Juice of 1/2 lemon

1 tablespoon all-purpose flour

Pinch of fine sea salt

1/2 cup unsweetened applesauce

1/4 cup Calvados, applejack, bourbon, or Cognac

1 tablespoon unsalted butter, chilled and cut into
  small pieces

1 tablespoon cold water, for brushing

1 cup heavy cream, chilled

On a silicone baking liner or parchment paper, roll out the pastry to 1/4 inch thick. Transfer to a baking sheet. If it cracks or breaks, simply pinch the dough to seal. Cover loosely with plastic wrap and refrigerate until firm, about 30 minutes.

While the pastry is chilling, peel and core apples, then cut into 1/8-inch slices. Toss the slices with the sugar, lemon juice, flour, and salt. Set aside. Combine the applesauce with 2 tablespoons of the Calvados. Set aside.

Preheat the oven to 425°F.

Place the baking sheet with the chilled pastry on a clean work surface. Spread the applesauce over the pastry, leaving a 2-inch border. Top the applesauce with the sliced apples, mounding them slightly. Fold the edges of dough over, partially covering the apples, and leaving the center uncovered. If the pastry cracks or breaks, simply pinch the dough to seal. Dot the apples with the butter. Brush the edge of the pastry with water and sprinkle with sugar.

Bake until the pastry is golden brown and the apples are tender, 40 to 45 minutes. Let cool on a rack to warm or room temperature.

Just before serving, beat the cream in a chilled bowl over ice using an electric mixer or chilled whisk until the cream holds soft peaks. Add the remaining 2 tablespoons Calvados and beat until incorporated. Slice the tart and serve the slices topped with dollops of the cream.

Brilliant: Short Recipe
Apple Chips

Release your inner pastry chef. Garnishing the Basic Country Apple Tart with oven-dried apple chips is Brilliant.

Preheat the oven to 200°F. Line 2 baking sheets with silicone baking liners; set aside. Using a chef's knife, cut off the bottoms of 2 apples. Using a mandoline, thinly slice the whole apples (with the seeds), making sure each slice is uniform in thickness. Place the apple slices in a single layer on the prepared baking sheets. Sift 2 tablespoons confectioners' sugar over the apple slices. Bake for 1 hour; then rotate the pans top and bottom. Continue baking until the apples are dry and crisp, 45 to 60 minutes. Transfer to a wire rack to cool. Store in an airtight container for up to 2 days.

Michele's Quick and Easy Fudge

MAKES 1 (8-INCH) SQUARE

Who doesn't like fudge? And, better yet, what busy cook doesn't like a Basic dump-and-stir candy made from essential pantry ingredients, with no candy thermometer required? Sign me up. This fudge will do duty for a school bake sale, is great to have around on for a family gathering or tailgating weekend, and, when Brilliant, is suitable for a grown-up supper club (pictured on page 232).

1 cup unsalted butter (1 stick) more for the pan

1/2 teaspoon fine sea salt

1 (16-ounce) box confectioners' sugar, sifted

1/4 cup low-fat or whole milk

1/2 cup unsweetened cocoa powder

1/2 cup chopped walnuts, peanuts, or pecans, toasted (see page 58)

1 teaspoon pure vanilla extract

Brush an 8-inch square baking dish with butter.

Melt the butter with the salt in a heavy saucepan over low heat. Whisk in the confectioners' sugar and milk until very smooth. Add the cocoa; stir until combined and remove from the heat. Add the walnuts and vanilla; stir until combined. The fudge will have a very smooth, shiny texture.

Spoon the fudge into the prepared dish. Transfer to the refrigerator until set, at least 2 hours. Or, if you just can't wait, slip it in the freezer. Run a knife around the edge of the pan and invert the firm block of fudge onto a clean work surface. Using a long utility knife, slice into $1^1/_3$-inch cubes. Heat the knife in hot water and pat dry before each cut for the smoothest slices. Store in an airtight container at room temperature for up to 1 week.

Brilliant: Presentation
Fudge-pops

Basic chocolate fudge is always welcome, but make it a fudge pop and it's Brilliant. Before the mixture has fully set, score the surface to make $1^1/_3$-inch-size pieces. Insert a wooden skewer (or a peppermint stick during the holidays) into the center of each square. Carefully cut into cubes. Refrigerate to set. Place 1 cup finely chopped nuts or crushed peppermint candy in a bowl. Firmly press each side of the block in the topping to coat. Makes about 3 dozen pieces.

Nut Brittle

In the South, peanuts are traditionally used for making brittle for gift giving at the holidays. Mama always has a tin on hand for company. Try a health-food store or grocery store with a robust health-food section for the raw nuts. I prefer using raw nuts because the nuts toast in the hot sugar; dry-roasted nuts can become too dark and taste burnt in the final brittle.

2 cups sugar

1 cup light corn syrup

1/2 cup cold water, plus more for brushing the pan

Pinch of fine sea salt

3 cups unsalted raw peanuts (Spanish or blanched), cashews, almonds, or macadamia nuts, or a combination of nuts, coarsely chopped

1 tablespoon unsalted butter, at room temperature, plus more for the baking sheet

1 teaspoon pure vanilla extract

1 teaspoon baking soda

Butter a rimmed baking sheet or marble slab, or line a rimmed baking sheet with a silicone baking liner.

In a heavy saucepan, combine the sugar, corn syrup, water, and salt and bring to a boil over medium-high heat, stirring until sugar has dissolved. Continue cooking, without stirring, until the mixture reaches the hard-ball stage on a candy thermometer (250°F to 266°F; see page 23) swirling the pan occasionally; wash down sides of pan with a pastry brush dipped in water to prevent crystals from forming. Stir in the nuts and continue cooking, stirring frequently to prevent the nuts from burning, until the mixture is light amber and the nuts are golden brown, about 5 minutes.

Remove the pan from the heat; stir in the remaining 1 tablespoon butter and the vanilla. Carefully stir in the baking soda; the mixture will foam up in the pan. As soon as it is combined, pour it onto the prepared baking sheet or marble slab.

Using an oiled offset spatula, quickly spread into an even layer about 1/2 inch thick. Slip the oiled spatula under the hot candy to loosen the edges and bottom. Let stand until completely cool, 45 to 60 minutes.

Break the brittle into large pieces, and layer between pieces of waxed paper in an airtight container. Store at room temperature up to 1 month.

Brilliant: Short Recipe
Chocolate-Dipped Nut Brittle

Line a baking sheet with waxed paper. Combine 6 ounces semisweet chocolate chips and 1 tablespoon vegetable shortening, in a microwave-safe bowl. Microwave, uncovered, on medium-high for about 1 minute. Remove and stir with a rubber spatula. Some chips may not have melted, so microwave again in 10-second intervals, stirring after each interval, until the chocolate and shortening are smooth and just melted. Let cool slightly. Dip the cooled brittle in the melted chocolate and shake off the excess. Sprinkle with additional chopped nuts, if desired. Place on the prepared baking sheet. Refrigerate until set.

Candy-Making Tips

- Have all the ingredients for your recipe measured and ready to go. Candy making requires that you react quickly. You do not have time to measure ingredients between steps.
- Make sure the kids know sugar mixtures are hot and can be dangerous. Candy is best made by older children.
- Wear oven mitts and a long-sleeve shirt.
- Use a large, sturdy pot or pan that won't overflow. If you think it might not be big enough, use a larger one.

- Keep a metal bowl of ice water on hand to plunge your hand into if caramelized sugar drips on it.
- The bowl of ice water also can be used for dipping the bottom of the saucepan to stop the cooking.
- Remove the saucepan of cooking candy when the candy thermometer registers at least 2°F below the temperature specified in the recipe. The temperature will continue to rise a little.
- To dissolve the sugar for easy cleanup, as soon as you've spooned the brittle out of the saucepan, fill the pan with hot water and return it to the stovetop over low heat with the spoon and thermometer.

Handwritten (top margin):
½"S + ...
½
2 egg plain
spoon plain
fork 375

Pecan Pie
3 egg
2 t butter ½ t salt
2 T flour ½ c sugar
½ t van 1 T Karo wh...
½ t 2 c nuts
10 min 425 + ... min

3 c
3/4 c
33/4
3 t
5 ...

Handwritten (left card, top):
3 c sugar ½ ...
3/4 BD ...
6 egg one at the ½ t P.C.
salt 2 egg 3 c flour Plain
1 tsp vin 3/4 salt ½ ...
½ soda 325 - 1½
Pound Cake

MUFFINS (clipping, upper left):
2 eggs
1 cup milk
4 tbs melted butter
2 tbs sugar
1½ cups *flour
2½ tsp baking powder
½ tsp salt

Beat eggs and milk, add sugar and
melted butter. Mix baking powder and
salt with flour, add to above. Mix but
do not overbeat. Bake in greased muffin tins 20 minutes in 450° oven.
Makes 12 Muffins.
*Flour: Muffin Master
For Highest Need of
Whole Wheat Flour

Quick Batter Rolls

2 packages active dry
yeast
1¼ cups warm water
3 tablespoons sugar
1 teaspoon salt
½ cup shortening
1 egg, beaten
3½ cups unsifted
flour

Soften yeast in water; stir until dissolved. Add sugar, salt,
shortening, egg and ½ the flour. Stir to combine ingredients, then beat vigorously 2 minutes. Blend in remaining
flour and beat well. Scrape batter down from sides of
bowl. Cover; let rise until doubled. Stir down batter.
Using large spoon, fill greased 2½-inch muffin cups ⅔ full.
Cover and let rise until almost doubled. Bake in 400° GAS
oven 10 to 15 minutes. Makes 1½ to 2 dozen rolls.

Handwritten (middle card):
1¼ C (cake flour)
½ c sugar) sift together
1½ C (12) egg whites beat
with ¼ tsp salt + 1¼ cream of T
1 tsp vin 1⅓ C sugar B. 350 30 mi

3 c flour 12 egg yolks
3 tsp B.P. 1 c hot water
1 t salt 2 c sugar
350°

SHORTCUT PAN ROLLS
Makes 3 dozen rolls
1 cup Quaker Instant Grits
½ cup sugar
1 tablespoon salt
2 cups hot water
⅓ cup vegetable oil
6 to 6½ cups sifted all-
purpose flour
2 pkg. dry yeast

Combine instant grits, sugar and salt in large bowl of mixer.
Add water, oil and 2 cups of the flour. Beat 2 minutes on low
speed. Add 1 cup additional flour and yeast. Beat 1 minute on
low speed. Stir in enough additional flour to mal...

...n on well floured board or canvas. Knead until
...c, about 10 minutes.
...ough in half. Shape e...
...8-inch round cake...
...until nearly double it...
...00° 30 to 35 minutes...
...brush with butter.

BUTTERMILK CORN BREAD
1 cup all-purpose flour
4 tablespoons SACO Buttermilk Powder
1½ teaspoons baking powder
½ teaspoon soda
2 tablespoons sugar
1 teaspoon salt
1 cup corn meal
2 tablespoons shortening
2 eggs, slightly beaten
1 cup water

Sift flour, SACO Buttermilk Powder, baking powder,
soda, sugar and salt into a mixing bowl. Add corn
meal. Cut in shortening with a fork until mixture is
like textured. Combine eggs and water and add to dry
ingredients. Stir just enough to moisten dry
ingredients. **Do not beat.** Pour into a well-greased
8 × 8 × 2-inch pan. Bake at 425°F for 25 to 30
minutes. Serve hot.

*For a crumbly, flakier corn-bread use 1¼ cups corn
meal and only ¾ cup of all-purpose flour. Proceed
as above.

BUTTERMILK PANCAKES
4 tablespoons SACO Buttermilk Powder
1 cup all-purpose flour
1 tablespoon sugar
1 teaspoon baking powder
1/2 teaspoon soda
1/4 teaspoon salt
1 egg
1 cup water
2 tablespoons melted shortening or salad oil

Sift dry ingredients together into a mixing bowl. Add
beaten egg, water and shortening. Beat just until
batter is smooth. **Do not overbeat.**

Drop from a spoon onto a hot greased griddle and
cook until top is full of tiny bubbles and the
underside is brown. Turn and brown the other side.

TEN 4-inch pancakes (recipe...)

LEMON...CAKE
(Makes ...)
1 package Duncan Hines Lemon
Supreme Deluxe Cake Mix
1 package lemon instant
pudding mix (4 serving size)
1/2 cup Crisco Oil*
1 cup water
4 eggs

Blend all ingredients in a large bowl, then beat at
medium speed for 2 minutes. Bake in a greased and
floured 10-inch tube pan at 350° for about 45-55
minutes, until center springs back when touched
lightly. Cool right side up for about 25 minutes,
then remove from pan.

BUTTERMILK BISCUITS
3 tablespoons SACO Buttermilk Powder
2 teaspoons baking powder
1/2 teaspoon soda
2 cups sifted flour
1 teaspoon salt
1/4 cup shortening
1 to 1/3 cup water

Preheat oven to 450°. Sift dry ingredients together
into a mixing bowl. Cut in shortening thoroughly until
mixture resembles corn meal. Add water and mix until...

Handwritten (bottom left):
Bonita
2 lb - 1 at
325°

Handwritten (bottom right):
use Che...
in ...
3 C O...
3 C P. flour
1 C...

Acknowledgments

Anyone who's talked to me for more than 5 minutes knows I love my Mama. Thank you, Mama for always loving me, supporting me, and believing in me. Always. If you ever had any worries about your bookish daughter, you never let on. I love you the most.

To Jona, my sister, who has more common sense than I ever will, but can't—or doesn't—boil water. Thank you for all your support.

To Lisa: Ah, Westchester, I love that my words nourish, nurture, and inspire you. Thank you for what we are building together. When you have faith, anything is possible.

Gena Berry has pretty much saved my life, it seems, on more than one occasion, and I'm sure she will again. And again. (If you ever need *anything* done in the kitchen, just call Gena.)

Claire and Ruby are my angels, too—as well as my sweet loves, recipe testers, and testing tasters. I feel at home in y'all's kitchen as well as at your table. I am not with you nearly enough in person, but I always, always am in my heart.

Thank you to Becky for being the first to encourage me to go to culinary school.

I believe Angie Mosier is one of the most talented women I have ever met. Thank you for your beautiful style, kind heart, and neverending support. You are a dear friend.

Nathalie Dupree, Anne Willan, and Martha Stewart all taught me so much, so much more than cooking. Thank you.

Jenni Coale: I can't thank you enough for My Southern Pantry® and helping build the plane as it sputtered and flew. I believe in you.

Mary Moore, owner of The Cook's Warehouse, and her colleagues Wendy Allen and Jim Brams are the hometown backbone and support I always need. Thank you.

To my web folk: Sue Anne Morgan of IdeaLand gets a very stern and special PM shout out; her colleague Sondra Landrum makes so many things seem seamless when I know they are not.

Big thanks to recipe testers Carlin Breinig and Natasha Mack. And the amazing support from photo shoot assistants Mallory deGolian, Donna Gustafson, Virginia Kerr, Junnie Lai, Shaquetta Maloney, Susan Slack, and Carol Varano.

Speaking of photo shoot: Hélène Dujardin, my French-born, history major culinary soul sister was the blessing I wanted. I had no idea she "came with" the handsome and kind Bill McSweeney. What an incredible team.

Thank you Whole Foods Market for the generous support. Having Cheryl Galway, Emily Shively, and Pam Fischette in your corner is, as my former employer would say, "a good thing." The bottom line is they think their support of efforts like mine may help bring about change in the marketplace. And they hope that will lead to good things for everyone and the planet. I hope so, too, and thank you.

Oh, what would a photo shoot be without drama, overnight deliveries, and "I need it yesterday" hurries? Thanks to Inland Seafood and Melissa's Produce for helping me make our photo shoot a success.

Many thanks to Steve and Marie Nygren of Serenbe for their support and use of their beautiful property.

Grateful thanks to the dedicated folks at Ten Speed Press: Aaron Wehner, Nancy Austin, Betsy Stromberg, Kristin Casemore, and especially my editor Melissa Moore. Y'all sure make pretty books.

To the Lisa Ekus Group staff who do so much: Jaimee Constantine, Sally Ekus, and Corinne Fay all do an amazing job and help in so many ways.

So many friends, supporters, and people who bring what I call heart equity have found their way to me. Evan Bernstein, Michele Minchew, Mike Thomas, Lloyd, Leslie, Beverly Seckinger, Rebecca Lang, the Berry Clan (by default). And there are so many supportive folks on Facebook and Twitter or my blog who I have met in my travels and teaching. Sometimes it renders me speechless that someone I don't know—much less haven't yet met in person—cares so much. It makes me a better person and I thank you for caring; thank you for helping me care.

Thank you to all the folks that bought *Bon Appétit, Y'all*. I could never have imagined the past few years. The part I love the most is when I meet someone with a dog-eared copy or one that's covered in spatters and spills. I love that what I write, helps feed someone—hopefully both body and mind.

Lastly, to my Meme and Dede, I say: I wrote this today, on the day I read that someone called me a "natural teacher." Meme, you always wanted that for me; I was stubbornly, ridiculously resistant. Thank you. You were right; deliciously, wonderfully, incredibly right.

Bon Appétit, Y'all!
VA

Index

MEASUREMENT CONVERSION CHARTS

Volume

U.S.	Imperial	Metric
1 tablespoon	1/2 fl oz	15 ml
2 tablespoons	1 fl oz	30 ml
1/4 cup	2 fl oz	60 ml
1/3 cup	3 fl oz	90 ml
1/2 cup	4 fl oz	120 ml
2/3 cup	5 fl oz (1/4 pint)	150 ml
3/4 cup	6 fl oz	180 ml
1 cup	8 fl oz (1/3 pint)	240 ml
1 1/4 cups	10 fl oz (1/2 pint)	300 ml
2 cups (1 pint)	16 fl oz (2/3 pint)	480 ml
2 1/2 cups	20 fl oz (1 pint)	600 ml
1 quart	32 fl oz (1 2/3 pint)	1 l

Temperature

Fahrenheit	Celsius/Gas Mark
250°F	120°C/gas mark 1/2
275°F	135°C/gas mark 1
300°F	150°C/gas mark 2
325°F	160°C/gas mark 3
350°F	180 or 175°C/gas mark 4
375°F	190°C/gas mark 5
400°F	200°C/gas mark 6
425°F	220°C/gas mark 7
450°F	230°C/gas mark 8
475°F	245°C/gas mark 9
500°F	260°C

Length

Inch	Metric
1/4 inch	6 mm
1/2 inch	1.25 cm
3/4 inch	2 cm
1 inch	2.5 cm
6 inches (1/2 foot)	15 cm
12 inches (1 foot)	30 cm

Weight

U.S./Imperial	Metric
1/2 oz	15 g
1 oz	30 g
2 oz	60 g
1/4 lb	115 g
1/3 lb	150 g
1/2 lb	225 g
3/4 lb	350 g
1 lb	450 g

Some of the recipes in this book include raw eggs, meat, or fish. When these foods are consumed raw, there is always the risk that bacteria, which is killed by proper cooking, may be present. For this reason, when serving these foods raw, always buy certified salmonella-free eggs and the freshest meat and fish available from a reliable grocer, storing them in the refrigerator until they are served. Because of the health risks associated with the consumption of bacteria that can be present in raw eggs, meat, and fish, these foods should not be consumed by infants, small children, pregnant women, the elderly, or any persons who may be immunocompromised.

Copyright © 2011 by Virginia Willis
Photographs copyright © 2011 by Hélène Dujardin
Back cover photograph copyright © 2011 by Angie Mosier

Published in the United States by Ten Speed Press, an imprint of the Crown Publishing Group,
a division of Random House, Inc., New York.
www.crownpublishing.com
www.tenspeed.com

Ten Speed Press and the Ten Speed Press colophon are registered trademarks of Random House, Inc.

Library of Congress Cataloging-in-Publication Data is on file with the publisher

ISBN 978-1-60774-009-4

Printed in China

Design by Betsy Stromberg
Food styling by Gena Berry
Prop styling by Angie Mosier

10 9 8 7 6 5 4 3 2 1

First Edition